ECONOMIC AND
OF ASIA AND THE PACIFIC 2022

BUILDING FORWARD FAIRER

Economic Policies for an Inclusive Recovery and Development

ESCAP 75
MOVING FORWARD TOGETHER

ECONOMIC AND SOCIAL SURVEY OF ASIA AND THE PACIFIC 2022

BUILDING FORWARD FAIRER

Economic Policies for an Inclusive Recovery and Development

United Nations publication
Language: ENGLISH
Sales no.: E.22.II.F.5

ISBN: 9789211208375
eISBN: 9789210013611
ISSN: 0252-5704
eISSN: 2412-0979
ST/ESCAP/2998

Photo Credits

Cover: Sasin Tipchai/Shutterstock
Chapter 1: Chetan Soni/ESCAP
Chapter 2: Kanawa_Studio/Istock
Chapter 3: Sasiistock/Istock
Chapter 4: Goc/Istock
Chapter 5: Janno Nivergall/Pixabay
Chapter 6: ProStock-Studio /Adobe Stock

FOREWORD

After two years of the COVID-19 pandemic, poverty is increasing, inequalities are widening, and daily life is becoming a growing struggle across every society – especially for those already on the social and economic margins.

In the Asia-Pacific region, more than 820 million workers in the informal economy and over 70 million children in low-income households have been hit hard by the pandemic's sweeping economic impacts. In 2021 alone, an additional 85 million people were pushed into extreme poverty.

Economic recovery, along with the core promise of the Sustainable Development Goals to "leave no one behind," are fast slipping beyond reach.

As the countries of Asia and the Pacific look to recovery prospects, they face fiscal constraints and difficult budgetary decisions.

The ***Economic and Social Survey of Asia and the Pacific 2022*** makes a strong case that now is the time for more investment and spending, not less.

Spurring sustainable recovery and development while countering rising inequalities across the region demands increased and inclusive spending to support human development. This includes strengthening health care, education, food systems and universal social protection. It also includes bold investments in job creation, the green transition, gender equality and opportunities for youth.

To help Governments make these urgent and necessary investments, the ***Survey*** offers a detailed blueprint to reorient fiscal and monetary policymaking, regulatory frameworks, and economic transformation processes across the region to ensure that all people are supported equally.

This includes ensuring more targeted and efficient social spending, improved revenue and tax collection, and putting inclusive finance and equitable development at the centre of decisions by central banks. Countries must plan wisely, spend smartly and tax fairly.

More broadly, the world can bolster these efforts by reforming the global financial system, so developing countries can readily access the debt relief, emergency financing, credit and foreign investment they need to support their people at this critical moment.

The findings and policy recommendations contained in this ***Survey*** remind us that the "Fairer Future" it envisions is not only necessary, but possible.

At this pivotal period in history, the United Nations looks forward to working with partners across Asia and the Pacific and beyond to shape a sustainable, inclusive and resilient recovery that belongs to, and is shared by, all.

António Guterres
Secretary-General of the United Nations

PREFACE

The developing economies in Asia and the Pacific rebounded robustly in 2021 after a year of contraction triggered by the COVID-19 pandemic. The recovery remains nascent and uneven; economic growth is projected to be moderate in 2022 amid continuing uncertainty about the pandemic and the likely unwinding of fiscal and monetary support in view of macroeconomic stability concerns.

A more fundamental challenge to sustained economic recovery and inclusive development is the K-shaped recovery among different sectors and the loss of jobs and incomes that pushed an estimated 85 million people in the region into extreme poverty since the pandemic. For developing countries in Asia and the Pacific, COVID-19 has also been a pandemic of inequality. Prolonged economic disruptions and school closures mean long-term scarring of productive skills and learning and, consequently, earning potential, all of which exacerbate inequalities.

"Leaving no one behind" is a core ESCAP strategic priority for 2022. This year's edition of the flagship ***Economic and Social Survey of Asia and the Pacific*** revisits macroeconomic and structural policies and lays out a road map for inclusive post-pandemic recovery and development – a "Building Forward Fairer" policy agenda. As developing countries in the region move ahead with learning to live with COVID-19, balancing the protection of public health and livelihoods, it is time to lay the foundations for a fairer future of equal opportunities and inclusive outcomes.

The *Survey* recommends the continuation of targeted public expenditures amid likely fiscal consolidations that tend to increase inequality and calls for efficiency in fiscal spending. The *Survey* shows that investments in health care, education and social protection significantly reduce inequality; however, there is much room for improvement in beneficiary targeting and spending efficiency. To ensure fiscal and debt sustainability, the *Survey* also highlights the importance of enhancing domestic fiscal revenues in a fair manner.

In taking a new perspective, the *Survey* highlights the role of central banking policies and argues that central banks can and should tilt their traditional monetary policy and official reserve management towards promoting inclusive development. The *Survey* also explores how a central bank digital currency can improve financial access as well as the role of innovative financial instruments in promoting inclusiveness.

The third pillar of the Building Forward Fairer policy agenda is Governments proactively guiding, shaping and managing the structural transformation and technological innovation process for more inclusive outcomes. Economic structure determines inequality dynamics, and the *Survey* outlines the path to "growing with equity". This requires learning structural transformation lessons from the past; promoting labour-intensive technologies and inclusive access to high-quality education and public services; reskilling; and strengthening social protection floors.

Following the global call for a major structural change set out in the Secretary-General's report Our Common Agenda, the efforts of the Asia-Pacific region towards building an inclusive future must also be based on a new social contract. The unprecedented human suffering caused by the COVID-19 pandemic has also created a generational opportunity to build a more equal and sustainable world. This is an opportunity that we cannot waste.

Armida Salsiah Alisjahbana
Under-Secretary-General of the United Nations
and Executive Secretary of ESCAP

EXECUTIVE SUMMARY

Sustaining a nascent recovery

After the pandemic-induced economic contraction in 2020, economic recovery in the developing Asia-Pacific counties in 2021 was driven by robust demand for exports from the region. The growth momentum was dented towards the latter half of the year as countries renewed lockdowns and restrictions in the wake of new COVID-19 variants, leading to supply disruptions. Border openings were further delayed, holding back employment recovery, particularly in tourism-dependent economies. Overall, economic growth in developing countries in Asia and the Pacific, estimated at 7.1 per cent in 2021, is projected to moderate to 4.5 per cent in 2022 and 5 per cent in 2023. Inflation has risen across the region, driven by rising food and fuel prices, affecting the poor disproportionately. Importantly, the unfolding of a K-shaped recovery among different sectors represents a major challenge for inclusive recovery and development, and is likely to further impede progress towards implementation of the 2030 Agenda for Sustainable Development.

In addition, policymakers need to be aware of impending risks, including the possible emergence of new variants of the COVID-19 coronavirus and the ongoing geopolitical conflict. Continued economic disruptions can have adverse impacts on productive capacities and long-term productivity through shorter working hours and lack of employment opportunities, which would erode worker skills. Within the region, women have been disproportionately affected by the pandemic as a large proportion of them were employed in sectors most severely affected by the pandemic and a large proportion of them are engaged in informal employment. Women's labour force participation has also been constrained by care responsibilities during closure of schools and care services. Prolonged school closures have long-term consequences for learning and, consequently, income-earning potential. Weakened economic prospects and balance sheets of businesses are likely to reduce incentives for productive investment and in research and development, resulting in medium- to long-term reductions in productivity.

Moreover, the diminishing fiscal space in many countries casts doubts over sustained fiscal support, while rising inflationary pressures and the prospect of higher interest rates may restrain monetary policy support, with implications for debt servicing, capital flows and currency depreciation. The structural shifts in China as it pursues its "Common Prosperity" agenda have triggered regulatory changes weighing on investor sentiment. Of particular importance are regulations to contain the highly leveraged property development sector, the slowdown in which will affect key trading partners and the demand for raw materials in the region. China's zero-COVID strategy will also have impacts on countries in the region that are highly dependent on tourist arrivals from China.

In looking ahead, the region should seek a balanced approach to coexist with the pandemic – one which is aimed at protecting public health but also enabling livelihoods to continue in order to ensure the economic and social well-being of people. For a sustained recovery, labour market policies, along with continuity in fiscal and monetary support, are needed. However, in the midst of constrained fiscal space, fiscal spending will have to be more targeted and efficient. With rising inflationary pressures, monetary policy can remain accommodative only in countries where inflation is expected to remain within targets, while timely increases in interest rates can help stem potential capital outflows and strengthen external position. Policies that are aimed at enhancing productive capacities and productivity, along with prioritizing spending on health care, education and social protection, can help to reduce inequalities and minimize scarring, thus contributing to sustained and inclusive economic recovery and development.

Spending smart and taxing fairly amid fiscal constraints

The COVID-19 pandemic and the consequent economic crisis pose a fiscal dilemma for countries in the Asia-Pacific region. The need to spend remains elevated, while the means to spend are reduced. Countries with sufficient fiscal space can continue to spend for an inclusive recovery. However, those that do not have the means will have to work on both improving the efficiency of spending and the collection of more revenues.

To ensure recovery at all income levels, instead of a K-shaped scenario, and lay firmer foundations for a more equal and resilient future, fiscal policies need to maintain spending in three major areas: health care, education and social protection. Moreover, Governments should "spend smart" by reducing or eliminating inefficiencies in expenditures and ensuring that basic health care services become increasingly universal, that all children receive high-quality education, especially girls and those in rural areas, and that social protection measures shield all throughout their life, in particular marginalized and vulnerable groups. These expenditures will not only minimize the negative long-term effects of the pandemic but will also help generate long-lasting returns. After all, expenditure on human capital is the best investment for our future.

However, "smart spending" will not be enough to address all the fiscal needs for "building forward fairer" towards achieving the Sustainable Development Goals of the 2030 Agenda. Support must come from the fiscal revenue side as well. "Taxing fairly", along with increases in tax collection efficiency and broadening of the tax base, should be the leading principles. In addition, there is a need to improve progressivity of personal income taxes, address persistent tax avoidance and evasion, close loopholes and cut unnecessary tax incentives. Improved multilateral cooperation for effective international taxation and for taxation of the emerging digital economy can go a long way in raising tax revenues of developing countries. Increases in domestic revenues through formalization of economic activities also provide an opportunity not only to increase fiscal revenues but also to expand critically needed social protection measures and access to universal health care.

Calls for implementation of the above-mentioned measures and significant systemic changes have been raised multiple times; however, they have been delayed not only because of lack of resources, but also lack of commitment, as well as administrative and operational barriers. As the pandemic has encouraged and facilitated innovation across all socioeconomic dimensions, the global transition towards digitalization should be of particular interest to policymakers in the coming years. For example, deployment of digital tools for fiscal management enhances expenditure control and results in much needed savings and efficiency gains. In supporting formalization of economic activities, new technologies generate further positive implications for accessibility of government services and revenue collection, ensuring that all contribute their fair share but also receive the support, as well as public goods and services, to which they are entitled.

Conducting central banking for a fairer future

The perceived failure of the "developmental" central banking approach, which was pursued until the 1980s and benefited only a few economic sectors, led central banks in developing countries to focus narrowly on achieving inflation stability. The ***Survey*** for 2022 argues that Asia-Pacific central banks can and should play an important, complementary role in promoting inclusive development.

Asia-Pacific central banks should step up their engagement with inclusive development amid mounting fiscal constraints to tackle pandemic-induced rises in inequality. Currently, only half of central banks in the region have taken up inclusive finance concerns, which is a missed opportunity given that financial access, financial education and consumer protection benefit the poor relatively more than the better off. Even when central banks have no clear mandate for inclusive finance or a development agenda, they should be concerned about high inequality because this undermines the effectiveness of their monetary policy.

The good news is that central banks in the region can support inclusive development through various policy strategies and tools. The ***Survey*** for 2022 examines how the central bank roles of monetary policymaking, official reserve management, currency issuance and financial sector regulation can promote more inclusive societies.

While monetary policy has indirectly helped the poor by striving to keep inflation low and stable, central banks can also consider the impact of monetary policy on income and wealth distribution, even raising ambitions to make economic equality a secondary goal and allocating part of asset purchases to domestic social bonds. Several Asia-Pacific central banks would likely achieve their core mandate of inflation stability in the coming years, so the pursuit of inequality-mindful monetary policy is possible.

The bulk of the estimated $9.1 trillion in Asia-Pacific official reserves is invested in bank deposits and money market instruments which offer no clear or direct social benefits. Changes in investment strategies and internal governance on investment decisions can mobilize more official reserves for social purposes. More ambitious central banks can deploy part of excess reserves as seed capital for local social projects. As official reserves are deemed more than adequate in several Asia-Pacific economies, there is room for more socially oriented reserve management.

Half of all central banks in the region are exploring how a central bank digital currency could foster financial inclusion. With certain design attributes, this digital currency could help reduce reliance on limited banking services and coverage of national personal identification systems. However, central banks need to be clear about the objective of issuing a digital currency and carefully consider operational issues, such as legal frameworks and risk mitigation. A central bank digital currency also needs a supporting Internet infrastructure and digital literacy.

To mobilize more financial resources for social purposes, Asia-Pacific countries could also promote social impact bonds and sustainability-linked bonds. Among others, these instruments enhance the effectiveness of development spending and attract more diverse bond issuers. To move beyond the current infancy stage, central banks and other financial supervisory authorities can conduct knowledge campaigns, create and harmonize social investment taxonomies and provide financial assistance partially to cover high project transaction costs.

Managing structural changes for a fairer future

While redistributive policies play a role in inclusive development, evidence shows that pre-distributive policies – meaning those that take place before taxes and transfers – are even more important. Structural transformation provides a unique lens for analysing pre-distribution dynamics over time.

The Asia-Pacific development experience to date suggests that pre-distribution dynamics driven by structural transformation are diverse, but inclusive economic development paths are still possible. The Kuznets' tension – the tendency of increasing inequality at an early stage of structural transformation – can be eased with faster job creation through labour-intensive manufacturing development, more inclusive access to public goods and services, rapid increases in skill supply through education and greater equity at the start of economic take-offs. On the other hand, pre-existing inequalities, the shift towards service-based economies and structural bottlenecks may lead to greater inequality pressures even in the presence of economic growth.

New technological revolutions may lead to paradigm shifts in structural transformation possibilities and modalities, with mixed implications for inequality. The combined effect of automation and industrial reshoring may limit the space for labour-intensive manufacturing and modern services, resulting in risks of slower job creation and polarization, and therefore, higher inequality. While the greater offshoring potential of services, enabled by the digital and robotic transformation, may create new job opportunities for low-income labour in developing countries in value chains for services, significant uncertainties in the direction, scale and speed of these transformations remain. It would thus be important for Asia-Pacific developing countries to adopt a balanced development strategy embracing both manufacturing and modern services for poverty reduction and to remain vigilant and be prepared for potential disruptions.

Meanwhile, structural transformation can be proactively guided, shaped and managed by Governments for more inclusive outcomes and smooth transitions. Governments can explore a number of policy options, including public funding and incentives for the development and adoption of labour-enhancing rather than labour-replacing technologies, empowering labour in compensation negotiations and corporate decision-making, ensuring fair competition and inclusive access to education and public services, and providing social protection floors and public support for reskilling and job-searching, among others.

INFOGRAPHICS

BUILDING FORWARD FAIRER SHOULD BE AT THE CENTER OF INCLUSIVE RECOVERY AND DEVELOPMENT

SPEND SMART on health care, education and social protection
TAX FAIR ensuring all pay their share

GUIDE labour-friendly technology
SHAPE the market distribution of economic rewards
MANAGE the labour market turbulences

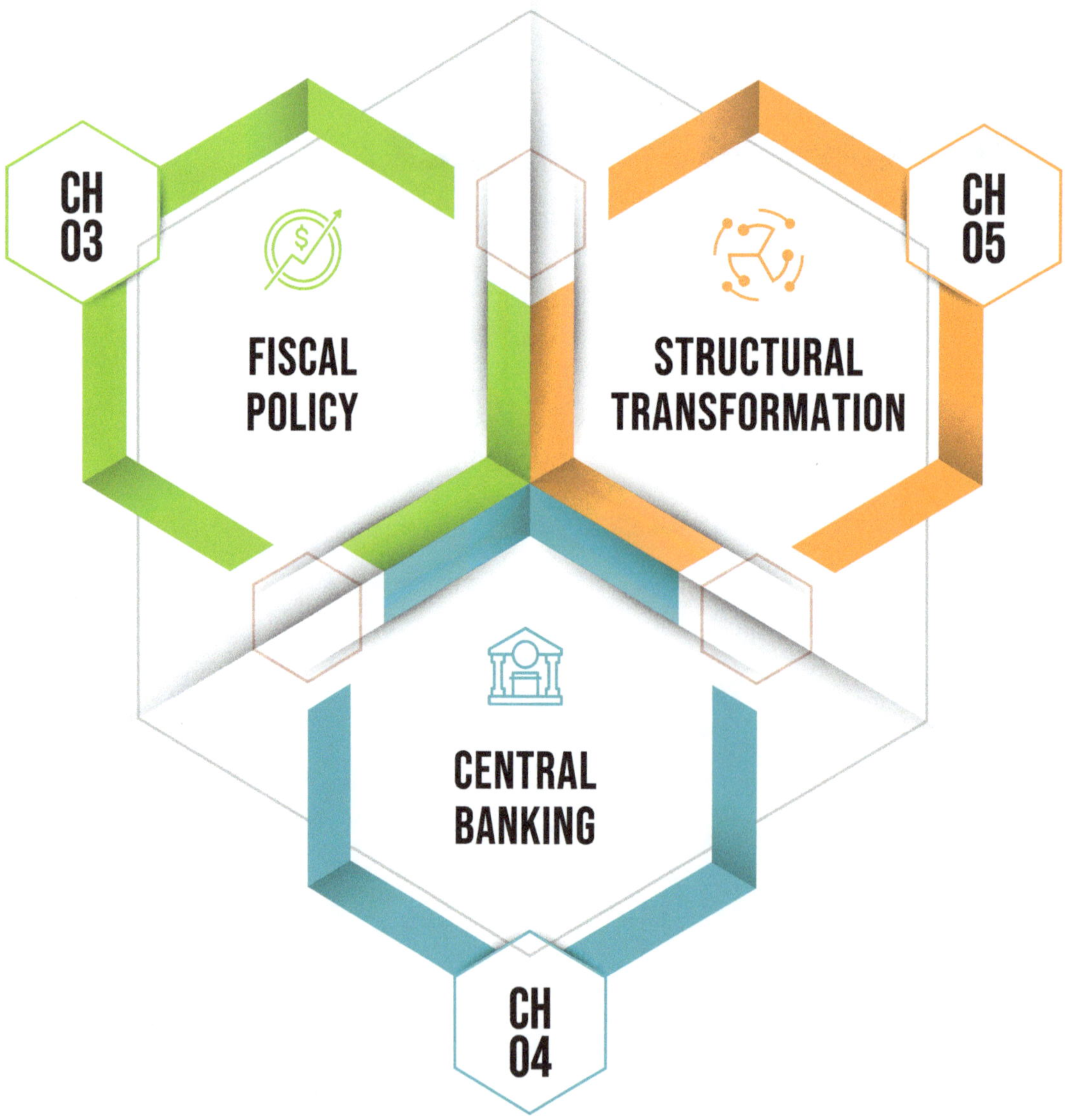

PROMOTE inequality-mindful monetary policy
INVEST official reserves with social gains
FOSTER financial inclusion through central bank digital currencies
SUPPORT innovative social-oriented financial instruments

A NASCENT AND UNEVEN RECOVERY IN ASIA AND THE PACIFIC

K-shaped recovery

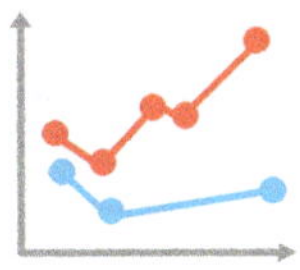

85 million

pushed into extreme poverty

01 UNEVEN RECOVERY

- Unfolded K-shaped recovery
- Uneven recovery across sectors
- Informal workers, women, youth suffer
- 85 million people pushed into extreme poverty since the beginning of the pandemic

inflation

02 RISKS TO RECOVERY

- New variants of COVID-19
- High food & oil prices, pandemic induced disruptions, currency depreciation
- Shrinking fiscal space
- Geopolitical tensions

03 INCLUSIVE DEVELOPMENT

- Co-exist with pandemic
- Counter adverse impacts of financial tightening
- Reduce inequality and minimize scarring
- Ensure targeted spendings

reduce inequality

SPEND SMART

INCLUSIVENESS IMPACT EFFICIENCY

HEALTHCARE

- Universal health coverage
- Flexibility in budget allocation
- Reduce wasteful and inefficient spending
- Deploy digial health technologies

EDUCATION

- Strengthen early age education for all
- Close digital divide
- Eliminate socio-economic barriers at all levels of education
- Inclusive tertiary education

SOCIAL PROTECTION

- Universal basic social protection
- Improve efficiency via digital technologies

INCLUSIVE FISCAL POLICIES

PAY FAIR SHARE

- Ensure all individuals and companies comply with existing tax regulations
- Close loopholes
- Fight illicit financial flows

EXPAND TAX BASE

- Formalize business activities
- Expand taxation of digital economy

SHIFT TAX BURDEN

- Take tax burden off from lowest-income households
- Make corporate and personal income taxes more progressive

TAX FAIR

ALL PAY A FAIR SHARE

CENTRAL BANKS SHOULD AND CAN PROMOTE INCLUSIVE DEVELOPMENT

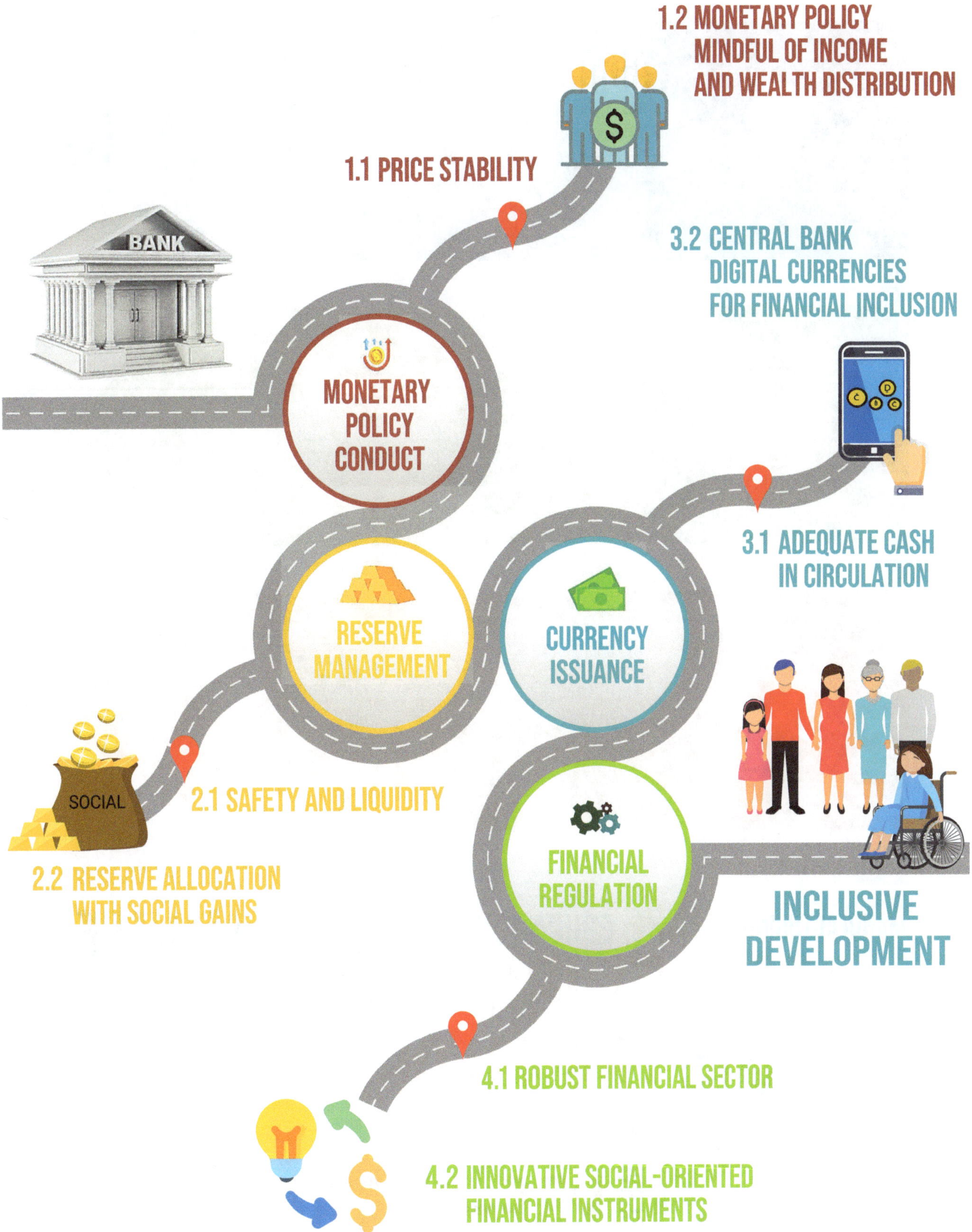

GEARING STRUCTURAL TRANSFORMATION FOR INCLUSIVE DEVELOPMENT

GUIDE

- Gear structural transformation towards a job-rich path
- Support job-friendly technological upgrading and innovation
- Establish correct market signals for private sector technological choices

SHAPE

- Empower labour in the job market
- Empower labour in corporate decision making
- Prioritize education for skill supply and ensure inclusive access

MANAGE

- Establish broad-based social protection as a first line of defense against future structural disruptions
- Strengthen public and private support for on-the-job training, lifelong learning and vocational education
- Keep technological changes at a more manageable pace

MANUFACTURING SHAPE EDUCATION INEQUALITY MANAGE
AI ROBOTIC STRUCTURAL GVC TELEMIGRATION
ACCESS TO OPPORTUNITIES JOB CREATION GUIDE
GLOBALIZATION DIGITAL TRANSFORMATION
POLICIES SERVICES TECHNOLOGIES UNCERTAINTIES EMPLOYMENT
KUZNETS TENSION PRE-DISTRIBUTION

ACKNOWLEDGEMENTS

The Economic and Social Survey of Asia and the Pacific is a flagship publication of the United Nations Economic and Social Commission for Asia and the Pacific (ESCAP). Published annually since 1947, the ***Survey*** has for decades been a valuable companion for policymakers, civil society, academia and other stakeholders in the Asia-Pacific region, providing forward-looking analyses and recommendations on economic conditions and key sustainable development challenges.

The ***Survey*** is produced under the direction of the Executive Secretary and the Editorial Board of ESCAP, with contributions of staff from its substantive divisions and subregional offices. It draws on expertise available from across the United Nations system.

This 2022 edition of the ***Survey*** was prepared by a core team led by Sweta C. Saxena, including Nixie Abarquez, Shuvojit Banerjee, Zheng Jian, Daniel Jeong-Dae Lee, Michał Podolski, Kiatkanid Pongpanich, Vatcharin Sirimaneetham and Lin Zhuo of the Macroeconomic Policy and Financing for Development Division.

Kaveh Zahedi, Deputy Executive Secretary of ESCAP, and Hamza Ali Malik, Director of the Macroeconomic Policy and Financing for Development Division, provided overall guidance and management.

ESCAP staff who provided valuable inputs and feedback include: Hongpeng Liu and Michael Williamson (Energy Division); Katinka Weinberger (Environment and Development Division); Tiziana Bonapace, and Sanjay Srivastava (Information and Communications Technology and Disaster Risk Reduction Division); Oliver Paddison and Yusuke Tateno (Office of the Executive Secretary); Patrik Andersson, Sabine Henning, Sayuri Okada and Weixun Hu (Social Development Division); Petra Nahmias

(Statistics Division); and Rupa Chanda (Trade, Investment and Innovation Division). Helpful comments and suggestions were also received from Sara Elder (International Labour Organization) and Zhenqian Huang (Department of Economic and Social Affairs).

The report benefited from extensive debates among and suggestions from a group of policymakers, scholars, private sector participants and development practitioners who acted as external peer reviewers and/or provided inputs at a virtual expert group meeting held from 1 to 3 December 2021 and on other occasions. ***From government ministries, national agencies, central banks, think-tanks, private organizations and academia***, they include: Md. Abul Bashar (Bangladesh Bank); Luying Gan (HSBC, Hong Kong); Carlos Gradín (World Institute for Development Economics Research of the United Nations University, Finland); Sang-Hyop Lee (University of Hawaii, United States); Ting Lu (Nomura); Darian McBain (Monetary Authority of Singapore); Thammarak Moenjak (Bank of Thailand); Saon Ray (Indian Council for Research on International Economic Relations, India); Nemat (Minouche) Shafik (London School of Economics and Political Science, United Kingdom); Andy Sumner (King's College, United Kingdom); Sally Torbert (International Budget Partnership, United States); Michiru Toda (Japan Social Innovation and Investment Foundation, Japan); Ulrich Volz (SOAS University, United Kingdom); Guanghua Wan (Fudan University, China); and Arief Anshory Yusuf (Padjajaran University, Indonesia). ***From the United Nations and other international organizations***, they include: Abdul Abiad (Asian Development Bank); Patrik Andersson and Alberto Isgut (ESCAP); Valerie Cerra and Jonathan D. Ostry (International Monetary Fund); Sukti Dasgupta (International Labour Organization); Cristina Duarte (United Nations); Peter J. Morgan (Asian Development Bank Institute); and Hassan Zaman (World Bank).

The following consultants provided substantive inputs: Freddy A. Rojas Cama, Shraddha Gautam and Sally Torbert.

Chawarin Klongdee provided excellent research and administrative assistance, including support for the publication's launch (Macroeconomic Policy and Financing for Development Division).

ESCAP Interns – Binvant Singh Broca, Elisa Campos, Xiang-li Lim, Giulia Mambrini, Alice Presotto and Haoyue Tan – provided inputs to the report and excellent research assistance.

The manuscript was edited by John Loftus. The graphic design and layout were created by Tatiana Kurbanova. The printing was provided by Ideol Digital Print Co., Ltd.

Mitch Hsieh, Raggie Johansen and Kavita Sukanandan, all from the ESCAP Communications and Knowledge Management Section, coordinated the media launch and dissemination of the report. Mahesh Uniyal supported the dissemination of the report.

EXPLANATORY NOTES

Analyses in the *Economic and Social Survey of Asia and the Pacific 2022* are based on data and information available up to 16 March 2022.

Groupings of countries and territories/areas referred to in the present issue of the *Survey* are defined as follows:

- **ESCAP region:** Afghanistan; American Samoa; Armenia; Australia; Azerbaijan; Bangladesh; Bhutan; Brunei Darussalam; Cambodia; China; Cook Islands; Democratic People's Republic of Korea; Fiji; French Polynesia; Georgia; Guam; Hong Kong, China; India; Indonesia; Iran (Islamic Republic of); Japan; Kazakhstan; Kiribati; Kyrgyzstan; Lao People's Democratic Republic; Macao, China; Malaysia; Maldives; Marshall Islands; Micronesia (Federated States of); Mongolia; Myanmar; Nauru; Nepal; New Caledonia; New Zealand; Niue; Northern Mariana Islands; Pakistan; Palau; Papua New Guinea; Philippines; Republic of Korea; Russian Federation; Samoa; Singapore; Solomon Islands; Sri Lanka; Tajikistan; Thailand; Timor-Leste; Tonga; Turkey; Turkmenistan; Tuvalu; Uzbekistan; Vanuatu; and Viet Nam.

- **Developing ESCAP region:** ESCAP region excluding Australia, Japan and New Zealand.

- **Developed ESCAP region:** Australia, Japan and New Zealand.

- **East and North-East Asia:** China; Democratic People's Republic of Korea; Hong Kong, China; Japan; Macao, China; Mongolia; and the Republic of Korea.

- **North and Central Asia:** Armenia, Azerbaijan, Georgia, Kazakhstan, Kyrgyzstan, Russian Federation, Tajikistan, Turkmenistan and Uzbekistan.

- **Pacific:** American Samoa, Australia, Cook Islands, Fiji, French Polynesia, Guam, Kiribati, Marshall Islands, Micronesia (Federated States of), Nauru, New Caledonia, New Zealand, Niue, Northern Mariana Islands, Palau, Papua New Guinea, Samoa, Solomon Islands, Tonga, Tuvalu and Vanuatu.

- **Pacific island developing economies:** All those listed above under "Pacific" except for Australia and New Zealand.

- **South and South-West Asia:** Afghanistan, Bangladesh, Bhutan, India, Iran (Islamic Republic of), Maldives, Nepal, Pakistan, Sri Lanka and Turkey.

- **South-East Asia:** Brunei Darussalam, Cambodia, Indonesia, Lao People's Democratic Republic, Malaysia, Myanmar, Philippines, Singapore, Thailand, Timor-Leste and Viet Nam.

- **Least developed countries:** Afghanistan, Bangladesh, Bhutan, Cambodia, Kiribati, Lao People's Democratic Republic, Myanmar, Nepal, Solomon Islands, Timor-Leste and Tuvalu. Samoa and Vanuatu were part of the least developed countries prior to their graduation in 2014 and 2020, respectively.

- **Landlocked developing countries:** Afghanistan, Armenia, Azerbaijan, Bhutan, Kazakhstan, Kyrgyzstan, Lao People's Democratic Republic, Mongolia, Nepal, Tajikistan, Turkmenistan and Uzbekistan.

- **Small island developing States:** American Samoa, Cook Islands, Fiji, French Polynesia, Guam, Kiribati, Maldives, Marshall Islands, Micronesia (Federated States of), Nauru, New Caledonia, Niue, Northern Mariana Islands, Palau, Papua New Guinea, Samoa, Singapore, Solomon Islands, Timor-Leste, Tonga, Tuvalu and Vanuatu.

Owing to the limited availability of data, selected small island developing States are excluded from the analysis. For the purpose of this ***Survey***, Singapore is not considered to be a small island developing State due to its high level of development and high-income status.

Bibliographical and other references have not been verified. The United Nations bears no responsibility for the availability or functioning of URLs.

Many figures used in the ***Survey*** are on a fiscal year basis and are assigned to the calendar year which covers the major part or second half of the fiscal year.

Growth rates are on an annual basis, except where indicated otherwise.

References to dollars ($) are to United States dollars, unless otherwise stated.

The term "billion" signifies a thousand million. The term "trillion" signifies a million million.

In the tables, two dots (..) indicate that data are not available or are not separately reported; a dash (–) indicates that the amount is nil or negligible; and a blank indicates that the item is not applicable.

In dates, a hyphen (-) is used to signify the full period involved, including the beginning and end years, and a stroke (/) indicates a crop year, fiscal year or plan year.

ACRONYMS

ACM	Association for Computing Machinery
ADB	Asian Development Bank
ADBI	Asian Development Bank Institute
AFI	Alliance for Financial Inclusion
AI	artificial intelligence
APO	Asian Productivity Organization
ASEAN	Association of Southeast Asian Nations
BEPS	base erosion and profit shifting
BIS	Bank for International Settlements
BSP	Bangko Sentral ng Pilipinas
CBDC	central bank digital currency
CEIC	CEIC Data (part of ISI Emerging Markets Group)
CEQ	commitment to equity
CIT	corporate income tax
COVID-19	coronavirus disease 2019
ENEA	East and North-East Asia
ESCAP	United Nations Economic and Social Commission for Asia and the Pacific

ESG	environmental, social and governance
FDA	Food and Drug Administration
FDI	foreign direct investment
4Ps	Pantawid Pamilyang Pilipino Program
G20	Group of Twenty
GDP	gross domestic product
GGDC	Groningen Growth and Development Centre
GNI	gross national income
GVC	global value chains
HANK	heterogeneous agent New Keynesian
ICMA	International Capital Market Association
ICT	information and communications technology
IFC	International Finance Corporation
ILO	International Labour Organization
ILOSTAT	International Labour Organization statistics and databases
IMF	International Monetary Fund
INFE	International Network on Financial Education
ISIC	International Standard Industrial Classification of All Economic Activities
ITU	International Telecommunication Union
MHA	Ministry of Home Affairs
NCA	North and Central Asia
NFSP	National Food Security Portal (India)
NGFS	Network for Greening the Financial System
OECD	Organisation for Economic Co-operation and Development
OMFIF	Official Monetary and Financial Institutions Forum
OPEC+	Organization of the Petroleum Exporting Countries Plus includes as members: Azerbaijan, Bahrain, Brunei Darussalam, Kazakhstan, Malaysia, Mexico, Oman, Russian Federation, South Sudan and Sudan

PER	public expenditure review
PFM	public finance management
PIT	personal income tax
PMI	purchasing managers' index
PPP	purchasing power parity
R&D	research and development
RCEP	Regional Comprehensive Economic Partnership
RMG	ready-made garment
SDG	Sustainable Development Goal
SEA	South-East Asia
SME	small and medium-sized enterprise
SOE	state-owned enterprise
STEM	science, technology, engineering and mathematics
SSWA	South and South-West Asia
SWIID	Standardized World Income Inequality Database
UBSOF	UBS Optimus Foundation
UHC	universal health coverage
UNCTAD	United Nations Conference on Trade and Development
UNDP	United Nations Development Programme
UNESCO	United Nations Educational, Scientific and Cultural Organization
UNICEF	United Nations Children's Fund
UNU-WIDER	World Institute for Development Economics Research of the United Nations University
UNWTO	United Nations World Tourism Organization
WDI	World Development Indicators
WFP	United Nations World Food Programme
WHO	World Health Organization
WTO	World Trade Organization

CONTENTS

CHAPTER 3: FISCAL POLICY CHOICES FOR INCLUSIVE RECOVERY AMID FISCAL SPACE CONSTRAINTS 55

CHAPTER 4: CENTRAL BANKING FOR INCLUSIVE DEVELOPMENT: THROUGH A NEW LENS 89

CHAPTER 5. GEARING STRUCTURAL TRANSFORMATION FOR INCLUSIVE DEVELOPMENT 119

FIGURES

CHAPTER 01

BUILDING A FAIRER FUTURE

1. INTRODUCTION

Economic growth in Asia and the Pacific has been the fastest in the world in the last decade. The region's economic success, however, has not been enjoyed by all. The failure of individual countries and areas to grow together at all income and social levels, as well as along urban-rural and gender lines, has led to scarring effects – especially during the pandemic, which brings the issue of inequality and fairness to the fore. These long-term scars are already setting the development agenda back.[1] The pandemic has had adverse impacts on some 829 million informal workers across the region as a result of lockdowns; subsequently, multidimensional poverty levels doubled, affecting 71 million children who have not had access to online learning during school closures. Our estimates suggest that additional 85 million people have been pushed into extreme poverty since the start of the pandemic, living on $1.90 per day or less. The number of people living in poverty would rise to 156 million and 160 million respectively if $3.20 and $5.50 per day thresholds are used. Hence, building a fairer[2] future – ensuring an inclusive recovery from the pandemic and building an inclusive development path – is an imperative.

Previous issues of the ***Economic and Social Survey of Asia and the Pacific*** have highlighted the role of high and sustained economic growth in lifting 1.2 billion people out of extreme poverty ($1.90 per person per day) since 1990 in Asia and the Pacific, mainly in China and India. However, raising the threshold to $3.20 per person per day means that some 800 million to 900 million people in the region still live below that line and experience serious economic insecurity. The Asia-Pacific region is still home to half of the world's poor people. Using the $5.50 per day threshold, the Asia-Pacific region's share in the global poverty headcount increases further to about 60 per cent of the global total, which is almost proportional to its population share in the world. By this standard, there are 1.8 billion people living in poverty in the region – and that was before the COVID-19 pandemic! Thus, the focus on rapid and high economic growth to reduce extreme poverty was misplaced.

1 For details on the scarring effects resulting from COVID-19, see Cerra, Fatas and Saxena (2021).

2 According to the Cambridge dictionary: fairness means the quality of treating people equally or in a way that is right or reasonable. For the purpose of the present Survey, the term fair will also reflect any policy or action that reduces income and wealth inequality.

2. CONSEQUENCES OF INEQUALITY

Even if reducing extreme poverty is considered as a measure of success, inequalities – of opportunities and outcomes – have remained persistent and have even risen in many economies in Asia and the Pacific. Income inequality increased in the Asia-Pacific region between the 1990s and 2010s when it was generally decreasing in other parts of the world (figure 1.1a). More recent estimates show that income inequality has increased for about 85 per cent of the region's population since 2000 (figure 1.1b). The income share of the top 10 per cent of people was close to 50 per cent of the total while the bottom 10 per cent account for only 0.2 per cent of that share (figure 1.1c).

This enormous gap in income share begs the question: why has economic growth been able to have beneficial impacts on poverty but not on inequality or inclusive development? Research suggests that the impact of economic growth on inequality depends on the underlying sources of growth (Cerra, Lama and Loayza, 2021) and the relationship between income inequality and economic growth is non-linear.

> For countries with low levels of inequality, especially low-income countries, some increase in inequality is integral to the effective functioning of a market economy.

Inequality can influence growth positively by providing incentives for innovation and entrepreneurship; by raising savings and investments as the rich save a higher fraction of their income; and by enabling a small proportion of the population to accumulate the minimum needed to start businesses and get a good education. For instance, when China

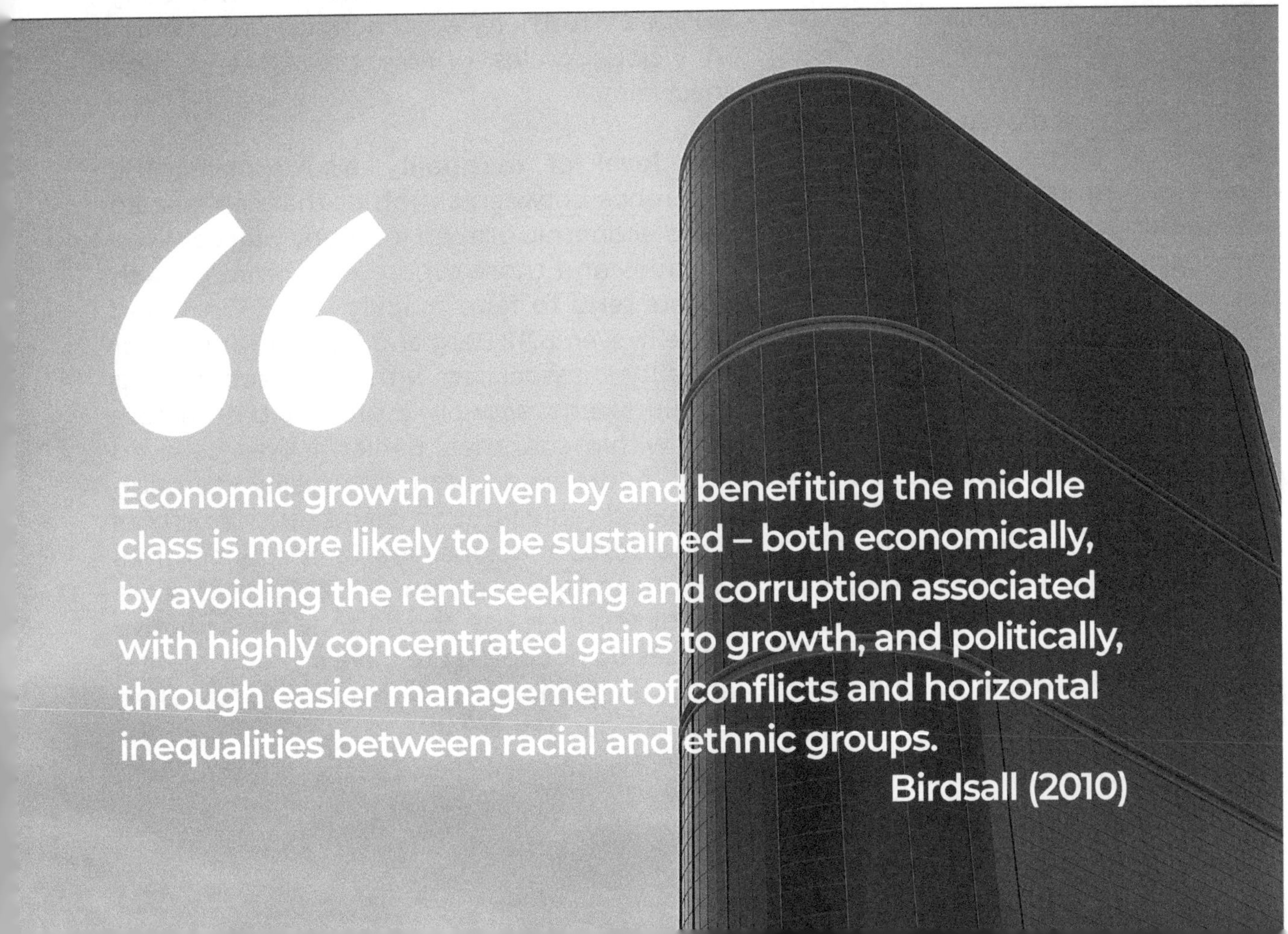

opened its economy, the then-leader, Deng Xiaoping, enjoined everyone to "let some people get rich first" so that "they could bring along others" and eventually achieve "common prosperity for the entire population".

It is also true that people are willing to accept some level of income inequality if there is **equality of opportunity** that gives everyone a fair chance to climb the economic ladder.

Intergenerational socioeconomic mobility encourages greater acceptance of policies that increase economic growth and prosperity in the long run with some trade-off in inequality in the short run.

Intergenerational mobility, however, has declined in the Asia-Pacific region for cohorts born between 1940 and 1980 (figure 1.2) (Huang and Saxena, 2021).

Nevertheless, **increases in inequality, beyond a certain threshold** and degree of persistence, **encourage rent-seeking, lower economic growth** and deprive the poor of the ability to stay healthy, acquire education and accumulate skills. Furthermore, high levels of inequality generate political and socioeconomic instability, which reduces the investment and social cohesion required to adjust to shocks and sustain economic development. The institutional, legal and social consequences of persistent inequality, thus, impair economic prospects. The persistence of high inequality has also been considered one of the causes of the global financial and economic crisis of 2008. For instance, Rajan (2010) pointed to the political and economic incentives that led high-income individuals to save and low-income individuals to borrow well beyond their ability to repay in order to sustain consumption; such low-income individuals were even encouraged to do so by financial institutions and regulators.

Widening inequality can also mean a hollowing out of the middle class (Kanbur, Rhee and Zhuang, 2014), which can have implications for macroeconomic policy. Birdsall (2010) argued that "economic growth driven by and benefiting the middle class is more likely to be sustained – both economically, by avoiding the rent-seeking and corruption associated with highly concentrated gains to growth, and politically, through easier management of conflicts and horizontal inequalities between racial and ethnic groups...". Birdsall (2014) also argued that the middle class is more likely to support market-friendly, poverty-reducing social and economic reforms. Additionally, higher levels of inequality mean that the majority of people will have a low marginal propensity to consume, which reduces the multiplier effect of both fiscal and monetary policies, further entrenching economies in vicious cycles of low growth and high inequality.

The **level of inequality** also explains the difference between countries that can sustain rapid economic growth for many years or even decades and those where **economic growth spurts tend to fade quickly** (Berg, Ostry and Zettelmeyer, 2011; Berg and Ostry, 2011). Greater equality is associated with faster subsequent medium-term economic growth, both across and within countries. Earlier, it was believed that addressing high inequality through increased redistribution could hurt growth as higher taxes and subsidies dampen incentives to work and invest (Okun, 1975). However, more recent research has shown that redistributive policies do not appear to have any detrimental effect on economic performance (Ostry, Berg and Tsangarides, 2014).

Worryingly, popularization of excessive economic integration and unfettered markets beginning in the 1990s (a phenomenon commonly termed as "**hyperglobalization**") **has intensified the persistence of inequality**. The use of integrated supply chains across borders to improve the efficiency of production processes indeed sparked economic growth in many regions. However, this system also gave companies a chance to exploit labour both at home and where they offshored jobs (Acemoglu, 2021). A fragmented supply chain system also discouraged workers from organizing for collective bargaining, while companies registered in low tax jurisdictions, which limited fiscal revenues in all locations of their real business activity. Both trends provided offshoring firms with windfall gains that were directly transferred to shareholders, further exacerbating income divides.

Another external force that can lead to increased inequalities between countries is climate change.

Recent research estimated that climate change has already increased between-country inequality by 25 per cent over the past half century. Within countries, climate change also disproportionately affects the poor. By 2030, it could push more than 100 million people into extreme poverty globally, primarily because of disrupted food production, lower labour productivity due to deteriorating health and natural disasters (World Bank, 2020a). South Asia is a subregion expected to be most adversely affected by climate change.

Lastly, inequality begets inequality. While high-income households are able to save a lot, the same is not true for their low-income counterparts and Governments.

The savings of already high-income households are funnelled into the financial sector, which has been growing over the past several decades, while physical investment has been falling (Mian, Straub and Sufi, 2021a; 2021b; 2021c).[3] Hence, increases in income inequality and excessive financialization, supported by financial deregulation, lead to indebted household demand, pushing down the natural rate of interest. Prolonged expansionary policies – such as accommodative monetary policy – generate debt-financed short-run booms at the expense of indebted demand in the future. This situation continues until the economy becomes stuck in a debt-driven liquidity trap. Escaping a debt trap requires consideration of less conventional macroeconomic policies, such as those focused on redistribution or those reducing the structural sources of high inequality (Mian, Straub and Sufi, 2021a). (Chapters 3, 4 and 5 of the present *Survey* explore these considerations in detail.) Finally, it should be recognized that rising income inequality is more than a distributional issue; it is likely a central force shaping broader macroeconomic trends (Mian, Straub and Sufi, 2021b).

3 Contrary to this view, Larry Summers (in a lecture at LSE www.lse.ac.uk/Events/2021/11/202111101400/stagnation on 10 November 2021 – Secular Stagnation After COVID-19) argues that the reason for secular stagnation is a dearth of investment and not a savings glut among the rich, as maintained by Mian, Straub and Sufi (2021a; 2021b; 2021c), because the European Union and Japan are experiencing sluggish growth and excess capacity but inequality is not considered a reason for those issues.

FIGURE 1.1
Asia and the Pacific region has experienced persistent and rising inequality

(a) Income inequality, by region, and changes between the early 1990s and early 2010s

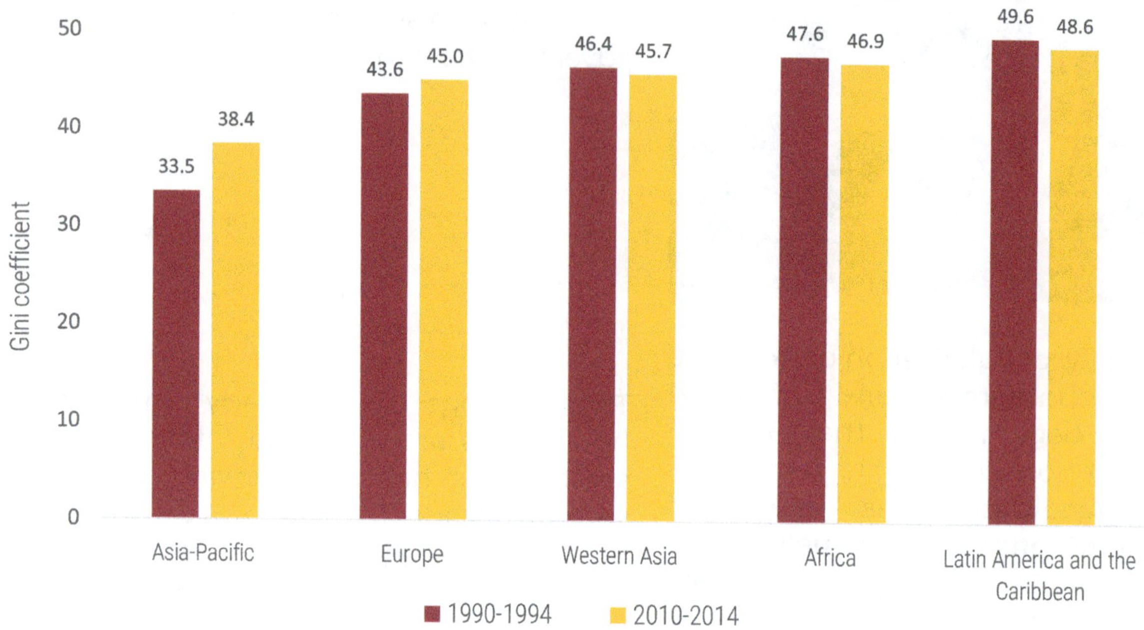

Source: ESCAP (2018a).

(b) Gini coefficient in Asia and the Pacific, by subregion, between the early 2000s and late 2010s

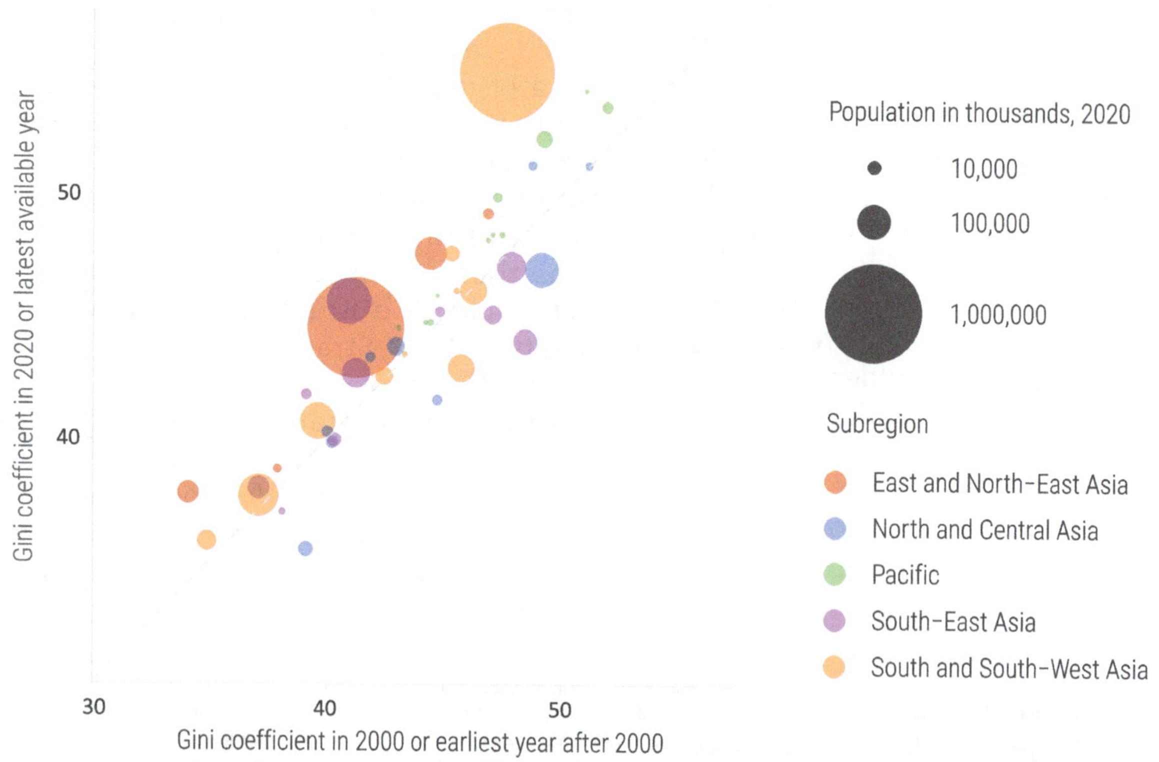

Source: The Standardized World Income Inequality Database, available at www.wider.unu.edu/database/world-income-inequality-database-wiid (accessed on 23 June 2021); and 2019 Revision of World Population Prospects, available at population.un.org/wpp/ (accessed on 23 June 2021).

Note: The dotted line is at a 45-degree slope.

(c) Pre-tax income share, by income groups in Asia

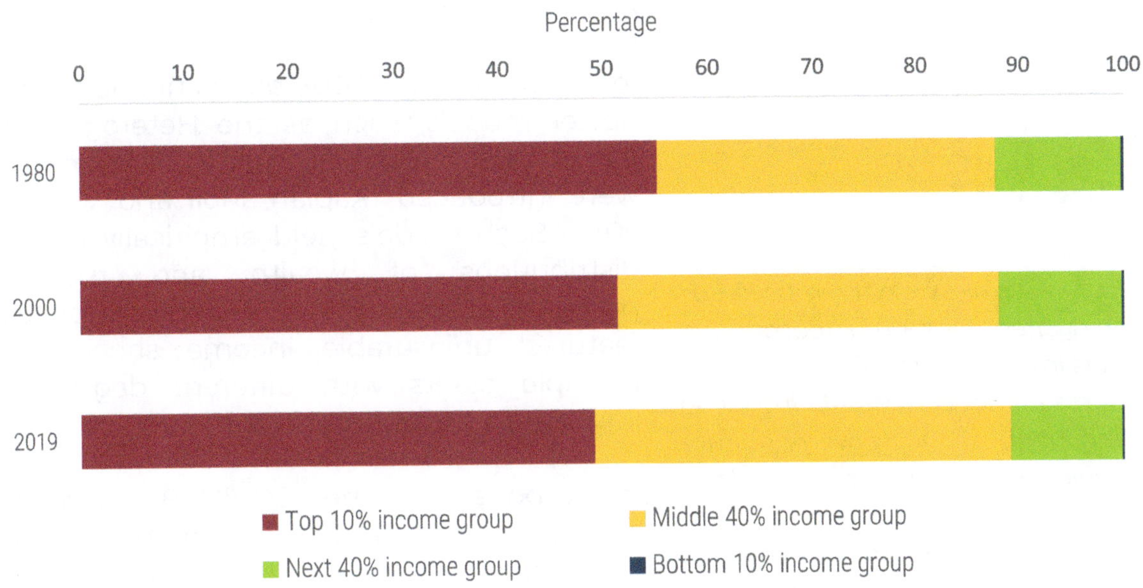

Source: World Inequality Database, available at wid.world/data/ (accessed on 7 June 2021).

FIGURE 1.2
Intergenerational mobility in Asia and the Pacific is declining: relative intergenerational mobility in education for 1940-1980 cohorts

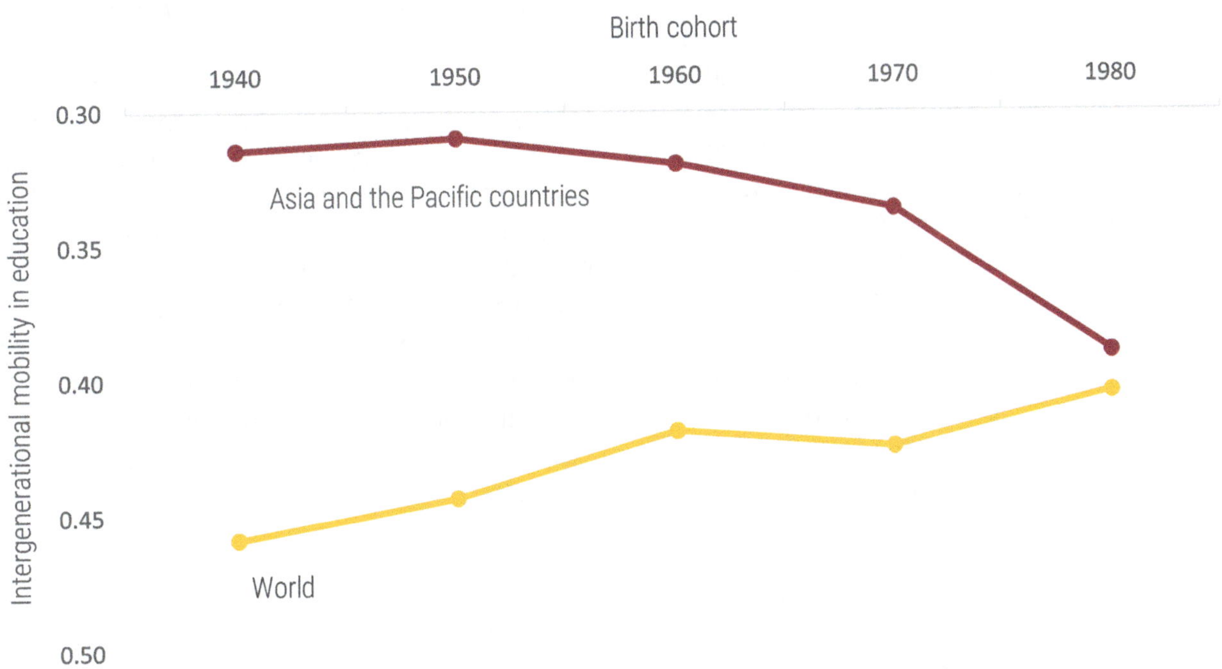

Source: World Bank (2018), Global Database on Intergenerational Mobility (accessed on 28 May 2021).

Note: The vertical axis shows intergenerational persistence, but in reverse order. Hence, if a line goes up, it means improved intergenerational mobility; if it goes down, it means worsened intergenerational mobility. The median value is taken to estimate intergenerational persistence/mobility for the Asia-Pacific region and the world.

3. BUILDING AN INCLUSIVE STAKEHOLDER ECONOMY

While we often must focus on aggregates for macroeconomic policy, it is impossible to think coherently about national well-being while ignoring inequality and poverty, neither of which is visible in aggregate data. Indeed, and except in exceptional cases, macroeconomic aggregates themselves depend on distribution.

Angus Deaton, Nobel Lecture 2016 [4]

Addressing the lack of inclusion in economic modelling...

Traditional economic policies have not addressed the **issue of inequality** well because **economic modelling, which informs policymaking, has paid insufficient attention to the issue of inequality** (Moll and Rickard, 2021). Macroeconomists from the 1930s, such as John Maynard Keynes, focused more on such aggregates as consumption, investment and government spending, rather than on individual behaviours. Even when economists started to model individual behaviours after the 1970s, the focus was on a "representative agent", which nullifies differences among individuals within an economy. Even when "heterogenous agent" models were introduced in the late 1980s and 1990s, the behaviour of all these "agents" remained the same after a shock. For instance, even if poor and rich people spend differently, their spending and saving behaviours were assumed to change in similar ways in the aftermath of a recession.

In response to the 2008 global financial crisis, newer models, such as the Heterogeneous Agent New Keynesian (HANK) models, were introduced (Kaplan, Moll and Violante, 2018). Such models yield empirically realistic distributions of wealth and marginal propensities to consume because of two features: uninsurable income shocks and multiple assets with different degrees of liquidity and different returns.

In response to the COVID-19 pandemic, microlevel empirical research has shown its disproportionately larger impact on poorer households than on others and the epidimiological model of virus transmission is being incorporated into the heterogenous agent model framework (Kaplan, Moll and Violante, 2020). Doing so provides a quantitative analysis of the trade-offs between health outcomes and the distribution of economic outcomes associated with alternative policy responses to the COVID-19 pandemic.

New research is also discussing long-term changes in inequalities related to wealth, race, gender and intergenerational mobility, and exploring the implications of such inequalities for macroeconomic policies: for instance, the impact of inequality on interest rates (Mian, Straub and Sufi, 2021a); the impact of changes in gender and racial equality of occupations on economic growth (Hseih and others, 2019); and the implications of demographic shifts on inequality and global balances (Auclert and others, 2021).

...and incorporating the political economy of stakeholder participation

As mentioned in section II, **some level of income inequality** has a positive economic function as it provides incentives for hard work.

4 www.nobelprize.org/uploads/2018/06/deaton-lecture.pdf

Indeed, **tolerance for such inequality is high**, according to Hirshman and Rothschild (1973), when people believe that **everyone has access to opportunities to do well** and the success stories are attributed to chance[5] as opposed to being the result of nepotism, favoritism, or other such unjust practices[6]. Acceptance of inequality is also more likely in societies that are more homogenous than those that are diverse in terms of ethnicity and religion. The tolerance for high levels of inequality can be expected to decline when a capitalist economy becomes more oligopolized and bureaucratized, and when perceptions grow that economic gains for the few come with losses for many.

Even when economic models and associated policies do not properly account for inequality, **unequal outcomes have political implications**. Research has found that high levels of inequality significantly depress interest in politics, the frequency of political discussion and participation in elections among all but the most affluent, providing compelling evidence that greater economic inequality yields greater political inequality (Solt, 2008). Also, initial distributions of power can lead dominant elites not only to preserve antimarket or anticompetitive institutions, but also to offset democratic pressures to redress social inequalities (Acemoglu and Robinson, 2006). This, in turn, leads to the persistence of inequalities over generations.

5 Indeed, Bergant, Weber and Medici (2022) show that bad luck" plays an important role in explaining why some people in the US are poor.

6 They coined the term "tunnel effect" to describe a situation when changes in the income of B lead to changes in A's welfare not only because A's relative position in the income scale has changed, but also because changes in B's fortunes will affect A's prediction of his or her own future income. In other words, a person may be happy to witness the success of someone else if he or she believes that person's success may lead to better chances for his or her own prosperity.

Much of the literature on the political economy of reforms blames **electoral cycles** for the inability of Governments to implement reforms, which usually have short-term adverse effects even when they are beneficial in the longer run. However, the two may be linked through the level of inequality and trust. There is increasingly more evidence that **high levels of inequality lead to decreased trust in Governments and undermine their ability to push for reforms** (Ortiz-Ospina and Roser, 2016). More recent research by Nunn, Qian and Wen (2020) found that countries with lower levels of trust in Government are also more likely to face political instability, especially in times of economic downturns. In fact, the effect is strongest in democratic countries. This illustrates that inequality in a society may not only degenerate trust but also worsen the chances of an incumbent Government getting re-elected, thus further delaying reforms.

Additionally, **the electorate in countries with high levels of inequality are also sharply divided on national policies needed to mitigate inequalities**, further complicating the job of policymakers, with electoral consequences. World Bank estimates, based on the World Values Survey Wave 7 (2017-2020)[7], show that preferences are highly polarized (figure 1.3a) – people either support the notion that "Incomes should be more equal" (statement 1) or "We need larger income differences as incentives for individual effort" (statement 10). The results further correlate with income, where high-income households are less inclined to support policies in favour of reducing inequality, as opposed to the low-income households (figure 1.3b). This correlation is particularly strong for East Asia and South Asia, where inequality is likely viewed by the rich as an important incentive.

However, on the optimistic side, recent research has also shown that **inequality** is linked to electoral cycles and **tends to fall in election years**, which also witness a rise in spending on education (Sever and Yucel, 2021). Hence, well-functioning democracies and increased political competition can be key in tackling inequality within countries.

7 For details, see www.worldvaluessurvey.org/WVSDocumentationWV7.jsp.

Not surprisingly, the growing levels of inequality in the region have made fighting it a political imperative. In 2014, the current Government of India ran on the platform of sabka saath, sabka vikas ("Leaving No One Behind") and was elected to power. In the next five years, delivering on the most essential Sustainable Development Goals, such as the ones that have targets to end such practices as open defecation, to provide clean cooking energy and to supply electricity to 173 million, 11.7 million and 230 million people, respectively, in rural area aided its re-election with an even larger majority than in the previous election.[8] In 2020, the Government of China launched its inclusive platform of "Shared Prosperity". About 50 years ago, Thailand conceived the notion of a "sufficiency economy"[9] as the basis for balanced and stable development. More recently, the "Bio-Circular-Green Economy" underpins the Thailand 4.0 policy as a strategy to drive economic and social development. Going even further back, the first country in the region to emphasize a more holistic approach to development by giving equal importance to non-economic aspects of well-being was Bhutan. In 1972, the-then King of Bhutan, Jigme Singye Wangchuck, famously declared, "Gross National Happiness is more important than Gross Domestic Product."[10]

As leaders and policymakers are beginning to think of a new development paradigm that is consistent with both their values and constraints, it is important to **avoid the mistakes of the past by continuing to rely on outdated economic models and policy thinking that are inconsistent with the growing political imperative of inclusiveness**. Hence, in going forward, policymakers need to ensure equitable access not only to opportunities ("distributive justice"), but also to "contributive justice", where all individuals are – and are seen to be – meaningfully contributing to society (Sandel, 2020).

A starting point is for leaders to define what the new inclusive stakeholder economy would look like and what is expected of all.

Incorporating environmental, social and governance (ESG) aspects into policy considerations is essential (ESCAP, 2020).

So is holding Governments and businesses accountable. The pandemic brought into focus the "S" of ESG, with calls for more humane treatment of workers and returning the dignity of work to labour. Earlier, there was already a spotlight on Asian CEOs whose salaries exceeded those of peers in the United States of America (Nagumo, 2019). The good news is that government leaders are defining their vision for the future. For instance, India is advocating a mass movement of "Environmental Conscious Life Style" and "Mindful and Deliberate Utilization, instead of Mindless and Destructive Consumption"[11] and towards "P-3 Pro Planet People" policies.[12] China wants to "adhere to a people-centered philosophy of development, place development and livelihoods front and center

8 Similarly, one Indian state (Assam), which first initiated implementation of the Sustainable Development Goals, also had visibly better socioeconomic results as well as the re-election of the incumbent party as a result (Chatterjee, 2018).

9 thaiembassy.se/en/monarchy/philosophy-of-sufficiency-economy/

10 ophi.org.uk/policy/gross-national-happiness-index/

11 From the translation of the statement made in Hindi on 1 November 2021 by the Prime Minister of India at the twenty-sixth session of the Conference of the Parties to the United Nations Framework Convention on Climate Change, held in Glasgow from 31 October to 12 November 2021. The full translated speech is available at pib.gov.in/PressReleseDetail.aspx?PRID=1768712.

12 From a statement made on 17 January 2022 by the Prime Minister of India at the World Economic Forum Virtual Session. The full statement is available at mea.gov.in/Speeches-Statements.htm?dtl/34754.

FIGURE 1.3

(a) Views on income inequality are highly polarized

Source: ESCAP calculations based on World Value Survey (Wave 7).

(b) Preference for inequality differs by income deciles, with high-income households less inclined to support policies in favour of reducing inequality

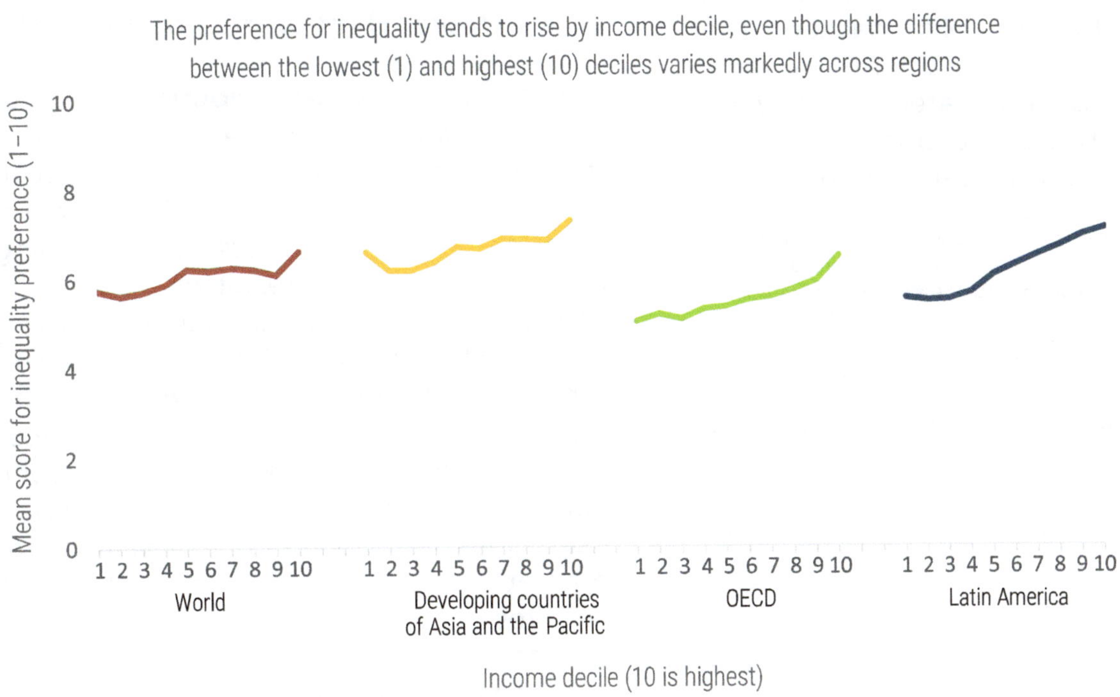

Source: ESCAP calculations based on World Value Survey (Wave 7).

in global macro-policies".[13] The Republic of Korea wants to "raise the quality of life" and be "a nation in which no one is left behind and everyone lives well and happily together".[14] Indonesia's "commitment to prove that there is no one left behind" is evident in its focus on inclusiveness as "a major priority for Indonesia's G20 Presidency".[15]

4. POLICY AGENDA FOR A FAIRER FUTURE

As countries in the region push forward their development strategies for the foreseeable future and focus on how to achieve the 2030 Agenda for Sustainable Development, the one assuring insight is that economic policies *can* help (Cerra, Panizza and Saxena, 2013; ESCAP, 2021a). The ***Survey*** for 2021 advocated for a "Building Forward Better" policy package that would include investments in social, digital and green areas, and would deliver better economic, social and environmental outcomes by 2040. For instance, if such a package were implemented, the region would have 180 million fewer poor people, and carbon emissions would be reduced by 30 per cent. This present issue of the ***Survey*** will highlight the roles that fiscal, monetary and structural policies can play in the quest for building an inclusive stakeholder economy.

Role of Governments and fiscal policies

As Governments in the Asia-Pacific region move beyond policy interventions just to respond to the pandemic and try to steer economies towards inclusiveness and building forward fairer, they could be guided by the following principles:

- **Replacing the Washington Consensus with the Cornwall Consensus:** There is need for a new paradigm – guided by the 2021 G7 Cornwall Consensus[16] to "Build Forward Better", with inclusion as a core pillar – that pivots the role of Governments from post-crisis repairing to preparing in advance against risks and shocks (Mazzucato, 2021). It also entails focusing public investment on the creation of long-term public value rather than short-term private profit.

- **Prioritizing pre-distribution over redistribution:** The debate is moving away from dealing with inequality ex post facto to preventing it in the first place. For instance, Europe's relative success in extending prosperity to all is a result of creating an economy that is less unequal before taxes and transfers (Sandbu, 2021), although this is not to say that taxes and transfers do not work. Similarly, public spending on services plays an important role even when everyone benefits equally from it. Redistribution in itself does not do much to create fairer market opportunities. Prosperity for all requires creating markets that support societal well-being, rather than just compensating for their inequitable results.

13 From the translation of the statement made in Chinese on 17 January 2022 by the President of China at the 2022 World Economic Forum Virtual Session. The full statement is available at www.fmprc.gov.cn/mfa_eng/zxxx_662805/202201/t20220118_10629754.html#:~:text=On%20January%2017%2C%202022%2C%20President,Better%20Post%2DCOVID%20World%22.&text=Xi%20Jinping%20stressed%20that%20the,changes%20unseen%20in%20a%20century.

14 From the translation from Korean of the New Year's Address of the President of the Republic of Korea, made in Seoul on 3 January 2022. The full translated statement is available at english1.president.go.kr/BriefingSpeeches/Speeches/1130

15 From the address of the President of Indonesia made on 23 September 2021 at the seventy-sixth session of the United Nations General Assembly held in New York. For the full statement, see setkab.go.id/en/address-of-president-of-the-republic-of-indonesia-at-the-general-debate-session-of-the-76th-general-assembly-of-the-united-nations-23-september-2021/

16 For the full Consensus, see www.g7uk.org/wp-content/uploads/2021/06/G7-Economic-Resilience-Panel-The-Cornwall-Consensus.pdf.

The ***Survey*** for 2021 showed that fiscal policies are helpful in recovering from shocks and supporting pursuit of the 2030 Agenda, and should continue to be used to avoid permanent development setbacks. Chapter 3 of the present issue of the ***Survey*** continues to advocate for inequality-reducing fiscal spending but in the light of reduced fiscal space due to the stimulus that has been needed for fighting the pandemic. Specifically, the chapter stresses the still untapped potential of more targeted and efficient fiscal spending. For instance, while spending on education may reduce inequality, its efficiency in reducing inequality is much higher when invested at the primary and secondary levels rather than the tertiary level. Similarly, tackling the wastefulness in the health care system currently might be more important than simple increases in health-related spending.

Role of monetary and other central bank policies

In many developed economies, conventional monetary policy reached its limit quickly during the global financial and economic crisis of 2008 when interest rates could not be lowered further. Various central banks, including some in emerging Asia-Pacific economies, thus adopted unconventional monetary policy tools, such as large-scale asset purchase programmes. However, these massive sovereign and corporate bond-buying schemes pushed up financial asset prices, which tended to benefit the rich, thus exacerbating existing inequalities (see section II). In the United States, the Federal Reserve started the conversation on inclusive monetary policy in August 2020 when it announced that it would maintain a loose monetary policy stance for longer in order to help marginal sections of the labour market. There have recently been further calls for a progressive monetary policy or "sustainable monetary tightening" (Varoufakis, 2021), where interest rates are raised and the money from quantitative easing programmes is used to support climate action and reduce inequality.

The ***Survey*** for 2022 looks at how Asia-Pacific central banks can move beyond their traditional role of stabilizing inflation and output to addressing economic inequality. As high inequality can reduce the effectiveness of monetary policy through a weaker monetary transmission mechanism, many central banks in the region have actively made inclusive finance a part of their mandate. However, central banks should and can do more, such as by making the conduct of monetary policy more mindful about inequality and pursuing socially tilted official reserve management (chapter 4). Issuing a central bank digital currency could also help with the objective of inclusive finance.

Role of structural policies

The ***Survey*** for 2022 also examines policies that can help flatten the trade-off between inequality and economic growth through growth-enhancing and inequality-reducing structural reforms and transformations (chapter 5). The development experience across the Asia-Pacific region suggests that, although pre-distribution dynamics driven by structural transformation are diverse, inclusive economic development paths are possible. For instance, the Republic of Korea, during its economic takeoff between the 1960s and early 1990s, was able to transform without any rise in inequality (thanks partly to its emphasis on universal access to education), while China achieved such a transformation alongside a significant rise in inequality. Chapter 5 teases out lessons from diverse regional experiences.

Current technological revolutions, however, are likely to lead to further structural tranformations, with attendant implications for inclusive development. Digital and robotic

The issue of inequality

Economic growth in Asia and the Pacific has been the fastest in the world in the last decade. The region's economic success, however, has not been enjoyed by all. The failure of individual countries and areas to grow together at all income and social levels, as well as along urban-rural and gender lines, has led to scarring effects – especially during the pandemic, which brings the issue of inequality and faireness to the fore.

Adverse impacts of the pandemic

The pandemic has had adverse impacts on some 829 million informal workers across the region as a result of lockdowns; subsequently, multidimensional poverty levels doubled, affecting 71 million children who have not had access to online learning during school closures. Our estimates suggest that an additional 85 million people have been pushed into extreme poverty since the start of the pandemic, living on $1.90 per day or less.

Policy agenda for a fairer future

The Survey for 2021 advocated for a "Building Forward Better" policy package that would include investments in social, digital and green areas, and would deliver better economic, social and environmental outcomes by 2040. For instance, if such a package were implemented, the region would have 180 million fewer poor people, and carbon emissions would be reducedby 30 per cent. This present issue of the Survey will highlight the roles that fiscal, monetary and structural policies can play in the quest for building an inclusive stakeholder economy.

transformations will lead both to challenges, as many current jobs will cease to exist, and to opportunities, as new jobs that do not exist now will be created. Therefore, policymakers will have to proactively guide, shape and manage this new structural transformation for inclusive outcomes and fewer socioeconomic disruptions. Governments can explore a number of policy options, including public funding and incentives for the development and adoption of labour-enhancing rather than labour-replacing technologies, empowering labour in compensation negotiations and corporate decision-making, ensuring fair competition and inclusive access to education and public services, and providing social protection floors and public support for reskilling and job-searching, among other policy options.

Building forward a fairer world

To build forward a fairer world, do we need a new social contract? Yes.

The region has less than a decade to fulfil the "No one left behind" 2030 Agenda. Yes, it is a monumental task. Yes, it is a challenge, but, if supported by collective will and political commitment, it can be done.

The challenges and the opportunities related to the achievement of the 2030 Agenda were encapsulated in part of a speech by the Secretary-General:[17] "The response to the pandemic, and to the widespread discontent that preceded it, must be based on a New Social Contract and a New Global Deal that create equal opportunities for all and respect the rights and freedoms of all", and in Our Common Agenda: Report of the Secretary-General[18], which points out that this new social contract must be "... anchored in a comprehensive approach to human rights, in the light of the pandemic and beyond, one that allows many more actors to tackle increasingly complex and interconnected problems".

17 The full speech, entitled "Secretary-General's Nelson Mandela Lecture: 'Tackling the Inequality Pandemic: A New Social Contract for a New Era'," made by the Secretary-General in New York on 18 July 2020, is available at www.un.org/sg/en/content/sg/statement/2020-07-18/secretary-generals-nelson-mandela-lecture-%E2%80%9Ctackling-the-inequality-pandemic-new-social-contract-for-new-era%E2%80%9D-delivered.

18 The full report is available at www.un.org/en/content/common-agenda-report/assets/pdf/Common_Agenda_Report_English.pdf.

MACROECONOMIC PERFORMANCE AND OUTLOOK: ASIA-PACIFIC REGION

CHAPTER 02

1. INTRODUCTION

After a significant contraction in 2020, economic activities in the developing countries in the Asia-Pacific region rebounded in 2021, thanks to robust external demand. The growth momentum moderated somewhat, however, towards the latter half of 2021 as countries grappled with renewed lockdowns and restrictions in the wake of the Delta variant of the severe acute respiratory syndrome coronavirus, which causes COVID-19 disease. Nevertheless, some encouraging signs did emerge towards the end of 2021 with COVID-19 infections receding and countries attempting to live with the pandemic. Economic recovery is likely to continue into 2022, albeit at a more moderate pace amid impending risks, including the possible emergence of new coronavirus variants, pandemic-induced supply disruptions, moderating exports, macroeconomic stability concerns and potential risks arising from moderation in economic growth in China and the ongoing geopolitical conflict. Policymakers should therefore not be overly optimistic. Moreover, risks to an inclusive recovery remain, as a K-shaped recovery has unfolded and is likely to leave long-lasting scars and set back progress in implementing the 2030 Agenda and achieving the Sustainable Development Goals. To avoid such scars, macroeconomic policies need to be fully employed. In this vein, the role of fiscal spending amid limited fiscal space and likely fiscal consolidation is analysed in chapter 3, while the role of central banks in supporting inclusive recovery and development, beyond their traditional role in stabilizing inflation, is the focus of chapter 4.

This chapter takes stock of the economic performance of Asia and the Pacific in 2021 and analyses the economic prospects for 2022 and 2023.

It provides insights on near-term economic risks and vulnerabilities and discusses relevant policy considerations.

The near-term outlook for developing countries in the Asia-Pacific region is riddled with uncertainty and downside risks. The chapter highlights that the lingering impact of the pandemic and associated socioeconomic disruptions could hamper a sustained recovery. Additionally, mounting concerns over global monetary tightening, limited fiscal space and likely spillovers from China's growth moderation will further exacerbate pre-existing inequalities as well as those that emerged due to the crisis.

In terms of policy recommendations, the chapter calls for a balanced approach to coexist with the pandemic – one which seeks to protect public health but also enables livelihoods to continue in order to ensure the economic and social well-being of people.

For a sustained recovery, labour market policies, along with continuity in fiscal and monetary support, are needed. However, in the midst of constrained fiscal space and rising inflationary pressures, providing continued support would be challenging and will need to be better targeted. External risks, including global monetary tightening pressures and the possible spillovers through China's property sector downturn, will require vigilance and prudent policies to prevent large capital outflows as well as those to avert any economic and social fallout. Policies that are aimed at enhancing productive capacities and productivity can minimize inequalities and long-term scarring. In going forward, the chapter also commends green and inclusive recovery initiatives proposed by countries in the region as pivotal steps towards a more inclusive and balanced post-pandemic development.

2. ECONOMIC PERFORMANCE AND OUTLOOK

2.1 Global context – strong recovery in 2021 is losing steam

Global economic growth experienced a substantial uplift in momentum in early 2021 as economic activities resumed in major developed economies. It is estimated to have expanded by 5.5 per cent in 2021; the highest growth in more than four decades in the backdrop of the 3.4 per cent contraction in 2020 (United Nations, 2022). Global economic recovery is expected to continue with GDP growth projected at 4 per cent in 2022 and 3.5 per cent in 2023, amid risks of new waves of COVID-19 variants, persistent labour market challenges, lingering supply-chain disruptions and rising inflationary pressures.

Resumption of activities in developed economies led to robust growth in trade and manufacturing. The United States and the European Union led the global growth momentum on the back of rapid vaccination rollouts and ample fiscal and monetary stimulus. As the economies reopened, demand for goods surged leading to robust growth in trade and manufacturing. Global export volume grew by 5.6 per cent in the first half of 2021 relative to the sharp contraction in 2020 while industrial production grew by 2.9 per cent (figure 2.1). Stronger demand for goods was accompanied by a shift in consumption towards services.

This nascent economic recovery nevertheless remains uneven across regions and countries, driven by persistent cross-country gaps in successful pandemic containment and unequal access to vaccines. In Latin America, economic rebound was supported by favourable external conditions, but soaring inflation and tighter fiscal and monetary policies are weighing on domestic demand. In Africa, recovery remains fragile with countries facing elevated debt levels, rising interest payments and limited fiscal space to support recovery.

Global growth momentum seems to have lost steam towards the second half of 2021. The European Union and the United States, both of which registered robust growth in 2021, faced headwinds in the second half of the year from supply constraints, shortage of labour and mounting inflationary pressure. The automotive industry, a crucial business of the European Union, scaled back production due to shortage of semiconductors. Another wave of the pandemic led to reintroduction of containment measures disrupting the services sector.

The global economic outlook depends upon major uncertainties, such as continued risk of new COVID-19 variants and recurring outbreaks and restrictions on economic activities. Moreover, the economic impacts of the Russia-Ukraine conflict will reverberate across the globe through slower growth, rising inflation, disrupted trade and remittance flows. Rising inflationary pressures in major developed economies, particularly the United States, the euro area and major developing countries in Latin America and the Caribbean, coupled with faster than expected tightening of global monetary conditions, could also impede recovery. While the European Central Bank has scaled back its asset purchase programme, it will likely maintain low interest rates to support recovery. Employment recovery is projected to remain below pre-pandemic levels in 2022 and beyond. While global poverty is projected to show a slight decrease to 876 million people in 2022, it is still well above pre-pandemic levels, thus exacerbating inequalities and its long-term consequences (United Nations, 2022).

FIGURE 2.1
Increased momentum in global trade and industrial activities

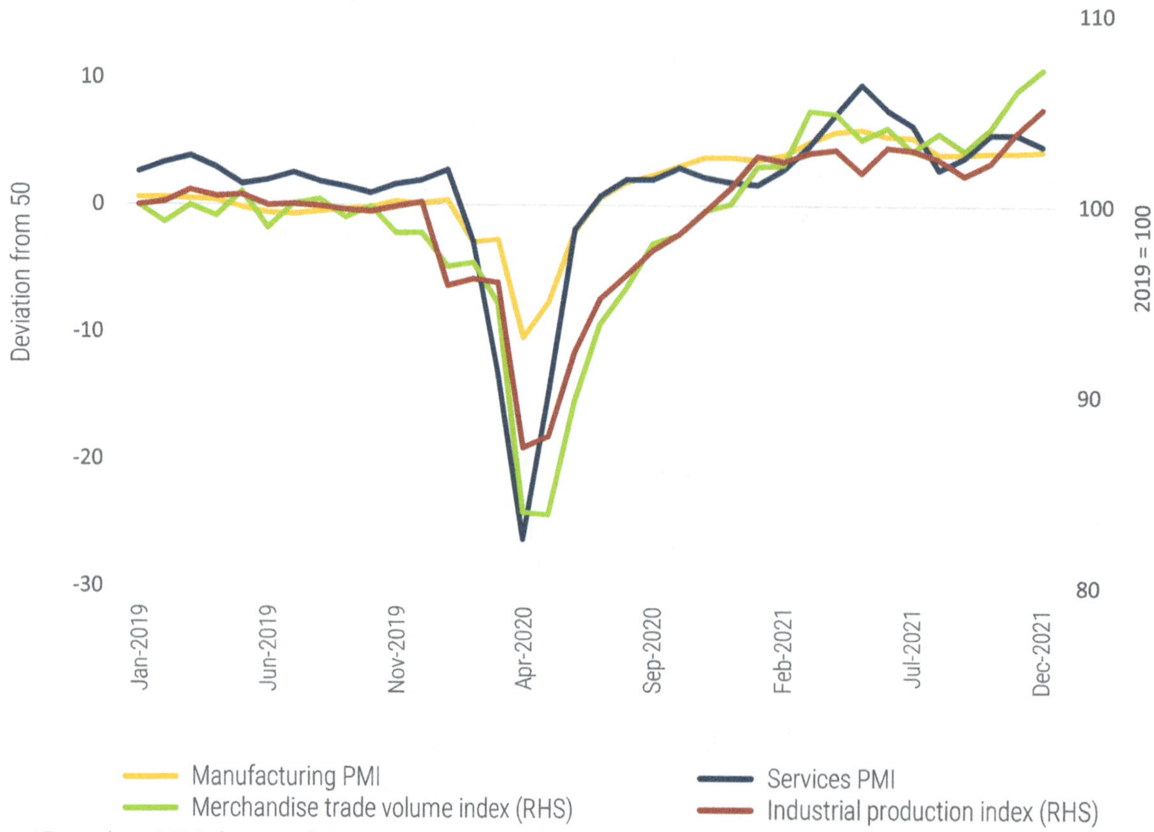

Source: Based on CEIC data and CPB Netherlands Bureau for Economic Policy Analysis (accessed on 4 March 2022).
Note: RHS - right-hand side.

2.2 Performance in the developing Asia-Pacific countries in 2021 – a strong rebound but recovery remains nascent and uneven

After experiencing a contraction in 2020 in the wake of the COVID-19 pandemic, developing countries in Asia and the Pacific recovered strongly in the first half of 2021, thanks to robust external demand for the region's exports and sustained monetary and fiscal support (figure 2.2). Despite setbacks caused by the Delta variant, developing countries in the Asia-Pacific region recovered from a contraction in economic activity of 0.3 per cent in 2020 to an estimated expansion of 7.1 per cent in 2021.

Robust demand from developed countries helped increase trade and manufacturing activities in Asia and the Pacific (figures 2.3a and 2.3c). Merchandise trade in the region returned to pre-pandemic levels in mid-2021, with export volumes from developing countries in the Asia-Pacific region increasing at approximately 15 per cent above pre-pandemic levels. Exporters of electronics, semiconductors, machinery and other consumer durables[1] benefited from increased demand and manufacturing, while demand for pandemic-related goods waned (figure 2.3b). On the other hand, latest data suggest that the export of services in developing countries in the Asia-Pacific region is 33.5 per cent below pre-pandemic levels. Resilient remittance flows supported consumption in Bangladesh, Nepal, Pakistan, the Philippines and Pacific island economies, while countries in North and Central Asia benefited from higher commodity prices.

Trade and manufacturing started to decline from May 2021 onwards, owing to mobility restrictions and economic disruptions caused by the Delta variant and the resulting supply shortages.

Renewed outbreaks of COVID-19, most evident in the third quarter, led to supply disruptions within the region and globally, and dented economic recovery. Particularly hard hit were countries in South and South-West Asia when the second wave of outbreaks of the more virulent Delta variant peaked in May 2021 after which the variant moved on to have impacts on South-East Asia for most of the third quarter. Renewed restrictions disrupted production and transport of goods, particularly of semiconductors, which constitute a large share of regional exports.

Such disruptions were exacerbated in key semiconductor production locations due to natural hazards – an earthquake in Japan and the drought in Taiwan Province of China. Shipping delays from port closures added to the costs. The ongoing technology and trade tensions between the United States and China further hampered production and exports of semiconductor chips. The resulting supply chain bottleneck halted electronics and automotive assembly lines and weighed on exports, contributing to the global supply chain disruptions.

Recent developments in China also weighed on sentiment and activities contributing to the moderation in region's economic growth. A deceleration in the Chinese economy, as seen in its fourth quarter GDP growth rate of 4 per cent, comes amid policy shifts towards good-quality growth based on its "Common Prosperity" agenda. Regulatory tightening on various sectors, including technology firms, education service providers, online finance and the property sector, has had negative

1 China, Malaysia, the Philippines, Singapore, the Republic of Korea, Thailand and Viet Nam

FIGURE 2.2
Strong growth rebound in developing countries in the Asia-Pacific region in 2021

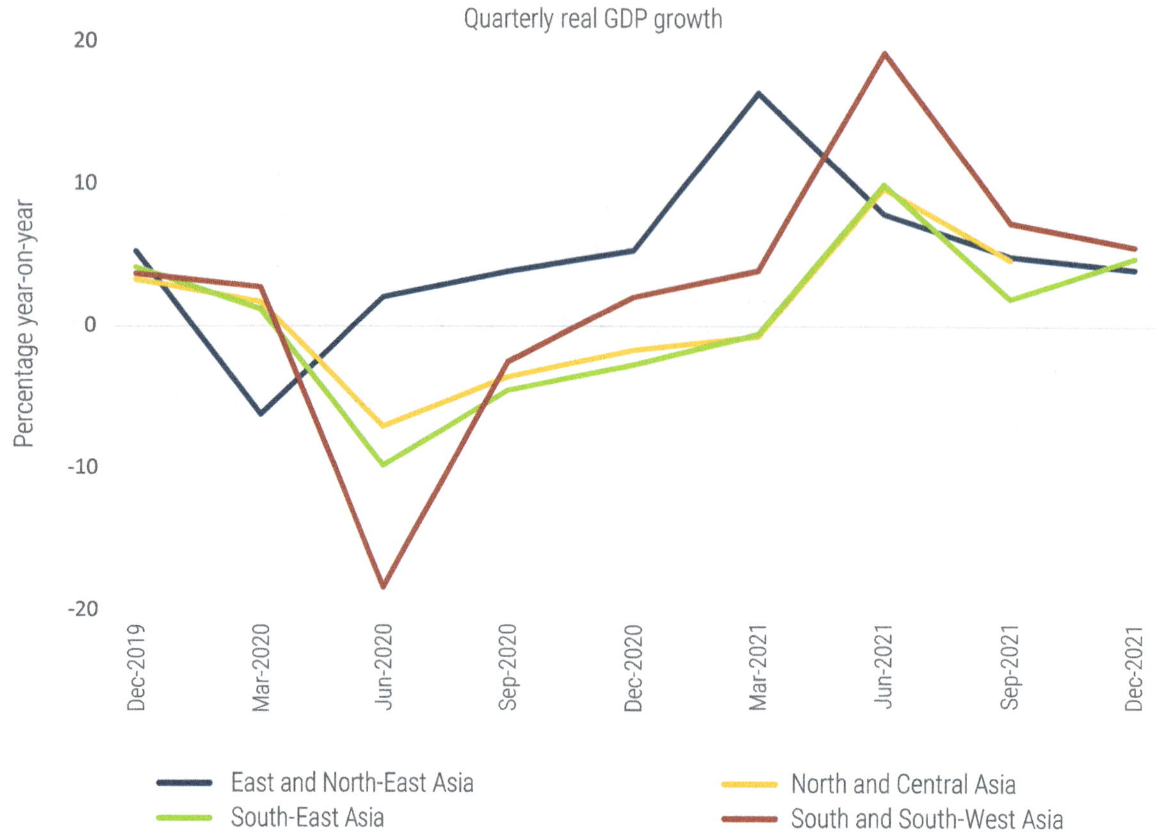

Source: Based on CEIC (accessed on 4 March 2022).
Note: Subregional aggregates are the weighted average, based on 28 economies in Asia and the Pacific for which quarterly GDP data are available.

FIGURE 2.3
Strong external demand led to upturns in trade and manufacturing in the region
(a) Monthly export volume index

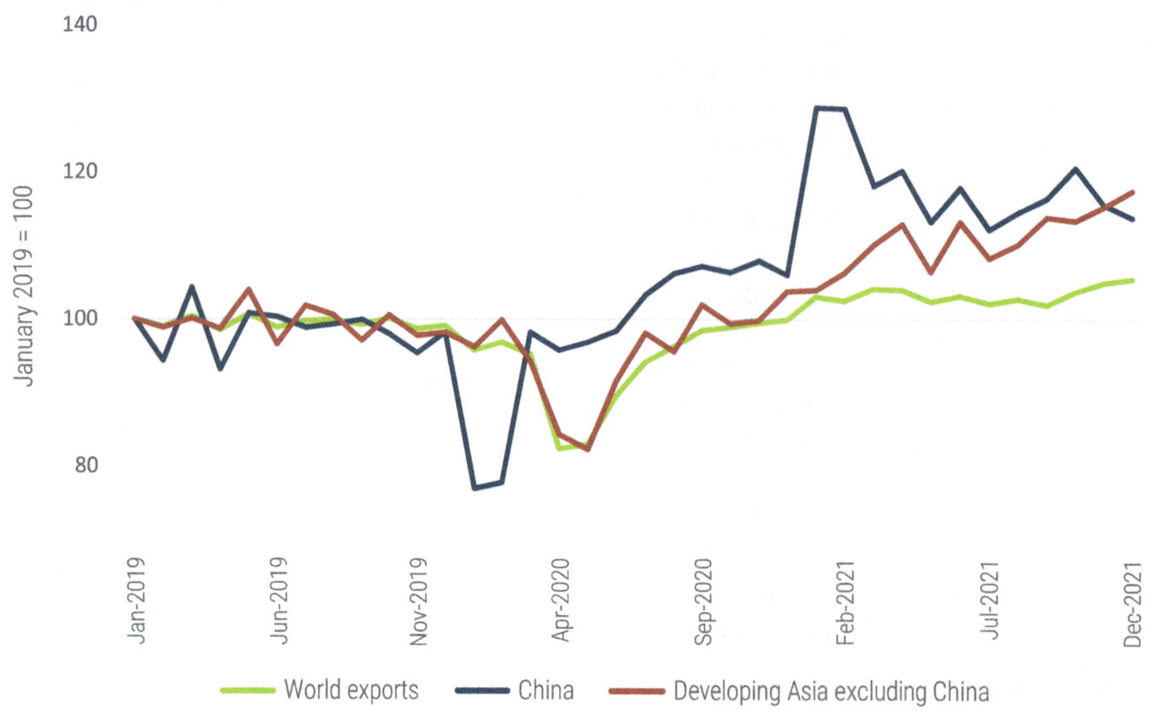

(b) Exports from developing countries in Asia to rest of the world

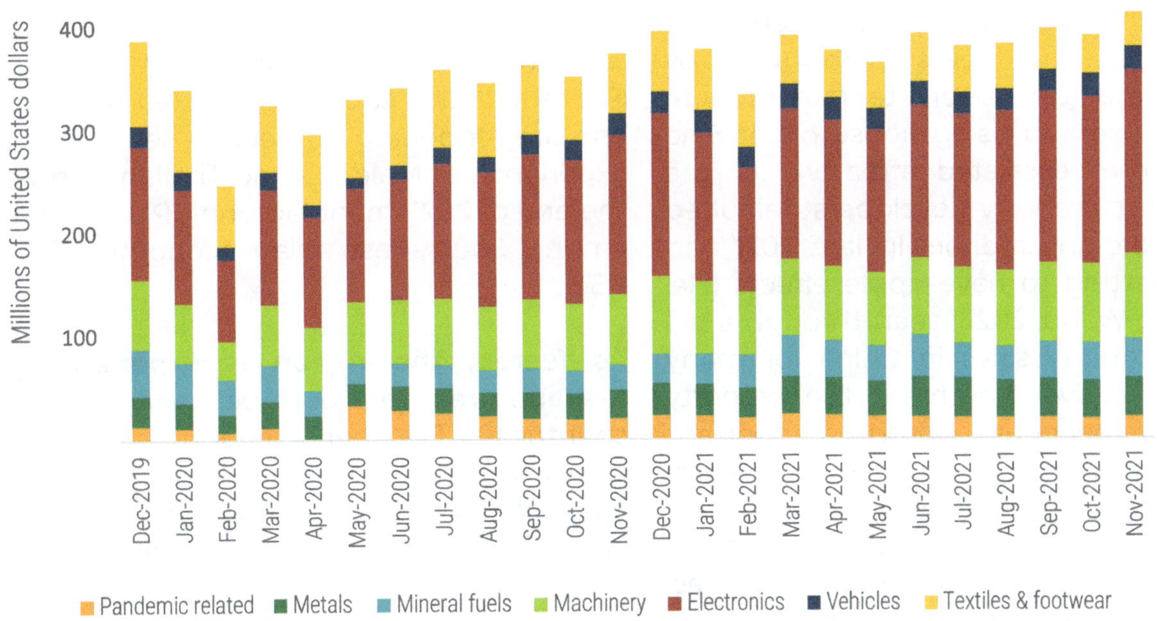

(c) Manufacturing purchasing managers' index for selected countries in the Asia-Pacific region[a]

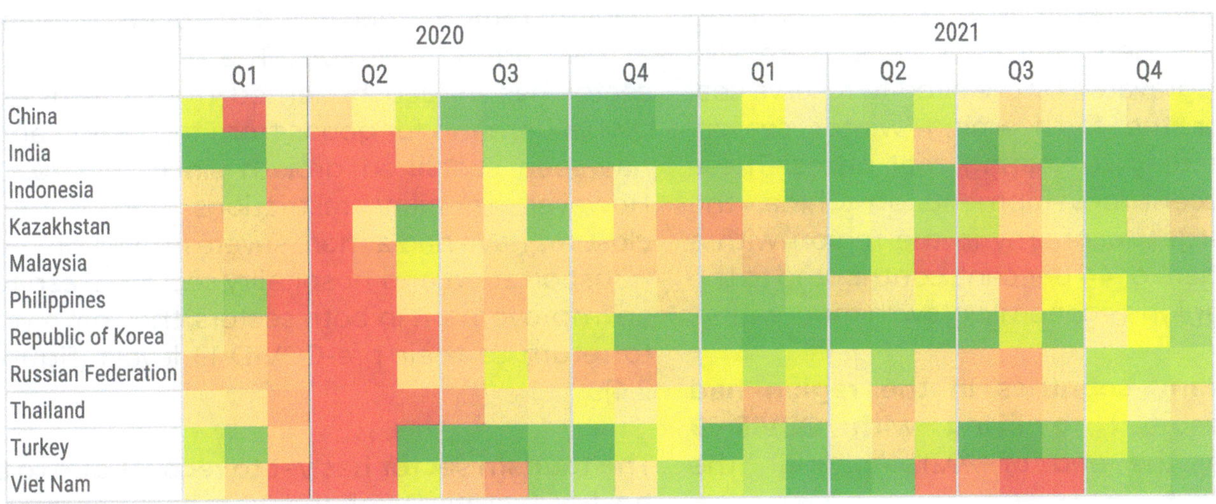

Source: ESCAP based on CEIC, CPB Netherlands Bureau for Economic Policy Analysis (as of 28 February 2022); and International Trade Centre, Trade map (accessed on 4 March 2022).

[a] Purchasing managers' index (PMI) reading above 50 indicates expansion (green). Readings below 50 indicate contraction where yellow indicates readings between 45 and 49, while red indicates readings below 44.

impacts on investment sentiments (ISI Emerging Markets Group, 2021). The property market slowdown is a concerning development as the sector accounts for up to 30 per cent of China's GDP.[2] The property market crunch began in 2020 when the Government tried to curb excessive borrowing by property developers to rein in high leverage and rising house prices. The problem escalated after two of the largest property developers defaulted on foreign creditors in late 2021 and is starting to have ripple effects (He, 2022; Webb, 2022) seen through a fall in property sales in China for many consecutive months as the property crisis deepens. Another important policy shift was the Government's aim to cut carbon emissions, which led to coal and power shortages, further disrupting manufacturing activities. China's target to lower carbon emissions means transitioning away from coal to cleaner options, such as gas, thereby lowering coal production. Yet, coal still dominates the energy mix, accounting for up to 60 per cent of electricity generation.[3] Dwindling coal inventories in 2021, in part associated with geopolitical tensions, were also aggravated by the need to reserve coal for the forthcoming winter season, leading to soaring coal prices. These recent developments in China, the largest economy in the region with a share of 44 per cent, contributed to the region's economic growth moderation.

Many countries in the region had resorted to living with COVID-19 by the end of 2021. Although the Delta outbreak has largely subsided in the region, the persistence of the pandemic across the globe continued to have adverse spillovers on the region through the virtual cessation of tourism and border closures. Most countries in the region have adapted to recurring outbreaks and resorted to targeted restrictions to facilitate living with COVID-19. Countries have cautiously relaxed restrictions and are reopening borders, as seen from the experience of Maldives and Thailand. Towards the end of 2021, manufacturing PMI picked up among South-East Asian economies (figure 2.3c).

As feared, the region is experiencing a K-shaped recovery both between and within countries. Between countries, different recovery trajectories, unequal vaccine access and differences in stimulus measures are observed. Within countries, vast differences in recovery among sectors and opportunity gaps among sections of society are contributing to increased poverty and inequalities, undermining progress on achieving the Sustainable Development Goal of ending extreme poverty.

In the developing countries in the Asia-Pacific region, recovery has been uneven across different sectors. The manufacturing sector has indeed benefited from the rising global demand for goods from the region and has seen sustained growth since mid-2020. However, mobility restrictions and border closures have had a more severe impact on the transportation and hospitality sectors. Despite an improvement in both sectors, they have yet to return to their pre-COVID-19 levels (figure 2.4).

The tourism sector has yet to recover due to a host of factors. As of end-2021, approximately 65 per cent of borders were still closed (UNWTO, 2021). Tourist arrivals in Asia and the Pacific are 92 per cent below pre-pandemic levels (figure 2.5), although improvements were seen in the last months of 2021. Rigid and inconsistent requirements for entry, such as

2 Some estimates put the sector's share in GDP at about 30 per cent, which takes into account construction and other property-related goods and services.

3 For additional details, see Our World in Data (www.ourworldindata.org) based on data from the BP Statistical Review of World Energy (www.bp.com/en/global/corporate/energy-economics/statistical-review-of-world-energy.html) (accessed on 8 October 2021).

FIGURE 2.4
Recovery in consumer-facing sectors is trailing behind

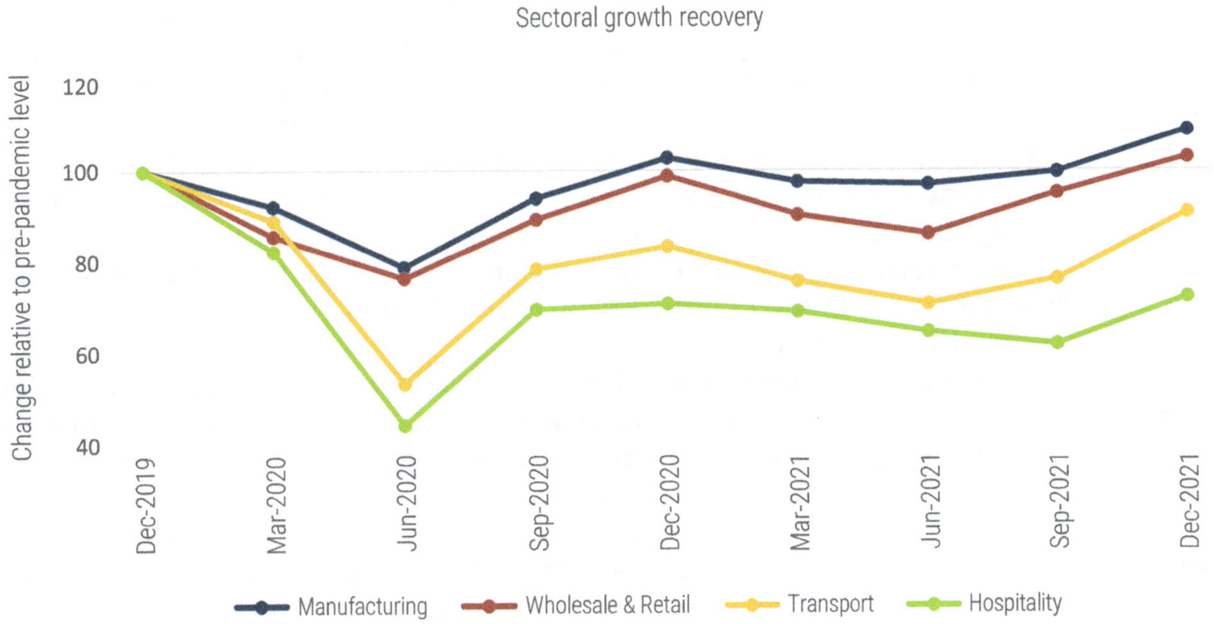

Souce: Based on CEIC (accessed on 4 March 2022).
Note: Median of 13 developing Asia-Pacific countries for which data are available.

FIGURE 2.5
International tourist arrivals remain significantly below pre-pandemic levels

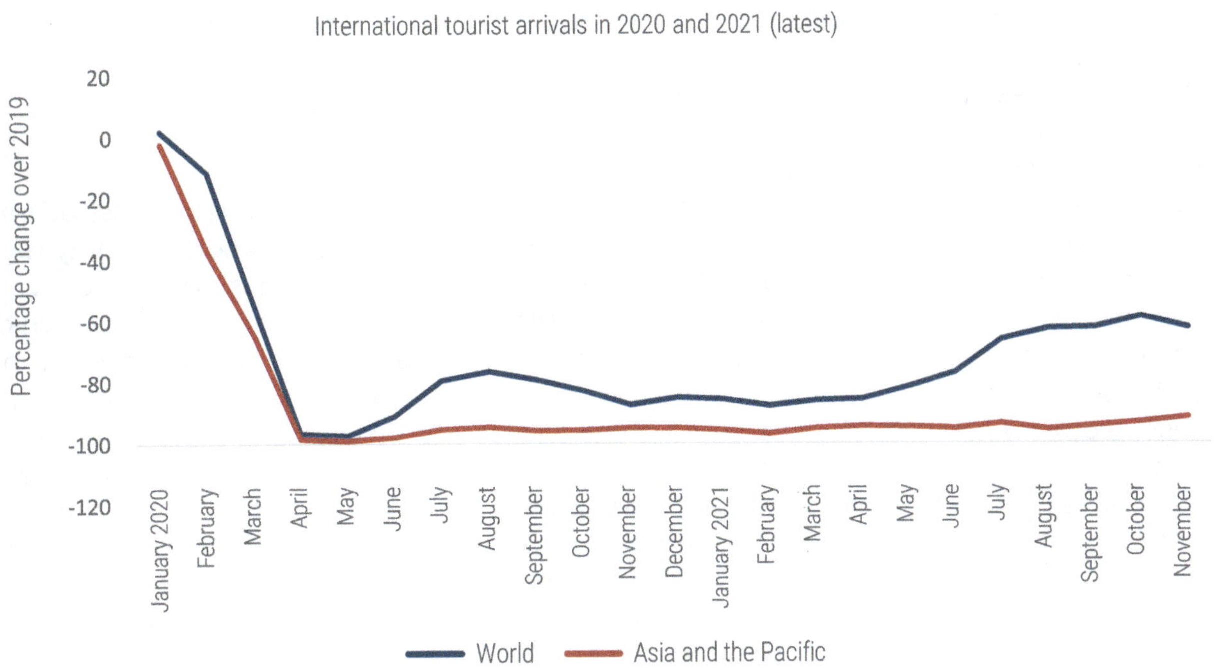

Source: UNWTO, World Tourism Barometer and Statistical Annex, January 2022.

proof and recognition of vaccination, costly pre- and post-arrival testing, contact tracing through applications and tokens, the need for COVID-19 insurance and certificates of entry are all impediments to non-essential travel (UNWTO, 2021; STR, 2021). Moreover, mandatory quarantine requirements for tourists in many countries or for citizens returning home are also a factor deterring travel. Economic factors, such as rising inflationary pressures in many economies, may also lead to a rise in airfare and accommodation costs and contribute to dampening of travel sentiments and recovery prospects of the tourism industry.

Since the onset of the pandemic, informal workers have been the first to suffer adverse impacts due to job insecurity, low skills and lack of social safety nets. Within the region, informal employment to total employment can be as high as 95 per cent. Within many countries, women make up a higher proportion of informal employment (figure 2.6). Such workers comprise a high share in such sectors as food services, tourism-related services, wholesale, and retail trade as well as construction. Women are disproportionately affected by job and income losses as they are often overrepresented in most of the aforementioned sectors along with domestic work, and labour-intensive segments of manufacturing, such as those related to garments. All these sectors were the most severely affected by the pandemic, resulting in women experiencing greater employment losses (ILO, 2021a). Based on ILO estimates, the pandemic led to a decrease of 3.8 per cent in women's employment compared with 2.9 per cent for men in Asia and the Pacific (ILO, 2021b). In 2021, the number of men in employment was projected to have offset the job losses in 2020, while that of women is likely to remain below pre-crisis levels (ILO, 2021b). Moreover, women are more likely to leave their jobs to care for families and children during prolonged closures of businesses, schools and care services. This phenomenon has been dubbed as "she-cession". Youth, on the other hand, faced fewer job prospects, lower pay and fewer opportunities for skill development, all of which will have impacts on their future productivity potential (Pritadrajati, Kusuma and Saxena, 2021).

Formal employment seems to have partially recovered in 2021, as losses in working hours declined. For instance, estimated working hour losses for Asia and the Pacific declined in 2021 to 4 per cent compared with 8.2 per cent in 2020, indicating some adjustments to pandemic-related restrictions (figure 2.7a). This translates into 71 million full-time job losses in 2021 compared with 145 million in the previous year (figure 2.7b).

The divergence in employment recovery is also seen in more rapid turnaround in sectors, such as information and communications technology, wholesale and retail segment and manufacturing. Contact-intensive sectors, such as accommodation and food services, have not seen a substantial increase (figure 2.8).

The number of poor people being pushed into extreme poverty remained considerably high in 2021. The uneven and sluggish recovery, particularly in the tourism sector, on which many economies in the region are highly reliant, as well as other sectors that employ a high share of informal workers, has contributed to millions of people being pushed into poverty across the region. According to latest estimates, an additional 85 million people[4] have been pushed into extreme poverty since the start of the pandemic based on the $1.90 per day threshold (figure 2.9). When considering the higher income criteria of $3.20 or $5.50 per day, poverty levels are at 156 million and 160 million,

4 For the methodology on poverty estimates, see annex I in ESCAP (2021a).

FIGURE 2.6
In many countries in the region, women account for a higher share of informal employment compared with men

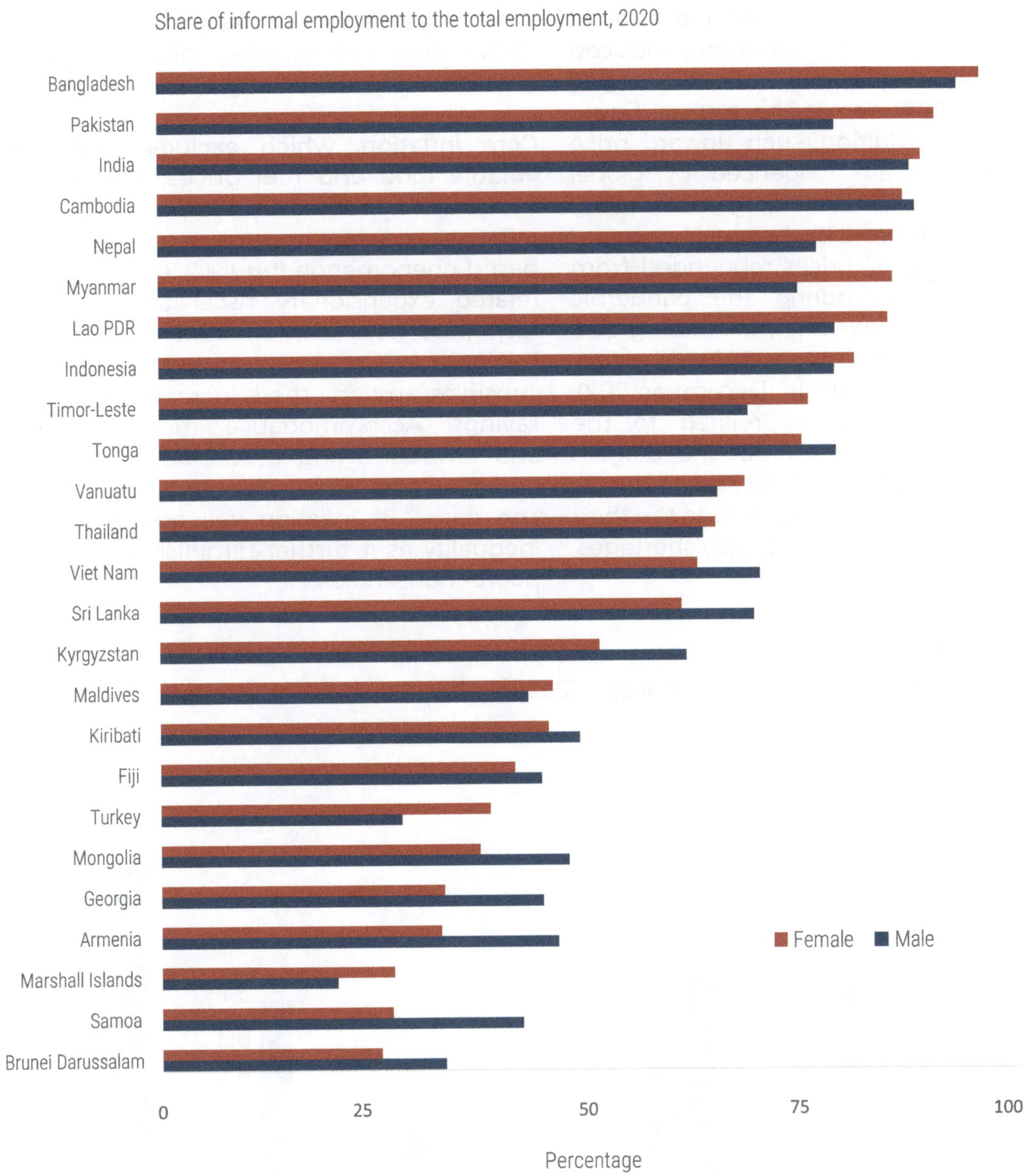

Source: ILOSTAT (20 January 2022).
Note: Data are for latest years between 2013 and 2020 for which data are available.

respectively. High and persistent poverty will erase years of progress in poverty reduction.

Against the backdrop of this strong yet nascent and uneven economic recovery and pandemic-induced supply disruptions, inflation edged up in 2021 across the region (figure 2.10). In addition, such upward price pressures are influenced by global factors, such as rising commodity prices (figure 2.11). As global demand recovered, oil prices rebounded from record lows during the pandemic to a three-year high, surpassing $80 per barrel in October 2021. Oil prices fell back slightly in December 2021, reflecting concerns related to the Omicron variant but rebounded again at the start of 2022. Coal and gas prices also surged to record levels in the third quarter of 2021 amid supply shortages. The overall food price index has reached a 10-year high and was up by 28 per cent above 2020 levels. Pandemic-induced disruptions in production and transport, including high shipping costs, also translate into higher costs of goods. Within many developing Asia-Pacific countries, currency depreciation also contributed to inflationary pressures.

Core inflation, which excludes the more volatile food and fuel prices, also showed moderate increases in 2021, indicating that inflation may be becoming a more broad-based phenomenon (figure 2.10b). Pandemic-related expansionary fiscal and monetary responses have also affected inflation. Cash handouts, wage-subsidy schemes, utility bill subsidies, among others, increased household savings. Accommodative monetary policy and low borrowing cost induced spending and investments, leading to rising inflation. The surge in inflation will adversely affect inequality as it further diminishes income of poorer households.

FIGURE 2.7
Employment did not fully recover in 2021

(a) Working hours lost due to COVID-19

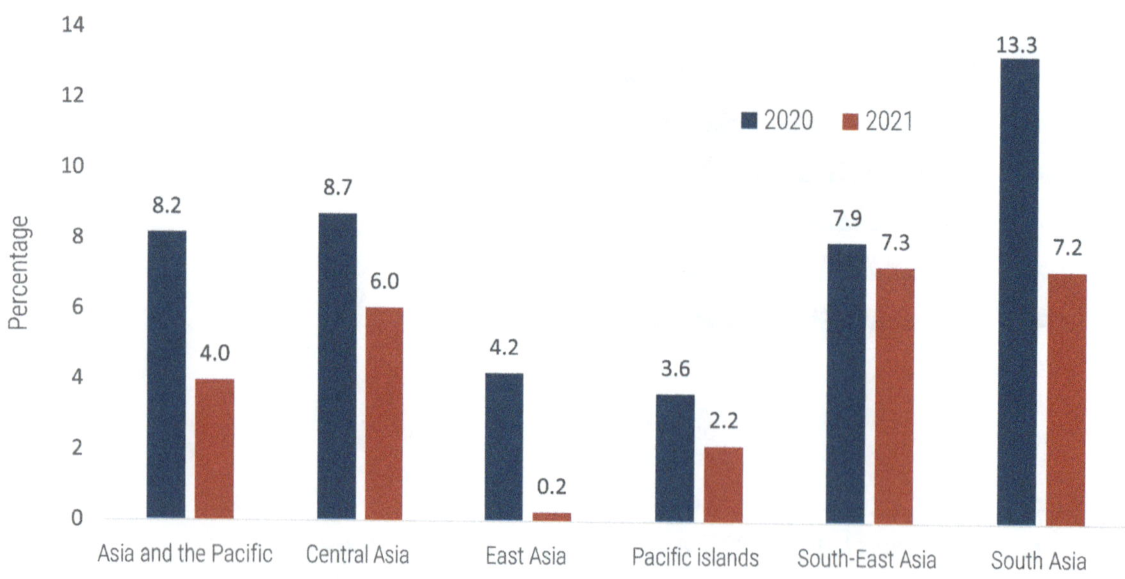

(b) Equivalent number of full-time jobs lost (48 hours/week)

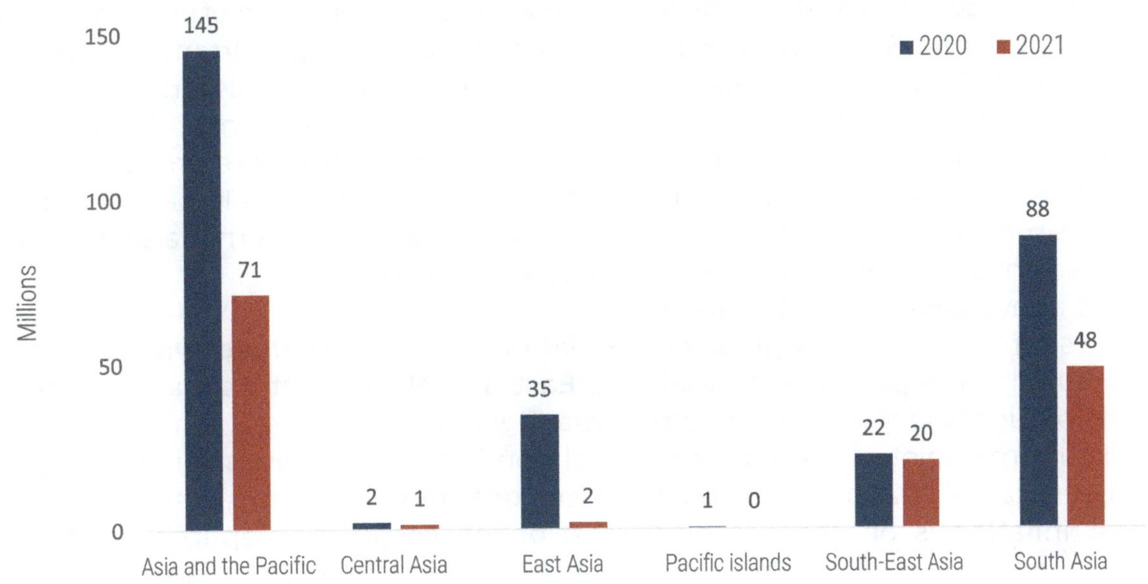

Source: ESCAP, based on ILOSTAT Database (16 February 2022).

FIGURE 2.8
Employment recovery is divergent across sectors in developing countries in the Asia-Pacific region

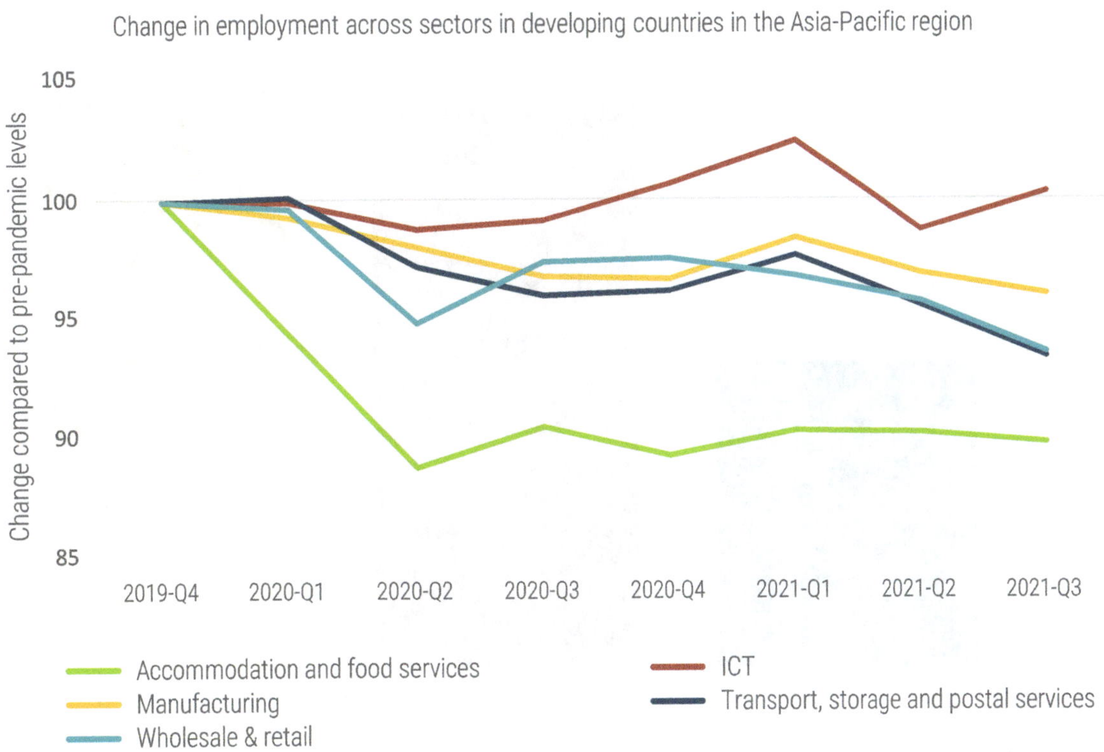

Source: Based on CEIC (accessed on 4 March 2022).
Note: Median of 15 countries for which data are available.

Rising inflation has also surpassed central bank targets in a number of countries in the region (figure 2.12) particularly those in North and Central Asia and South and South-West Asia. In North and Central Asia, inflation was influenced by rising food prices, currency depreciation and higher demand for goods as restrictions were relaxed. Similarly, inflation in major economies in South and South-West Asia was above central banks' targets due to rising food and energy prices. Easing supply disruptions and weak demand brought India's inflation down towards the midpoint of the target in the second half of 2021 but latest data suggest inflation is on the rise and signs of price pressures in non-food segments, such as clothing, health and transport, are evident (Verma, 2022). In Pakistan, withdrawal of tax exemptions on a host of items has pushed up inflation along with currency depreciation concerns, prompting the central bank to raise the interest rate. In Sri Lanka, there are signs of inflation becoming more broad-based with core inflation rising above 10 per cent coupled with depreciation concerns, also leading to interest rate hikes.

Inflation is more subdued within countries in East and North-East Asia and South-East Asia (figure 2.10). Domestic factors, such as the typhoon in the Philippines bumping up food prices or rising domestic housing rentals and cost of services in the Republic of Korea, are also influencing inflation dynamics.

FIGURE 2.9
Increase in poverty due to the pandemic

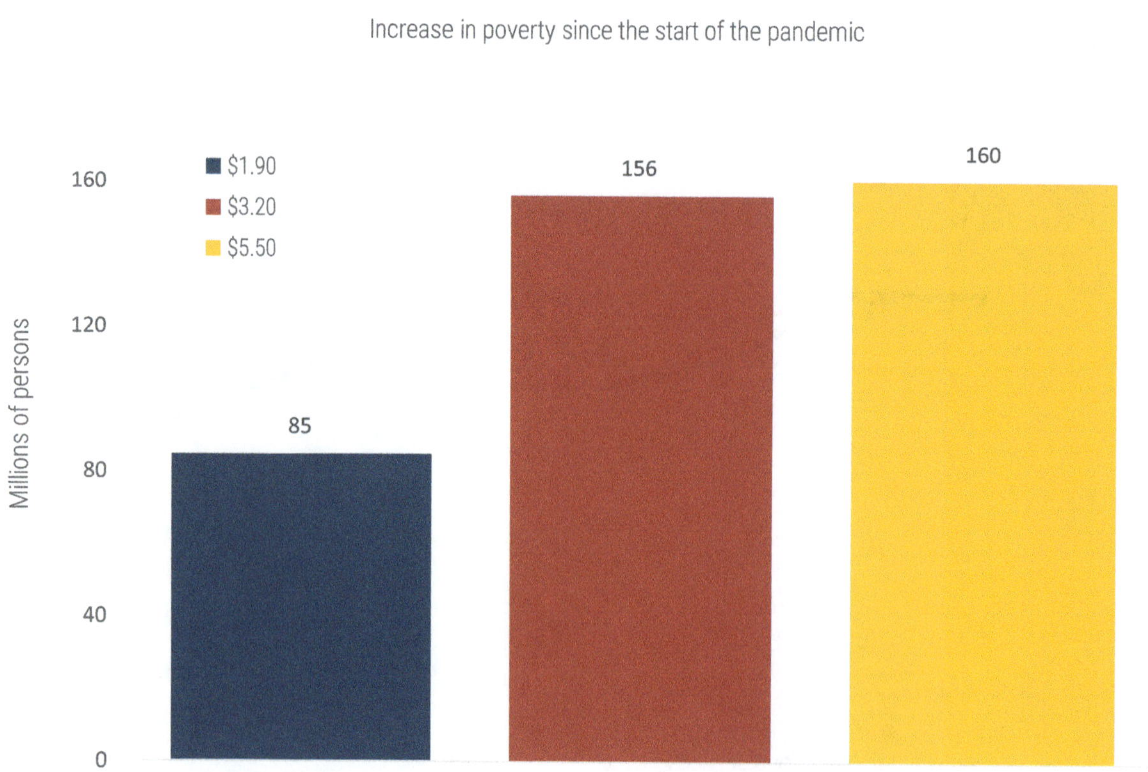

Source: ESCAP estimates.

FIGURE 2.10

Inflation rose across developing countries in the Asia-Pacific region in 2021

(a) Headline inflation by subregion

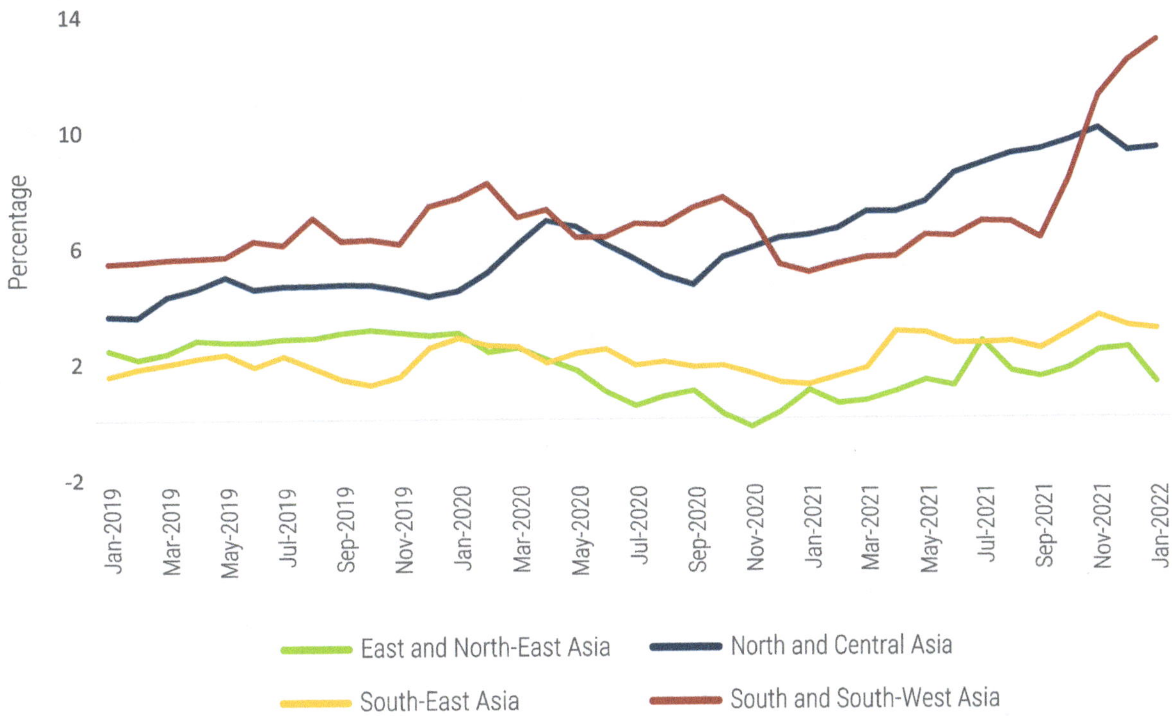

(b) Headline, core and food inflation

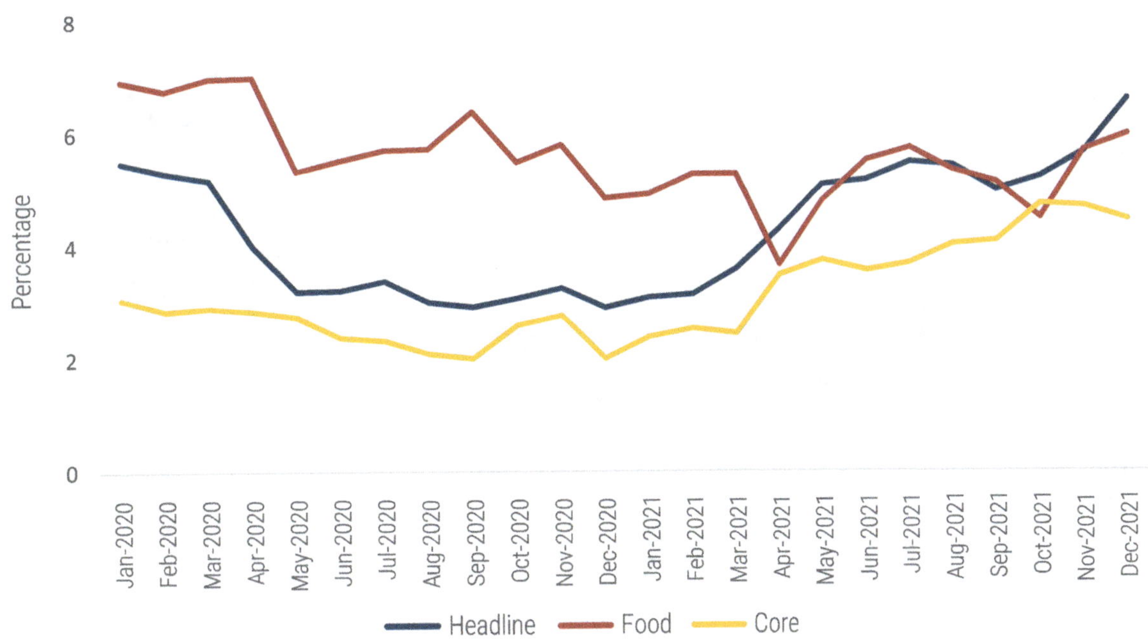

Source: CEIC (accessed on 4 March 2022).
Note: Developing Asia-Pacific headline and food inflation is based on median of 30 countries; core inflation is based on a median of 19 countries.

FIGURE 2.11
Global commodity prices have risen
(a) Global oil and commodity prices

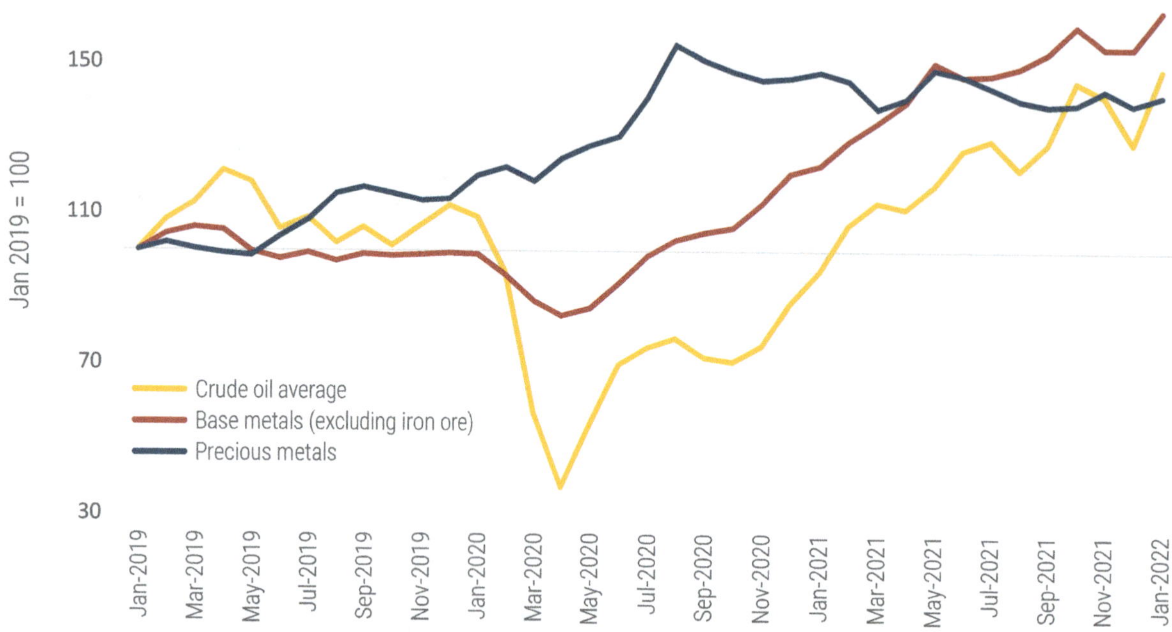

(b) FAO world food price index

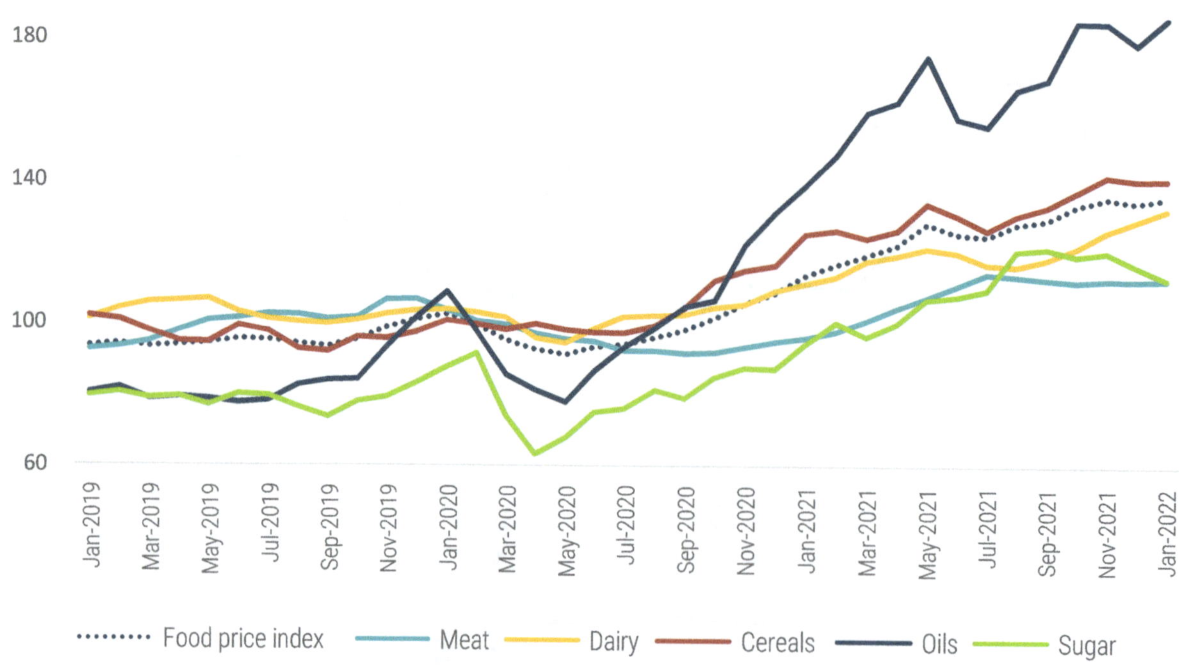

Source: CEIC and FAO (accessed on 4 March 2022).

FIGURE 2.12
Inflation surpassed targets in many countries in the region

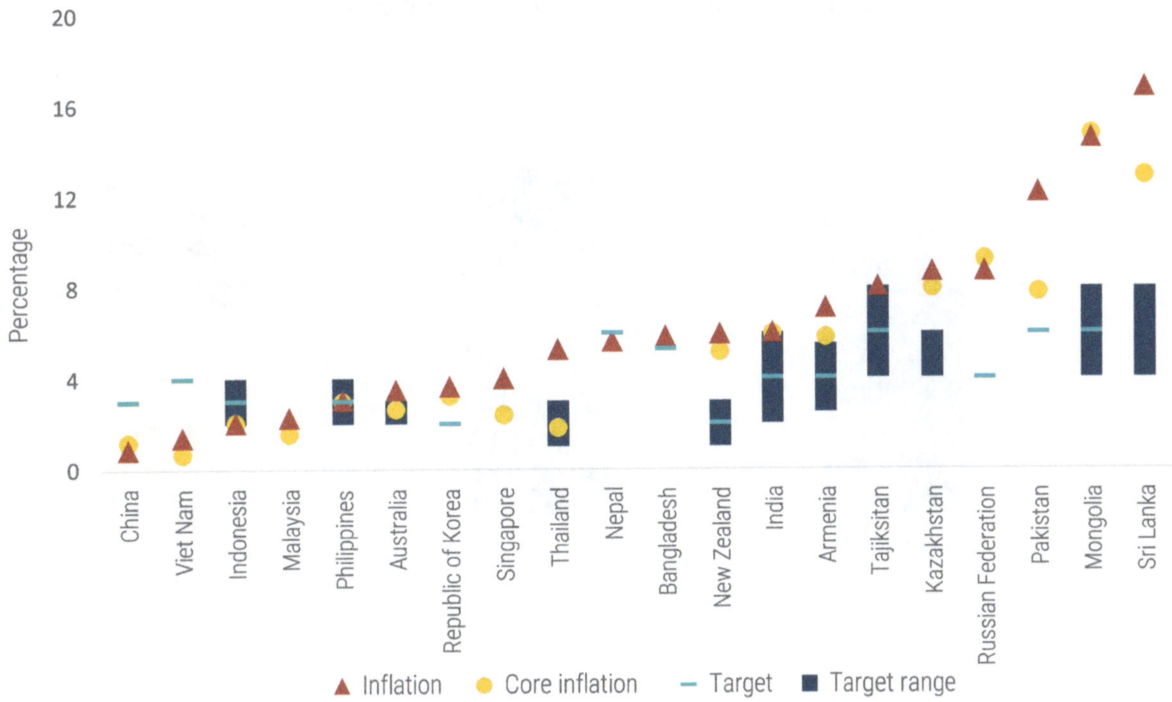

Source: CEIC (accessed on 4 March 2022) and Central Bank News, CentralBankNews.info.
Note: Inflation and core inflation are for the latest month available between December 2021 and February 2022.

In response to rising inflationary pressures, monetary policy has become less accommodative in the region, with most central banks either having increased policy interest rates or kept them unchanged during 2021(figure 2.13a). Nevertheless, China reduced its reserve requirement ratio in early December 2021 to inject $188 billion for business and household loans (Choudhury, 2022). Later in December the central bank reduced its loan prime rate by 5 basis points for the first time since April 2020 in order to reduce the interest burden, reinforcing the notion that it is open to keeping rates accommodative. In Thailand, despite a recent rebound in inflation, the central bank has left the policy rate unchanged in view of the fragile economic recovery and sluggish tourism sector recovery.

Fiscal policy remained supportive across developing countries in the Asia-Pacific region in 2021 (figure 2.13b). The average fiscal deficit in 2021 at 5.2 per cent of GDP remained relatively unchanged from the deficit of 5.3 per cent in 2020. Spending on health measures remained a priority in most of the countries as they were affected by successive waves of COVID-19 infection along with additional spending on vaccinations. Responses, such as unemployment benefits, wage subsidies, measures to support firms and small businesses, or cash handouts, continued or were expanded through 2021. Spending on emergency relief or crisis response has been reduced in some countries while some have shifted spending towards supporting recovery in such areas as job training, digitization, boosting tourism recovery, or to support safe reopening.

FIGURE 2.13
Fiscal and monetary policies remained accommodative in 2021

(a) Central bank interest rate decisions in developing Asia-Pacific countries

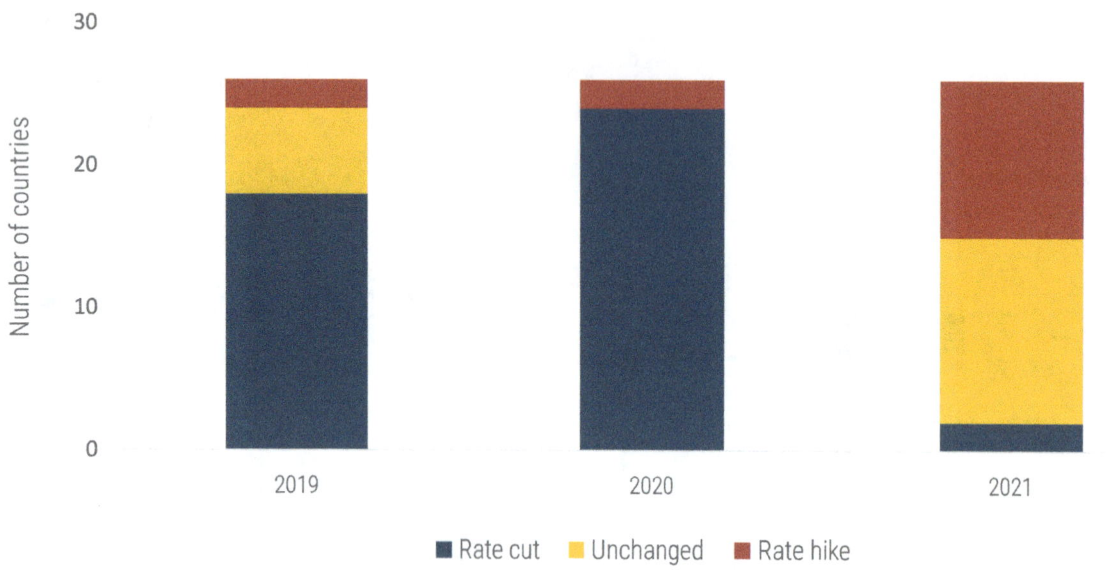

(b) Fiscal balalance in developing Asia-Pacific countries

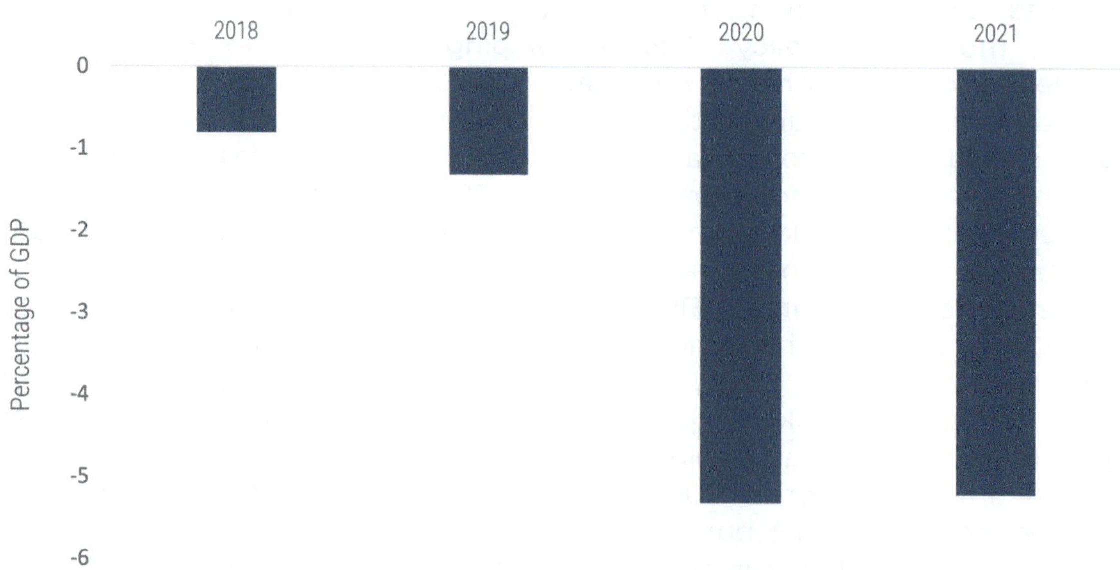

Source: IMF, Fiscal Monitor Database, October 2021, and CEIC (accessed on 4 March 2022).
Note: Central bank interest rates decisions are based on policy rate data for 26 countries in developing countries in the Asia-Pacific region, and fiscal balance for developing Asia-Pacific countries is based on a median of countries in developing Asia-Pacific countries.

BOX 2.1

Subregional perspectives

East and North-East Asia: Economic growth rebounded strongly in early 2021 as major countries, China and the Republic of Korea, were well ahead in terms of pandemic management, with shorter lockdowns or having avoided lockdowns entirely in the case of the Republic of Korea. Both countries also benefited from the global recovery, which led to a surge in export demand for consumer goods, electronics, semiconductors and automobiles. Manufacturing activities surged in line with export demand. Border closures have caused a challenging environment for Hong Kong, China, as a business and financial hub and have had severe impacts on tourism in Macau, China. Mining recovered strongly in Mongolia on the back of higher global commodity prices. China's growth moderated in the second half of 2021 due to regulatory tightening in various sectors, which weighed on sentiments and economic activities. China grew by 8.1 per cent in 2021 despite moderation in the last two quarters. Investments and private consumption are expected to pick up towards the end of 2022 as countries move closer to normalization. Inflation edged up broadly among countries in East and North-East Asia primarily driven by supply-side pressure from elevated food and fuel prices. Inflationary pressures are expected to continue in 2022 and will ease towards the latter half of the year as supply-side pressures ease. Demand-side pressures will be contained by elevated unemployment and weak wages.

North and Central Asia: Countries in the subregion rebounded in 2021 from contractions in 2020 underpinned by higher commodity prices and increased global demand for commodities. Private consumption was the main driver of growth in the majority of economies. The Delta variant and restrictions also weighed on the pace of recovery in 2021. In Kazakhstan, higher oil prices, expansion of industry and services supported growth in domestic demand as restrictions eased. In the Russian Federation, growth expanded in the first half from a low base, but the Delta variant wave constrained growth in the latter half. The growth outlook for countries in the subregion will be significantly influenced by the ongoing

Russia-Ukraine conflict. The Russian Federation is likely to suffer the largest impact due to various sanctions being imposed, with significant spillovers to countries in the North and Central Asian subregion through trade and remittance linkages. Countries that have a higher dependency on trade and remittances with the Russian Federation will see their growth moderate in 2022 while net oil exporters will benefit from higher oil prices. Inflation increased above central bank targets across the subregion, driven by high global food prices and rising domestic demand, prompting interest rate increases in almost all countries throughout 2021. Inflation will likely remain high within the subregion due to higher costs for food, fuel, and shortages of goods due to trade disruptions. A provisional assessment of potential economic impact of the Russia-Ukraine conflict is provided in box 2.3.

South and South-West Asia: The Delta variant outbreak around May 2021 disrupted manufacturing and trade in Bangladesh, India, Nepal and Sri Lanka. The economic setback in countries in the subregion was brief. This was particularly the case in India, as the country resorted to more localized and targeted restrictions compared with the hard lockdowns of 2020. Manufacturing PMI in India moved into expansionary territory in July after only a month of decline. Private consumption was the main driver of growth in India, which also influenced activities in its trading partners. Tourism recovery is still tepid but did somewhat support activities in Bhutan, Maldives and Nepal. Hydropower projects supported growth in Bhutan and investments in infrastructure projects supported growth in Pakistan and Sri Lanka. Resilient remittance flows propped up domestic consumption in Nepal and Bangladesh, which also benefited from strong global demand for apparel. Growth is expected to pick up in 2022 as a result of improved tourism prospects, robust exports and improving private consumption. Inflation in the subregion increased slightly in 2021 reflecting supply chain bottlenecks and higher food prices, with larger impacts on Pakistan and Sri Lanka due to their weak currencies. Monetary tightening and easing supply disruptions will help moderate prices. Record high inflation in the Islamic Republic of Iran and Turkey are due to sanctions-related shortages and steep depreciation in the former and currency volatility in the latter. The sharp reduction in foreign aid, a banking crisis and soaring food prices will mean growth contraction and high inflation in Afghanistan.

South-East Asia: South-East Asia's exports benefited from strong global demand for electronics, auto parts and chemicals in the first quarter of 2021. The subregion grappled with the Delta variant during most of the second and third quarter of 2021 through lockdowns and disruptions to tourism and manufacturing, resulting in a global supply bottleneck. As the Delta variant receded in the last quarter of the year, countries gradually lifted restrictions and started to live with COVID-19. Continued recovery will be seen in 2022, with a weaker than expected first quarter due to the Omicron variant triggering a brief round of restrictions. Demand for exports from the subregion will continue to drive growth while border reopening, as pioneered by Thailand, is an encouraging sign for tourism recovery. With many of the restrictions expected to be lifted, private consumption will strengthen. Inflationary pressures have been influenced by high global food and oil prices. Typhoon Rai drove up food prices in the Philippines along with the African Swine Flu, which also raised meat prices in Thailand and Viet Nam. As inflation is more muted in South-East Asia and core inflation remains modest, central banks within the subregion will keep rates low to support recovery.

Pacific islands: The Pacific weathered another year of contraction in 2021 due to the adverse impact of the pandemic and border restrictions, which have had adverse impacts on tourism-dependent economies, such as Cook Islands, Fiji, Palau, Samoa, Tonga and Vanuatu. Travel bubbles were implemented in early to mid-2021 between Palau and Taiwan Province of China; Cook Islands and New Zealand; and New Zealand and Australia, among others. Some were able to resume towards the end of 2021 or are planned for early or mid-2022. Fiji opened its border to fully vaccinated tourists from about 50 partner countries in December 2021. Inflows of international tourists and resumption of the seasonal workers programme with Australia and New Zealand will boost private consumption through tourism receipts and remittance inflows for Kiribati and Tuvalu. Growth is expected to rebound in 2022 as tourism resumes while ongoing public infrastructure projects will also drive growth in Fiji, Samoa and Tonga, as will a liquified natural gas project in Papua New Guinea. Inflation in the Pacific is heavily influenced by food and transport costs, while weak currencies and the rebound in domestic demand will drive up inflation in 2022.

Despite strong rebounds in the growth of output in developing Asia-Pacific countries in 2021, supported by monetary and fiscal policies, the level of output was still about 2 per cent below the pre-pandemic path as of end-2021 (figure 2.14). The strong recovery momentum in the growth rate in 2021 is partly a reflection of the low base and low level of output in 2020.[5] Nevertheless, from a policy perspective, the focus should be not just on trying to boost the level of output through rapid economic growth; rather, policymakers need to think beyond GDP and also try and improve the quality of growth by improving inclusiveness and sustainability aspects of economic activities.

2.3 Outlook for developing countries in Asia and the Pacific – riddled with uncertainty

Developing Asia-Pacific economies are projected to grow, on average, by 4.5 per cent in 2022 and 5 per cent in 2023, a more moderate pace compared with 2021 as the base effect gradually disappears (table 2.1). As discussed in the previous section, economic recovery remains nascent and uneven, and economic growth in the developing countries in the Asia-Pacific region is likely to remain below pre-pandemic trends in 2022 and 2023 as well (figure 2.15). The near-term prospect is constrained by a new outbreak of the Omicron variant, having triggered another round of restrictions and border closures. At the same time, diminishing fiscal space in many developing countries is putting a question mark on the prospects of continued fiscal support. Rising inflationary pressures, along with the likelihood of increases in interest rates, may also put the brakes on support coming from the monetary policy stance. All in all, the output loss for the region is estimated to be at $2 trillion between 2020 and 2022.

Renewed restrictions and delayed border openings will set back employment and demand-side recovery (figure 2.16). Physical distancing and mobility restrictions will further dampen the consumer-facing sectors while delayed border openings have repercussions on employment in countries where the share of jobs in travel and tourism are higher than 20 per cent, many of which are small island developing States and least developed countries (WTTC, 2021).[6]

The region's exports are likely to continue to support economic growth but at a more moderate pace given declining demand in other regions of the world. The extent and duration of the ongoing supply shortages is still uncertain but is anticipated to recede as more countries reopen and demand shifts away from goods to services and back orders are filled.

The full resumption of economic activities will be influenced by many factors, including the availability of vaccines, the stringency of restrictions, workplace closures, and monetary and fiscal policy positions that have supported enterprises and the labour force so far. Nevertheless, labour markets will take time to recover. On the demand side, firms remain reluctant to hire new workers as repeated outbreaks prevent full reopening, and workers remain concerned about returning to work due to health risks and uncertainties. Labour

5 Owing to economic contraction, the level of output was much lower in 2020. Because the growth rate for 2021 is calculated as the change in level of output between 2021 and 2020 (the numerator) over the level of output in 2020 (the denominator or base), it will be higher due to the statistical definition of growth rate. Thus, while the rate of economic growth in 2021 may seem to have recovered, it is the level of output that should matter from the policy standpoint. In this vein, the level of output in 2021 remained lower than pre-COVID-19 levels (see figure 2.14)

6 Cambodia; Fiji; Macau, China; Maldives; the Philippines; Thailand; and Vanuatu.

FIGURE 2.14
Output levels in the majority of economies were still below pre-pandemic levels and trend

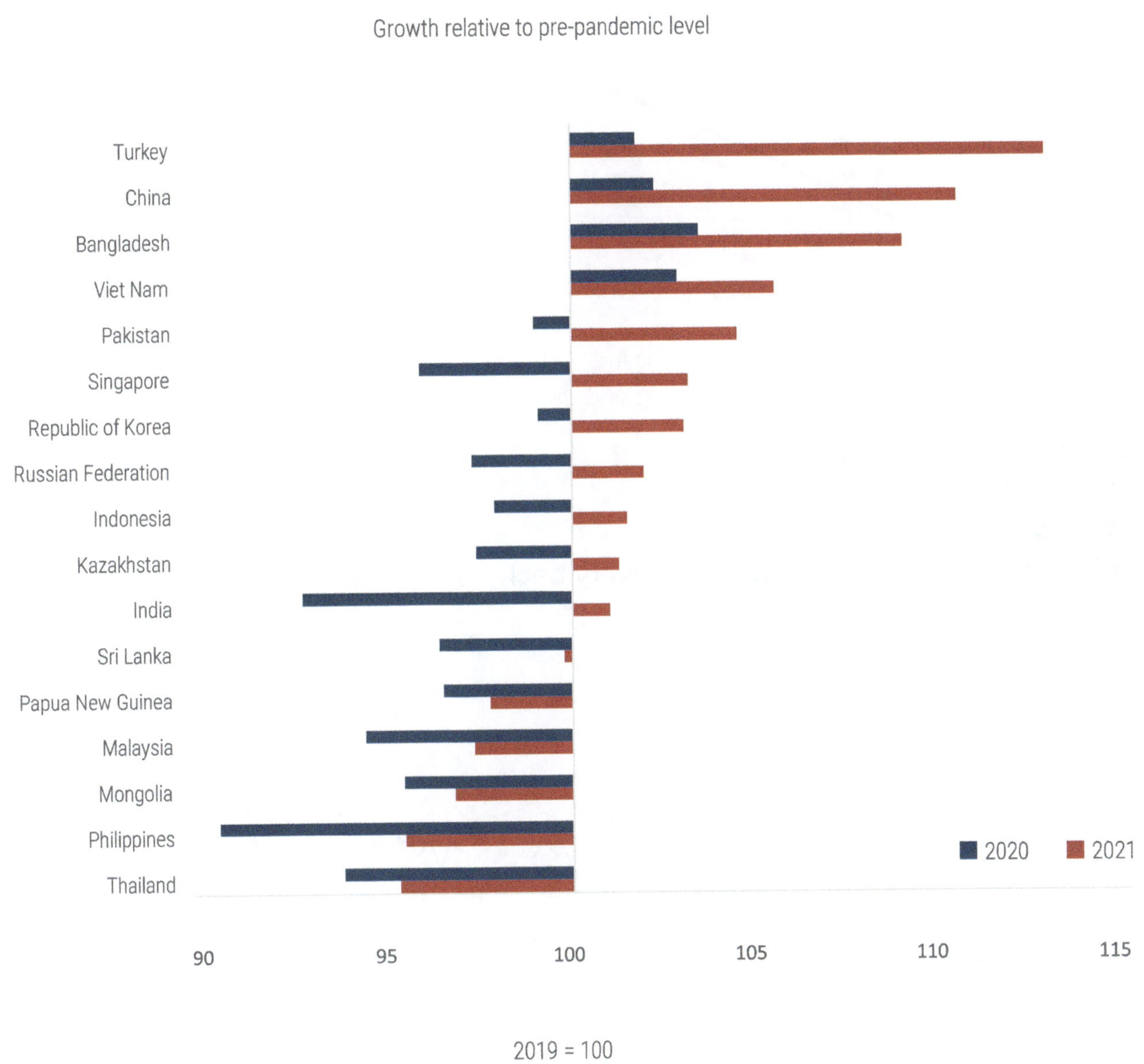

Source: Based on ESCAP estimates and projections.

FIGURE 2.15
The pandemic has shifted the economic output trend downwards

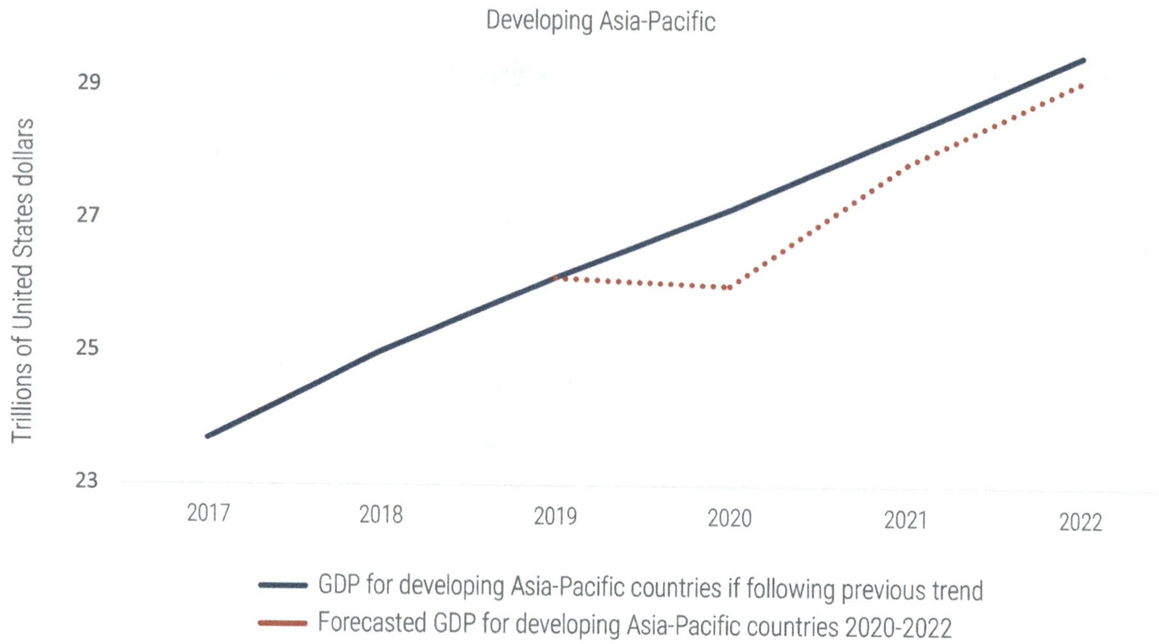

Source: ESCAP estimates and projections.

FIGURE 2.16
Mobility restrictions will set the recovery back

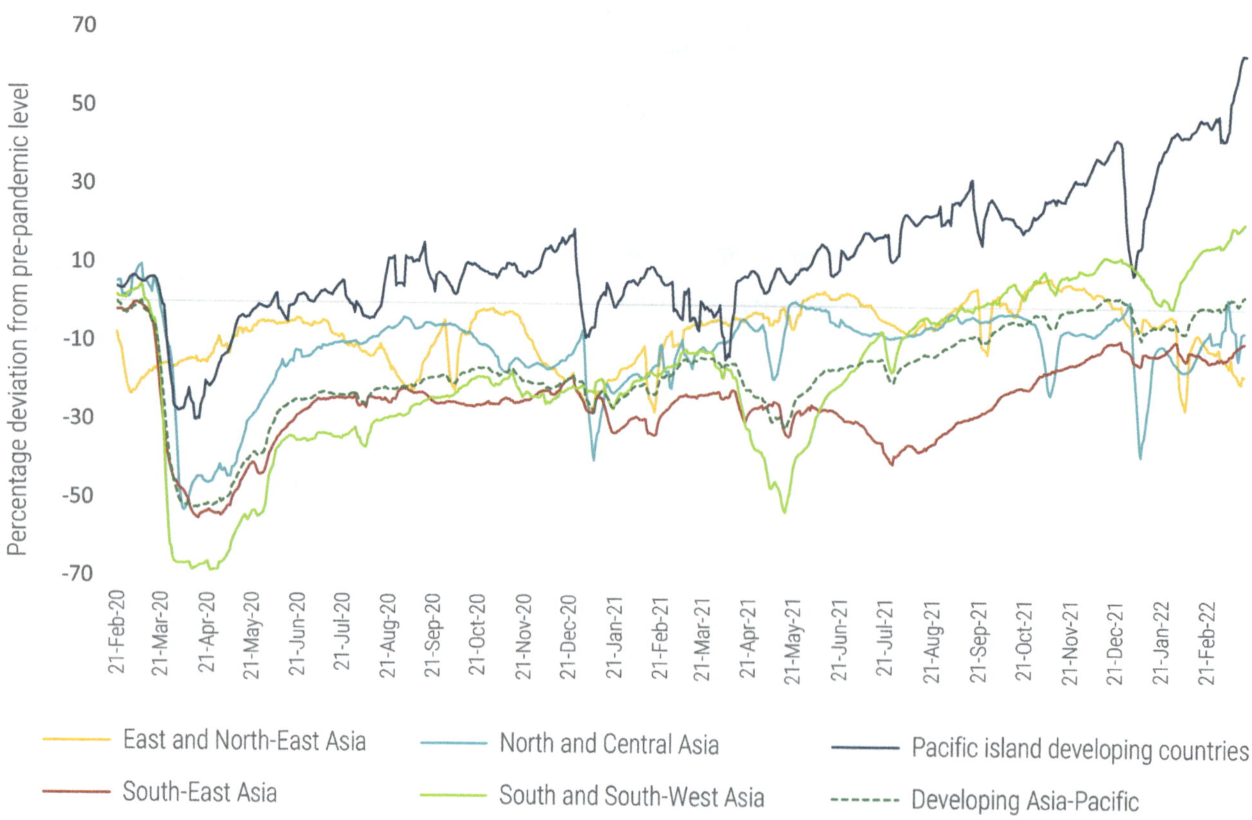

Source: CEIC, based on Google mobility index (accessed on 16 March 2022).
Note: The mobility index shows a seven-day moving average of an equally weighted index of retail and recreation, transit and workplaces.

TABLE 2.1
Selected economies in the ESCAP region: rates of economic growth and inflation, 2020-2023

	Real GDP growth				Inflation[a]			
	2020	2021	2022[b]	2023[c]	2020	2021	2022[b]	2023[c]
Total ESCAP region	**-1.0**	**6.2**	**4.3**	**4.4**	**3.1**	**3.0**	**4.5**	**3.6**
Developing ESCAP economies[d]	**-0.3**	**7.1**	**4.5**	**5.0**	**3.8**	**3.6**	**5.2**	**4.1**
Developed ESCAP economies[e]	**-3.8**	**2.5**	**3.5**	**2.0**	**0.3**	**0.7**	**1.7**	**1.5**
East and North-East Asia[f]	**0.3**	**6.4**	**4.6**	**4.3**	**1.8**	**0.8**	**1.9**	**2.0**
East and North-East Asia (excluding Japan)[f]	**1.6**	**7.7**	**5.0**	**5.1**	**2.3**	**1.1**	**2.1**	**2.2**
China	2.3	8.1	5.2	5.3	2.5	0.9	2.0	2.2
Democratic People's Republic of Korea	..	..	..	..	..	..	..	..
Hong Kong, China	-6.5	6.4	3.0	3.3	0.3	1.6	2.1	3.3
Japan	-4.5	1.7	3.3	1.6	0.0	-0.2	1.0	1.1
Macao, China	-54.0	33.5	36.6	26.0	0.8	0.0	2.0	2.2
Mongolia	-4.6	1.4	5.6	6.1	3.7	7.1	8.5	9.0
Republic of Korea	-0.9	4.0	3.0	2.7	0.5	2.5	3.1	2.2
North and Central Asia[f]	**-2.3**	**4.9**	**-5.2**	**2.6**	**4.5**	**7.3**	**13.7**	**10.1**
North and Central Asia (excluding Russian Federation)[f]	**-1.1**	**5.4**	**5.5**	**4.6**	**7.9**	**9.3**	**9.8**	**7.3**
Armenia	-7.4	5.7	4.2	4.6	1.2	7.2	7.0	6.0
Azerbaijan	-4.3	5.6	4.5	4.0	2.8	6.7	11.0	6.5
Georgia	-6.2	10.1	5.5	5.0	5.2	9.6	12.0	8.0
Kazakhstan	-2.6	4.0	5.6	4.5	6.8	8.0	8.6	6.0
Kyrgyzstan	-8.6	3.6	2.6	4.1	6.3	11.9	12.0	5.0
Russian Federation	-2.7	4.8	-8.6	2.0	3.4	6.7	15.0	11.0
Tajikistan	4.5	6.0	4.0	3.4	8.6	8.0	9.0	7.0
Turkmenistan	5.9	5.3	6.0	3.7	10.0	15.2	14.0	13.0
Uzbekistan	1.9	7.4	6.3	5.6	12.9	10.9	9.6	8.1
Pacific[f]	**-2.1**	**4.6**	**4.1**	**3.0**	**1.0**	**3.0**	**3.4**	**2.5**
Pacific island developing economies[f]	**-5.4**	**-0.3**	**4.8**	**3.6**	**3.3**	**3.4**	**3.7**	**3.2**
Cook Islands	-5.9	-26.0	7.1	6.0	0.7	1.0	0.7	0.5
Fiji	-15.7	-4.1	7.0	6.0	-2.6	0.2	3.0	2.3
Kiribati	0.6	0.3	2.3	3.0	1.0	1.1	1.5	2.2
Marshall Islands	-2.6	-3.3	3.5	3.0	0.3	1.0	1.7	2.0
Micronesia (Federated States of)	-1.8	-3.2	1.0	3.0	1.6	1.9	2.0	2.0
Nauru	0.7	1.5	1.0	0.8	0.9	1.1	2.0	2.0
Palau	-10.3	-16.0	10.5	12.0	0.7	-0.3	1.0	1.5
Papua New Guinea	-3.5	1.3	4.6	3.0	4.9	4.5	4.1	3.6
Samoa	-2.6	-8.1	1.7	2.8	-1.6	-3.0	2.7	2.7
Solomon Islands	-4.3	1.0	4.5	4.5	3.0	2.6	3.5	2.1
Tonga	-0.8	-5.1	1.8	3.1	0.2	1.3	2.5	2.0
Tuvalu	1.0	2.5	3.3	3.6	1.6	4.0	4.5	4.5
Vanuatu	-6.8	1.2	3.0	4.1	2.9	4.1	3.6	2.5

	Real GDP growth				Inflation[a]			
	2020	2021	2022[b]	2023[c]	2020	2021	2022[b]	2023[c]
Developed countries in the Pacific subregion[f]	**-2.1**	**4.7**	**4.1**	**3.0**	**1.0**	**3.0**	**3.4**	**2.5**
Australia	-2.2	4.7	4.2	3.0	0.9	2.9	3.3	2.5
New Zealand	-1.0	4.4	3.3	3.3	1.7	3.9	4.3	2.5
South and South-West Asia[f,g]	**-3.5**	**8.3**	**6.6**	**5.7**	**10.2**	**11.5**	**13.4**	**8.9**
Afghanistan	-8.9	-5.8	4.8	5.6	5.6	5.9	4.7	3.9
Bangladesh	3.5	5.4	6.5	6.7	5.7	5.6	5.8	5.5
Bhutan	-0.8	-2.3	5.0	5.0	4.5	6.8	6.6	5.6
India	-7.3	9.0	9.0	7.1	6.2	5.5	5.0	4.7
Iran (Islamic Republic of)	3.4	3.0	3.5	2.6	35.9	41.0	26.0	22.0
Maldives	-33.5	31.6	12.0	9.5	-1.4	0.6	2.3	2.2
Nepal	-2.1	4.0	4.7	4.3	6.2	3.6	5.5	5.4
Pakistan	-1.0	5.6	4.5	4.1	10.7	8.9	10.5	6.5
Sri Lanka	-3.6	3.5	3.7	4.1	6.2	7.0	6.1	5.5
Turkey	1.8	11.0	2.4	3.6	12.3	19.4	35.0	17.5
South-East Asia[f]	**-3.9**	**3.3**	**5.0**	**5.2**	**1.2**	**2.3**	**3.3**	**2.8**
Brunei Darussalam	1.1	-1.5	3.0	5.0	1.9	2.0	1.5	1.0
Cambodia	-3.1	2.7	5.5	6.2	2.9	2.9	2.5	1.6
Indonesia	-2.1	3.7	5.2	5.6	2.0	1.6	3.2	2.9
Lao People's Democratic Republic	3.3	2.1	4.2	4.8	5.1	3.7	5.0	4.1
Malaysia	-5.6	3.1	5.8	4.9	-1.1	2.5	2.8	2.0
Myanmar	-3.3	-18.0	-0.8	2.5	3.9	6.1	7.5	6.5
Philippines	-9.6	5.6	6.3	6.7	2.4	4.5	3.3	3.0
Singapore	-4.1	7.6	4.1	3.3	-0.2	2.3	3.5	2.5
Thailand	-6.2	1.6	4.0	4.2	-0.8	1.2	3.0	2.5
Timor-Leste	-7.6	1.8	3.8	2.6	0.5	1.6	2.5	2.8
Viet Nam	2.9	2.6	6.5	6.7	3.2	1.8	2.9	3.2
Memorandum items:								
Least developed countries	**0.8**	**0.0**	**4.7**	**5.6**	**5.2**	**5.3**	**5.8**	**5.3**
Landlocked developing countries	**-1.3**	**4.5**	**5.4**	**4.7**	**7.6**	**8.6**	**9.1**	**7.0**
Small island developing States	**-9.1**	**3.8**	**5.7**	**4.3**	**2.5**	**3.0**	**3.5**	**3.0**

Source: ESCAP estimates and projections.

[a] Changes in the consumer price index.
[b] Estimates.
[c] Forecasts.
[d] Developing Asia-Pacific economies consist of all countries and areas listed in the table, excluding Australia, Japan and New Zealand.
[e] The group of developed Asia-Pacific economies consists of Australia, Japan and New Zealand.
[f] Aggregate growth rate calculated using GDP in 2015 United States dollars as weights.
[g] The estimates and forecasts for countries relate to fiscal years. These are defined as follows, 2021 refers to fiscal year spanning the periods 1 April 2021 to 31 March 2022 in India; 21 March 2021 to 20 March 2022 in Afghanistan and the Islamic Republic of Iran; 1 July 2020 to 30 June 2021 in Bangladesh, Bhutan and Pakistan; and 16 July 2020 to 15 July 2021 in Nepal.

supply will also be constrained by lower international labour mobility (migrants returned home, limited and higher cost of travel with additional health procedures, paperwork and quarantine may limit international labour mobility). Those who have lost their jobs and have been pushed into poverty may resort to informal employment, which has negative impacts on their future earning potential (Pritadrajati, Kusuma and Saxena, 2021).

Inflation for the region is expected to remain elevated in the near term, averaging 5.2 per cent in 2022 and subsiding to 4.1 per cent in 2023 (table 2.1). This assumes that high food and energy prices will persist amid lingering supply chain disruptions in 2022[7], further exacerbated by the Russia-Ukraine conflict (box 2.3). On the supply side, continued pandemic-related disruptions, which delay production and transport and extend the global supply constraints, are one factor that is likely to keep upward pressure on prices. Moreover, as 90 per cent of the world's merchandise is shipped by sea, the high cost of shipping by sea is likely to remain elevated due to backlogs, a strained hiring market, high fuel prices and ports struggling with labour shortages, all of which will be factors fuelling inflation (Rao and Saul, 2021).

Nevertheless, some encouraging signs are already taking shape in early 2022 with easing concerns over Omicron and several countries in the region preparing to reopen their borders to support tourism recovery, shift demand away from goods towards services and ease other constraints, such as labour mobility and transport. On the other hand, country reopenings can contribute to demand-side inflation as observed in developed countries where pent-up demand and large fiscal stimulus led to overwhelming increases in demand for goods and services. However, the magnitude of increase in demand may not be as substantial in developing Asia-Pacific countries as excess savings may not be as large due to more modest stimulus packages, weak wage growth and subdued labour market conditions. Inflationary pressures are expected to gradually decline as supply-demand imbalances diminish. However, this is contingent upon the monetary policy stance.

7 The World Bank Commodities Market Outlook (October 2021) projects crude oil prices to remain elevated in 2022 at an average of $74 per barrel before declining to $65 in 2023. Likewise, food price projections remain high in the current year and will decline slightly in 2023 but will still be higher than pre-pandemic levels.

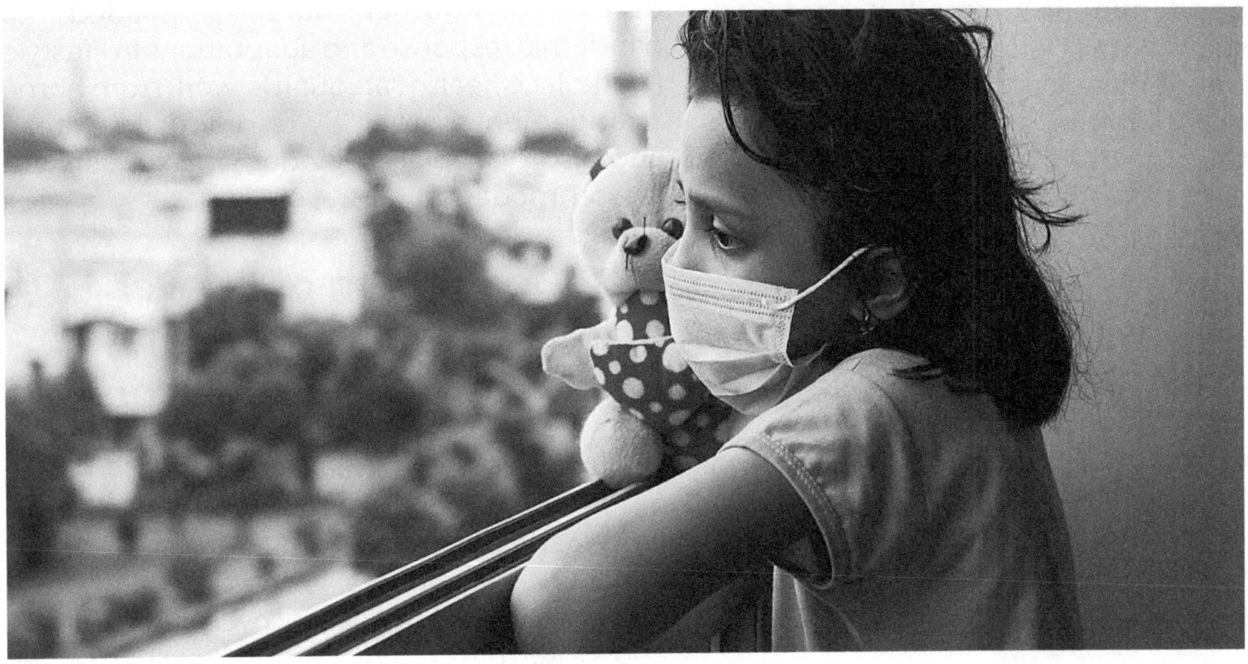

3. RISKS AND UNCERTAINTIES TO THE OUTLOOK

The region's near-term economic outlook is subject to several downside risks from pandemic-induced disruptions to mounting inflationary and macroeconomic stability concerns. The likely spillovers from China's moderation and property sector decline and the still-evolving geopolitical conflict between the Russian Federation and Ukraine cannot be ignored either.

3.1 Pandemic-related headwinds can set back the nascent recovery

COVID-19 remains the greatest threat

The emergence of more virulent variants could prolong the pandemic and derail progress as seen with Delta and Omicron. As the efficacy of vaccines remain questionable against new variants, the pandemic will linger on with some form of restrictions and distancing remaining in place. Vaccines, however, have not ensured sustained economic recovery as seen in the sharp rise in cases in developed countries with high vaccination rates. Continuation of cases, despite vaccinations, is likely to prolong restrictions on economic activity, causing uncertainty and dampening the near-term economic outlook.

Lingering supply shortages

Pandemic resurgence and continuation through new variants can disrupt economic activities and prolong supply shortages. Semiconductor shortages can have negative impacts on vehicle exports (Republic of Korea, Thailand) and economies where electronics account for more than 20 per cent of exports (China; Hong Kong, China; Philippines; Viet Nam) as seen in recent production halts. Fast-rising demand and supply disruptions in coal can disrupt factories in China and India through power outages. Supply shortages could persist even longer, leading to inflationary pressures.

Moderating export growth

Headwinds on exports are possible as a gradual recovery of production in other parts of the world may replace some of the demand for goods exports from the region. Supply bottlenecks can drive up shipping costs where global freight cost has already quintupled since early 2020 (The Economist, 2021; Rao and Saul, 2021). A surge in prices of raw materials is starting to drive up production costs and causing local production disruptions. At the same time, demand for pandemic-related goods, such as medical supplies, electronic devices and other durables needed for pandemic response and adaptations in lifestyle (workplace health safeguards, work from home arrangements) are likely to gradually plateau and also be replaced by demand for services (accommodation, air travel).

3.2 Deepening of uneven progress in recovery may lead to long-lasting scars

Prolonged pandemic disruptions may exacerbate the K-shaped recovery and cause long-lasting scars. Along with other pandemic induced disruptions, postponed border reopenings will delay recovery in tourism, and intermittent restrictions will hamper

BOX 2.2

Potential scarring effects of COVID-19

All recessions lead to long-term scars (Cerra and Saxena, 2005) and pandemics are no different (ESCAP 2021a; Ostry, Loungani and Furceri, 2020; Jordà, Singh and Taylor, 2020; Ma, Rogers and Zhou, 2020). Globally, long-term damage to potential output from previous episodes is estimated at close to 3 per cent. The impacts of the current pandemic could be larger because of its global scale and complexity.

The extent of scarring will vary across countries and sectors. Recent attempts to gauge potential medium-term output losses caused by COVID-19 range from 6 to 12 per cent of GDP.[a] Barrett and others (2021) estimated that economies more reliant on tourism and those with large service sectors are expected to experience higher persistent losses, which is consistent with the current period of prolonged border closures, while countries with larger fiscal measures are projected to suffer smaller losses.

Channels of scarring

Pandemic-induced disruptions in labour markets

Protracted labour market disturbances leave scars on the quality of the workforce and future productive potential. Large and sudden unemployment resulted from supply shocks following lockdown measures and economic and demand contraction arising from uncertainty in the early days of the pandemic. Resurgence of new COVID-19 variants and related disruptions prolong the duration of unemployment, resulting in erosion of workers' skills that will discourage them from returning to the workforce. As a result, many workers have fallen into poverty, which will exacerbate pre-existing inequalities and reduce future economic growth prospects.

Lack of capital investment

Weakened economic prospects and balance sheets may lead to an extended period of low investment, which in turn reduces productivity. Sizable stimulus measures introduced in developed countries and to a lesser extent in developing economies to alleviate adverse economic and social impacts have raised future concerns on increased debt and leveraging. Uncertain economic prospects and less availability of credit reduce incentives to invest in capital or R&D, thus reducing productivity.

Loss of productivity

Productivity loss from fewer working hours, lack of investments and loss in school hours will also be coupled with other structural changes brought about by the pandemic. These include digitization, decarbonization and demographic changes, which may have adverse impacts on production potential (Grömling, 2021). Reallocation of resources will take time and firms will need to adapt to restrictions.

A unique effect of the COVID-19 pandemic is the learning and earning loss from prolonged school closures. Full and partial closure of schools varied across countries in the region with the highest full closure being up to 63 weeks[b] (see figure below). The digital divide also meant that those lacking access to the Internet were deprived of learning opportunities as teaching was shifted to online formats. Earning loss for developing countries in the region is estimated at $1.25 trillion or 5.4 per cent of GDP in 2020 (ADB, 2021a). The impact of short-term disruptions, such as school closures and postponed or cancelled assessments and qualifications, are likely to have long-term consequences on learning and earning potential (Burgess and Sievertsen, 2020).

FIGURE

Pandemic-induced school closures in countries and areas in Asia and the Pacific

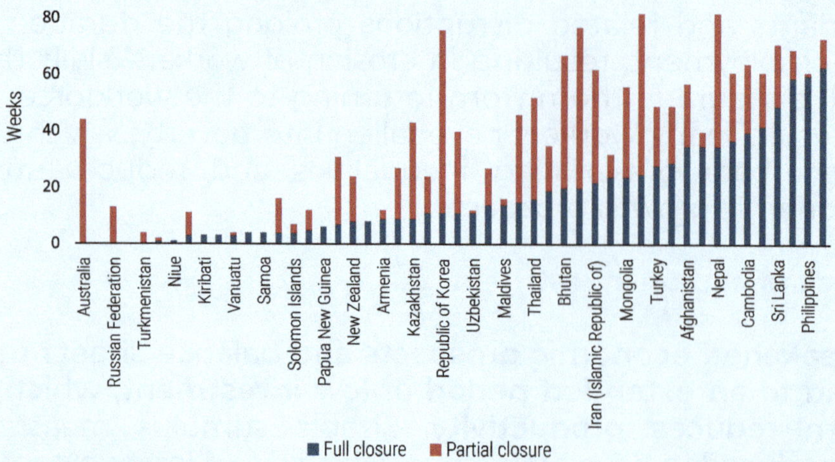

Source: UNESCO global dataset on school closures.

Some non-economic impacts specific to COVID-19 include effects on perception of risks and trust in institutions. Firms and individuals are likely to put higher weight on similar risks in future decisions that may affect spending patterns. Moreover, eroding public trust in institutions and leaders due to adverse impacts of the pandemic can affect their ability to deliver any change where public support is needed (Cerra, Fatas and Saxena, 2021; Aksoy, Eichengreen and Saka, 2020).

Aggressive expenditure response and continued macroeconomic stimulus, where policy space allows, will lower declines in output growth, according to Cerra, Fatas and Saxena, (forthcoming), compared with countries having a smaller fiscal response. Tailoring and targeting responses are also important to facilitate speedy and sustained economic recovery. Policies to help reduce the long-term effects of scarring are also discussed in section 4.3.

[a] Barro, Ursúa and Weng (2020) attempted to gauge potential effects of COVID-19 on mortality and economic activity through outcomes of the "Great Influenza Pandemic" (the so-called Spanish Flu), which showed a decline in GDP by 6 per cent and a decline in private consumption by 8 per cent. The use of the death rate during the great influenza pandemic, which translates into approximately 150 million deaths relative to the world's population of 7.5 billion in 2020, may seem remotely higher than the 6 million global deaths from COVID-19 and approximately 1.7 million deaths in Asia and the Pacific (as of March 2022 based on WHO COVID-19 explorer).

[b] For details, see UNESCO Institute for Statistics, global monitoring of school closures caused by COVID-19 dashboard (covid19.uis.unesco.org/global-monitoring-school-closures-covid19/regional-dashboard/).

growth in the services sector. Shorter working hours, extended business closures and extended unemployment can erode worker skills. Prolonged school closures can have long-term impacts on children's learning potential. Uncertainties regarding economic prospects lower incentives for investments in capital and research and development (R&D), thus reducing productivity. These effects will have impacts on future productive capacities, earning potential and productivity growth (box 2.2).

3.3 Macroeconomic stability concerns are rising

On the fiscal front, shrinking fiscal space, particularly in South and South-West Asian economies, amid tightening financial conditions, is likely to challenge the progress of the recovery. Premature withdrawal of fiscal support measures can halt the recovery's momentum. According to latest projections by IMF, fiscal consolidations are on the horizon (figure 2.17a), which are likely to have a negative impact on recovery and inequalities. While Governments should spend as long as needed for the recovery to become sustained, contracting fiscal space will have implications for financing recovery in the near-term and will adversely affect progress on sustainable development, including through a likely increase in inequalities. This crucial implication is explored in detail in chapter 3.

FIGURE 2.17
Shrinking fiscal space will challenge the progress of economic recovery

(a) Fiscal balance projections

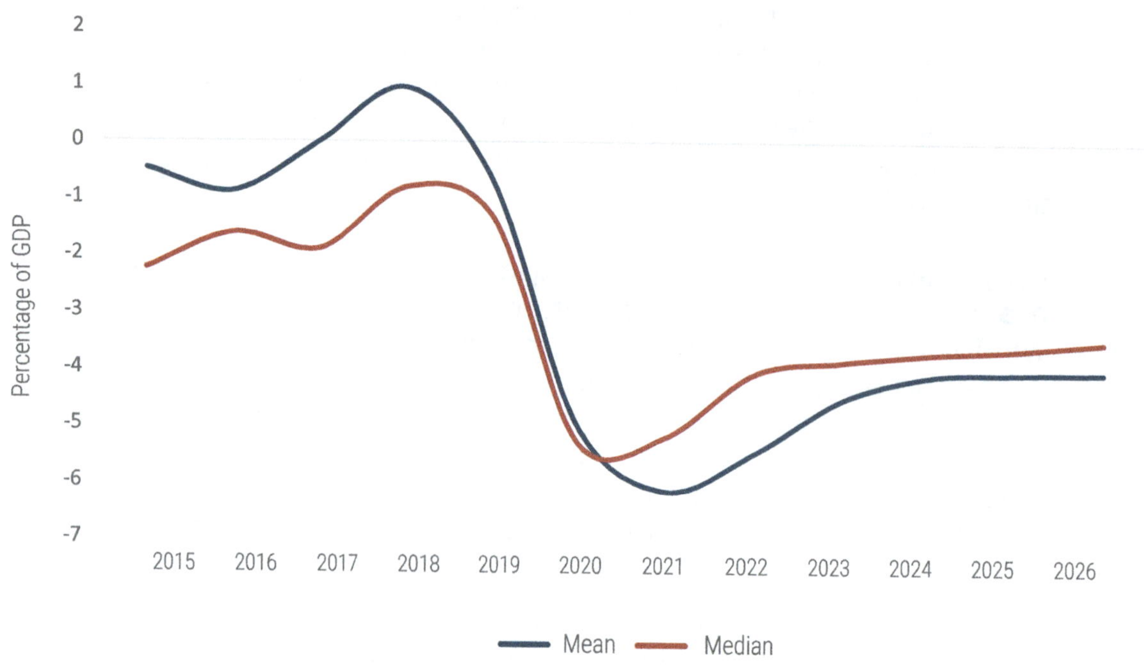

(b) Public debt to GDP ratio projections

Source: IMF, Fiscal monitor, October 2021.

Public debt to GDP ratio in developing Asia-Pacific countries will remain persistently high in the near term. The average public debt to GDP ratio for developing Asia-Pacific countries for 2021 is estimated at 50 per cent, which is higher than the pre-pandemic level by 20 percentage points. Debt levels are projected to remain elevated well into 2023 as the pandemic lingers on and recovery has yet to become sustained (figure 2.17b). In going forward, this would keep fiscal space constrained and servicing such debt will require additional fiscal resources that could otherwise be channelled towards supporting efforts to achieve the Sustainable Development Goals. Although debt levels for the region remain manageable, based on the commonly used 60 per cent debt to GDP benchmark, debt sustainability is still a concern in a number of countries. In Maldives for example, public debt to GDP remained higher than pre-pandemic levels by almost 60 percentage points in 2021. In Bhutan, Fiji, India and Sri Lanka, the increase in debt since the onset of the pandemic ranges from 17 per cent of GDP to 38 per cent of GDP. About a third of developing Asia-Pacific countries will be at high risk of debt distress over the coming years as the potential rise in interest rates may have negative impacts on debt servicing. In a scenario of prolonged economic stagnation, fiscal sustainability is likely to become a serious policy challenge for a large number of developing countries.

High and persistent fiscal deficits and rising public debt basically mean national dissavings, which are reflected in current account deficits. If current account deficits are not financed adequately, then there are risks for the overall balance of payments and for rapid exchange rate depreciation. Similarly, countries with weak capital markets and stagnant revenues run the risk of fiscal/debt sustainability risks, which may adversely affect credit ratings and thus financial flows to that country, forced contractions in fiscal positions (through ad hoc increases in taxes and reductions in critical fiscal expenditures) with several adverse consequences for recovery and development.

The expected monetary tightening in the United States due to record high inflation may put pressure on central banks across the globe to begin tightening as well, thus choking the recovery's momentum. Several Asia-Pacific economies are already facing rising inflationary pressure. In these circumstances, keeping interest rates low for long may be difficult. Monetary tightening will have implications for debt servicing in economies with high debt obligations and low foreign exchange reserves. This, in turn, would exacerbate debt sustainability risks.

Furthermore, risks of capital outflows and currency depreciation may lead to exchange rate pass-through and thus higher import prices. Growing price pressures from higher material costs driven by supply chain bottlenecks and surge in demand due to reopening may also pass on price inflation to consumers, thus reinforcing the need to initiate monetary tightening. Understanding such dynamic relationship between the inflation/interest rate outlook and fiscal/debt positions is important to fully appreciate the risks to macroeconomic stability.

3.4 China's moderation may have adverse spillover effects on other countries in the region

Moderation in China's consumption, exports and industrial activities will no doubt weigh on the region's growth momentum, given the interlinkages of its economy with several other economies in the region.

A potential contraction in China's property development sector could have significant impacts on the country's economic growth with possible spillovers to the rest of the region. Disruption would have wide repercussions for home buyers, property developers, suppliers, contractors, banks and financial institutions and will cause a slowdown in construction.

A slowdown in China is likely to spill over to the rest of Asia through lower trade, particularly for capital goods, machinery and electrical goods with key partners, such as Indonesia, Malaysia, the Philippines, Singapore, Thailand and Viet Nam.[8] Exporters of raw materials, such as Australia, which export iron ore for steel production will suffer adverse impacts from lower demand for steel because of declines in new construction, and China's target to lower carbon emissions which is aimed at lowering steel output as it involves a high-polluting and high-energy-intensity processes. Continued supply constraints and power shortages in China will prolong global supply disruptions, halting production in numerous factories and causing delayed delivery of goods.

China's Zero-COVID strategy is also a risk not only to its domestic demand, investment and tourist arrivals but also to countries highly reliant upon tourist arrivals from China, such as Cambodia, the Philippines and Thailand.[9]

8 ASEAN-6 (Indonesia, Malaysia, the Philippines, Singapore, Thailand and Viet Nam) have surpassed the European Union as China's largest trading partner in 2020. A slowdown in China will have impacts on trade with these countries.

9 Tourist arrivals from China contribute up to 28 per cent of tourism receipts in Thailand.

BOX 2.3

Potential economic impact of the Russia-Ukraine conflict on the Asia-Pacific region

The impacts of the Russia-Ukraine conflict are wide ranging and being felt globally. However, as the situation is fast evolving, it is difficult to assess its full implications for the Asia-Pacific region. The information contained in this box provides a provisional assessment. The most significant impact on the Asia-Pacific region will be inflation, and thus adversely affect people in lower-income groups, primarily through rising prices for oil and food. The Russian Federation is likely to suffer the largest impact due to various sanctions being imposed, with significant spillovers on countries in the North and Central Asian subregion through trade and remittance linkages.

Sanctions imposed on the Russian Federation will disrupt the country's trade and financial linkages, particularly through reducing exports of oil and natural gas which contribute about 15 per cent to the country's GDP.[a] Such sanctions will increase the cost of trade and cause shortages of goods, pushing up inflation and triggering currency depreciation and interest rate increases. These will further add to existing inflationary pressures, lower consumer and business confidence and thus aggregate consumption and investments, and eventually result in a significant decline in economic growth.

The impact on North and Central Asian economies is likely to be significant as well through trade ties and remittance linkages with the Russian Federation. North and Central Asian countries are more reliant on imports from the Russian Federation (5 to 7 per cent of GDP) and to a lesser extent on exports (2 to 5 per cent of GDP), while trade dependency with Ukraine is much lower (2.5 per cent of GDP and lower) (see figure below). Sanctions coupled with shipping and transport disruptions will add to trade costs and goods shortages, increasing the price of goods and services in countries in North and Central Asia. Moreover, the decline in economic growth and sentiments across the globe will likely lower trade and export revenues for export-oriented economies. For the rest of Asia and the Pacific, trade ties with the Russian Federation account for about 1 per cent of GDP or lower and approximately 0.1 per cent of GDP for trade with Ukraine. Such weak trade linkages should shield the rest of the Asia-Pacific region from direct large impacts, such as the collapse of Russian imports or any other trade barriers imposed on the country.

Figure
Trade dependency of economies in the Asia-Pacific region on the Russian Federation and Ukraine

Source: Capital Economics (2022). Available at data.capitaleconomics.com/lfqnbec/russia-ukraine-global-exposures (accessed on 16 March 2022).

The high dependence of many countries in North and Central Asia on remittances from the Russian Federation will leave them vulnerable. This is more so where remittances contribute between 10 and 30 per cent of GDP, and a significant percentage is from the Russian Federation, such as in the case of Kyrgyzstan (more than 80 per cent) and Armenia, Tajikistan and Uzbekistan (more than 50 per cent) (Ratha and Kim, 2022).

Weakening economic activities in the Russian Federation will dampen employment and incomes of migrant workers and their ability to send remittances home. A depreciated rouble will reduce the value of earnings and savings, and the overall value of remittances in 2022, despite increases in oil prices. Sanctions on the Russian banking system will disrupt remittance flows through formal channels. The decline in remittances will lead to economic and social pressures because they support household consumption and investments in workers' home countries. Based on an initial assessment of effects of the decline in economic activity in the Russian Federation and its weakening currency, remittances are likely to decline in countries in North and Central Asia in 2022 by as much as 33 per cent in the case of Kyrgyzstan (Ratha and Kim, 2022).

As the Asia-Pacific region is a net oil importer,[b] the impact of rising oil prices will be significant, particularly for large oil importers.[c] Although the Russian Federation is not the main source of energy and commodity exporter to the Asia-Pacific region, countries such as China and the Republic of Korea had been importing more than 10 per cent of their oil from the Russian Federation (Aljazeera, 2022). Oil prices are expected to remain above $100 per barrel until at least the second half of 2022, with energy exporters gaining considerably. Provisional ESCAP estimates show that compared to the baseline scenario of no-conflict, an average oil price at $100 per barrel would lead to a 0.4 per cent reduction in real output and an estimated increase in inflation by 2.3 percentage points.

The cost of food and agricultural commodities is also being pushed up. The Russian Federation and Ukraine together account for a quarter of the world's wheat exports, along with other grains. Higher costs for global wheat will likely push up the price of grain substitutes and animal feed, thus adding to the cost of livestock production. Higher energy prices will also push up the price of fertilizers, which may result in lower fertilizer use and lower crop yields. Food and feed prices may rise by 8 to 22 per cent in 2022/23 based on projections (FAO, 2022) and will have strong impacts on net food importers,[d] the majority of which are least developed countries (UNWTO, 2022).

Higher food, oil and agricultural commodity prices will weigh on consumption and growth as the weight of food and energy in the CPI basket are as high as 40 per cent or more in many countries in the region. This will hamper consumption at a time when countries are just recovering from the pandemic and labour markets remain weak. Consumption will also be constrained by the expected tightening of monetary and financial conditions, where global interest rate rises, in response to higher global inflation, may lead to interest rate increases in the region.

Lastly, as Russian citizens are unable to travel abroad, loss of tourism revenues will set back tourism recovery in countries dependent on arrivals from the Russian Federation. Russian tourists account for almost 20 per cent of international arrivals in Sri Lanka and approximately 4 per cent for Thailand, among other tourism-dependent economies in the region. In Thailand, the potential loss of tourism revenue from arrivals from the Russian Federation is equivalent to 0.2 per cent of GDP (Thai PBS, 2022).

[a] Current sanctions broadly include freezing assets of Russian banks, an export ban on specific oil-refining technologies to the Russian Federation from Europe and other strategic items from elsewhere, halting exports of such goods as semiconductors, cutting high-technology imports to stall development of military capabilities and stemming Russian companies and State from their ability to raise or borrow funds (Nolsoe and Pop, 2022; Funakoshi, Lawson and Deka, 2022).
[b] With the exception of net fuel exporters in the region: Azerbaijan, Brunei Darussalam, Indonesia, the Islamic Republic of Iran, Kazakhstan, Malaysia and Turkmenistan.
[c] Such as China, India, Japan, the Republic of Korea, the Philippines, Singapore and Thailand.
[d] Afghanistan, Bangladesh, Cambodia, the Lao People's Democratic Republic, Mongolia, Myanmar, Nepal, Pakistan, Samoa, Solomon Islands, Sri Lanka and Vanuatu.

3.5 Geopolitical tensions

Most recently, the conflict between the Russian Federation and Ukraine will have impacts on the region's growth prospects. As the situation is still evolving, a preliminary assessment is provided in box 2.3.

4. POLICY CONSIDERATIONS

4.1 Coexisting with the pandemic

Countries will need to adopt a policy mix that facilitates coexistence with the virus. While border closures, hard lockdowns and stringent quarantines have proven to slow the spread of outbreak, they have also been highly detrimental to economies and the well-being of people. Hence, countries will need to strike a balance between avoiding economic and social fallouts while maintaining public health, livelihoods and lower burdens on the health system. For instance, travel bubbles with appropriate testing and containment have given hope to tourism-dependent economies. The experience of border openings in Maldives and Thailand have set some examples which can be revisited under the Omicron and any future outbreaks. Coordinated action among countries on entry requirements, travel documents and related protocols may encourage increased international travel. Preparedness, clear communication and adaptability to a rapidly changing environment are important to establish credibility and trust.

4.2 Avoiding macroeconomic instability through prudent fiscal and monetary policies

Fiscal policies need to remain accommodative to support the nascent recovery in the region. However, with shrinking fiscal space, spending will have to be more targeted and efficient, while essential areas of spending will need to be maintained. A major shift in fiscal management will be needed to increase efficiency of spending through better prioritization, curtailing unnecessary spending and subsidies, improving direct tax collections through strengthened tax administrations and stemming tax evasion and controlling leakages. Chapter 3 explores priority spending areas and how to ***spend smarter.***

Similarly, given the rising inflationary trends, maintaining an accommodative monetary policy stance may be difficult for many countries. Monetary policy can remain accommodative only in countries where inflation is expected to remain within targets. In such countries as the Republic of Korea and Singapore, where inflation is rising rapidly while recovery has been more advanced than in other parts of the region, the central banks have raised interest rates to counter inflationary pressures. Pakistan and Sri Lanka have raised interest rates to check rising inflation, although economic recovery is not yet stable. A timely increase in the interest rate can help with stemming potential capital outflows, attracting portfolio investments and warding off unnecessary depreciation pressures, thus strengthening external positions.

Countries should consider some measures to counter adverse impacts of financial tightening, including debt rescheduling where possible to alleviate debt repayments or putting into place capital flow management and macroprudential measures to prevent large capital flow reversals.

4.3 Policies to reduce inequality and minimize scarring

Measures to address productive capacity of the current and future labour force along with increasing productivity through investments to promote innovation and technology adoption could help to reduce inequalities and minimize scarring.

Boosting labour market recovery and labour market adjustments through active labour market policies, such as trainings, job search and facilitating reallocation of workers, would be of particular benefit to vulnerable groups, such as those with low skills and limited work experience, such as youth. As a higher proportion of women worked in the most severely affected sectors and faced greater job losses, coupled with new care responsibilities during the pandemic, which forced many to leave the workforce, job retention schemes, provision of childcare and elderly care support, or policies to keep schools open, could facilitate labour market participation for women. To address future earning potential, policies to mitigate negative outcomes of school closures, such as rebuilding loss learning and investing in unlocking digital learning opportunities, would promote productive capacities.

Policies to boost investment, promote innovation and adoption of technology can increase productivity, particularly as COVID-19 has induced rapid adoption of digitalization and automation.

To minimize long-term scarring, Governments should prioritize spending on certain areas: examples would include health care to hasten recovery from the pandemic and lower burden of disease and care; spending on education could improve learning and the earning potential of students and the future workforce; and spending on social protection, which will protect millions from falling into poverty (see chapter 3 for details).

4.4 Building resilience into the system

The pandemic has exposed inherent vulnerabilities in the region's economies, which have relied too much on boosting short-term economic growth at the expense of long-term sustainability. In going forward, recovery should be green and inclusive; in this regard, a few countries in the region are already stepping up. Some examples include the Republic of Korea's New Deal, which is focused on improved quality of life and carbon neutrality. Singapore Green Plan 2030 (n.d.) describes how the country is striving to transition towards sustainability and establish a hub for green finance and carbon trading. China, India, Japan and the Republic of Korea have also announced plans to achieve carbon neutral targets: by 2050 for Japan and the Republic of Korea, by 2060 for China and

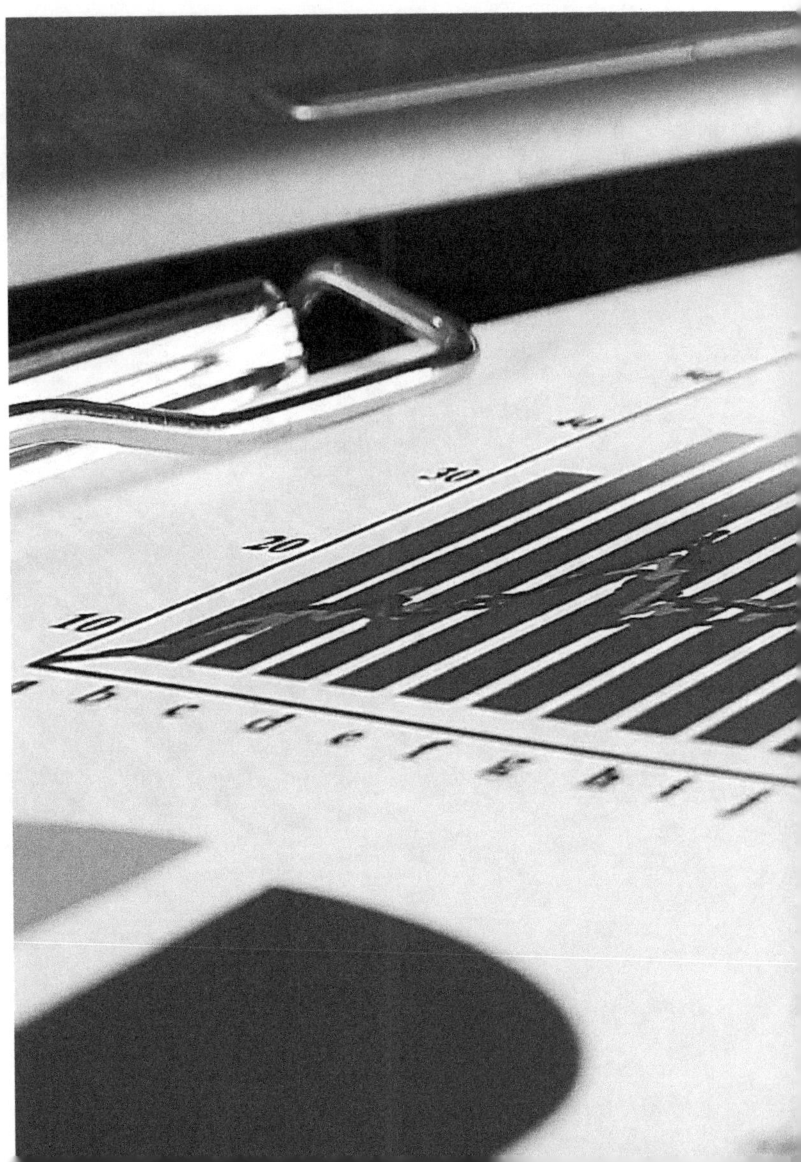

by 2070 for India. The Philippines and Viet Nam on the other hand have committed to move away from coal. These initiatives are helping to lay foundations for resilient economies to serve the well-being of both people and the planet.

ESCAP also proposed a "build forward better" policy package in the *Survey* for 2021 in order to build resilience and to avoid a potential K-shaped recovery and further damage to long-term development prospects. This could be accomplished through affordable investments in basic social services, such as universal health coverage and a social protection floor, closing the digital divide and taking stronger climate and clean energy actions.

5. CONCLUSIONS

The pandemic has indeed caused unprecedented socioeconomic disruptions in Asia and the Pacific. The region has emerged from the sudden and severe stage of the crisis. Yet, the recovery is incomplete as the pandemic lingers and considerable uncertainty on multiple fronts cloud the near-term outlook. An uneven recovery is likely to result in long-term scarring. A sustained recovery is contingent upon targeted fiscal, monetary and labour market policies, and strategies to coexist with the coronavirus. The region should continue to implement policies and initiatives that help transition towards an inclusive, green and resilient economy and thus lay a firm foundation to better withstand future shocks.

FISCAL POLICY CHOICES FOR INCLUSIVE RECOVERY

AMID FISCAL SPACE CONSTRAINTS

CHAPTER 03

1. INTRODUCTION

The COVID-19 pandemic has pushed countries in the region into a fiscal bind. The need to spend remains elevated, while the means to spend have been reduced. Those countries with sufficient fiscal space[1] should continue to spend to achieve an inclusive recovery, while those in a bind need to work on both improving the efficiency of spending and looking for more revenue.

As argued in chapters 1 and 2, the pandemic has brought the issue of inequality to the fore. Looking back, the pains of the pandemic, which have strengthened drivers of inequality, could have been partially mitigated if more people-oriented investments had been made prior to the start of the pandemic, in particular in health care, education and social protection programmes. In learning from the past, similar mistakes should be avoided this time around.

1 "Fiscal space" denotes "room in a government´s budget that allows it to provide resources for a desired purpose without jeopardizing the sustainability of its financial position or the stability of the economy" (IMF, 2005).

Two years into the pandemic, the fiscal outlook remains tough. The initial fiscal response included substantial spending on health systems to fight the pandemic and support workers and small businesses to prevent an even deeper crisis. While ameliorating the social and economic impact of the pandemic, the median fiscal spending increased from 28 per cent of GDP in 2019 to 29 per cent in 2021 (figure 3.1a). However, with large declines in economic output (chapter 2), fiscal revenues did not catch up with growing expenditures. As a consequence, median fiscal balances have deteriorated during this period from a deficit of 1.3 per cent of GDP in 2019 to 5.2 per cent of GDP in 2021.

The economic outlook also remains uncertain and challenging.

The permanent loss in output is estimated at $2 trillion dollars over the period 2020-2023 (chapter 2). With much of the fiscal space used up to fight the pandemic, there is reduced ability for many developing economies to spend their way out of the pandemic. According to the latest IMF projections, consolidations are expected over the medium term. A median reduction in the fiscal deficit for Asia-Pacific developing countries, from 5.4 per cent in 2020 to 3.5 per cent in 2025, is on the horizon (figure 3.1b). As discussed below, such a

FIGURE 3.1
Fiscal outlook looks tough as fiscal space shrinks

(a) Fiscal space, Asia-Pacific developing countries, median values as a percentage of GDP

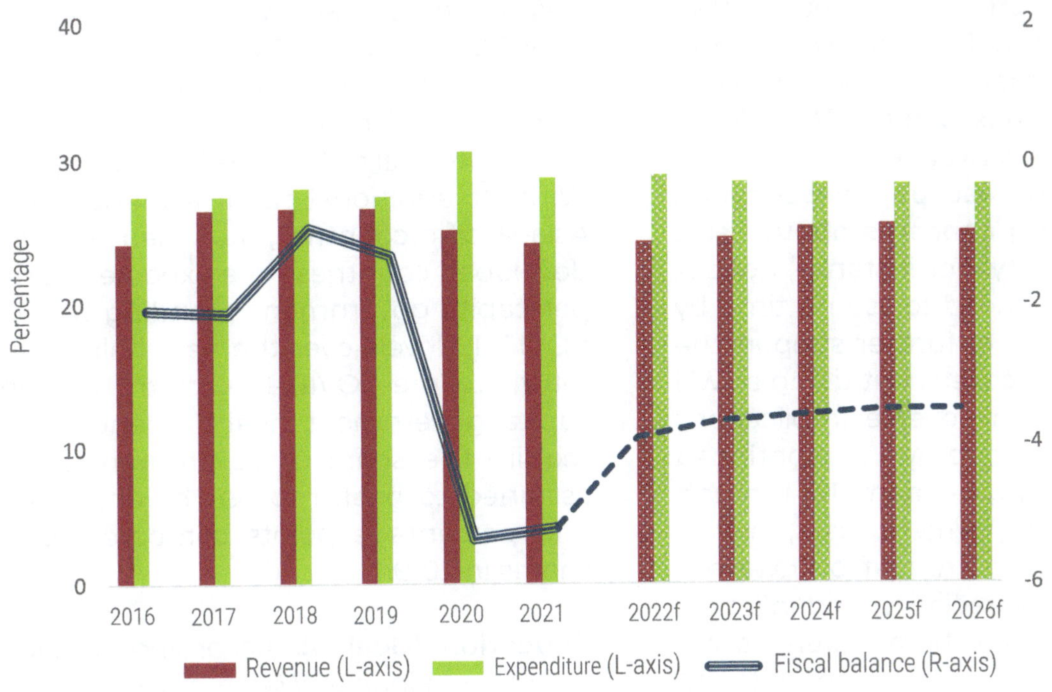

(b) Median debt, Asia-Pacific developing countries, as a percentage of GDP

Source: ESCAP estimates based on IMF data.

Note: The suffix "f" after some years means "forecast"; these years are depicted in shaded bars.

degree of consolidation is expected to have a negative and possibly long-term impact on inequality (section 2).

While Governments should strive to support their economic recovery through proactive fiscal policies for as long as possible (ESCAP, 2021a), it might eventually become very difficult to escape consolidation given rising concerns about fiscal sustainability. For instance, deficits can be financed for some time by issuing debt to further support the COVID-19 recovery, but doing so will have its own adverse implications for the economy if continued for too long – namely through balance of payment risks, higher risk premiums, retreat of investors, currency depreciation and inflation. At some point, fiscal revenues will have to be increased in order to safeguard continuation of needed expenditures. Determining that point in time is not easy, however. If steps are taken too soon, economic activity may slow down, reducing tax revenues even further. If delayed for too long, other adverse implications may start to bear down on the economy, again reducing tax revenues.

In the light of reduced fiscal space and to avoid deeper fiscal consolidation, Governments will also need to consider how to get the most "bang for the buck" from their spending. This would mean ensuring that the most essential expenditures are maintained and their efficiency of delivery improved. Typically, during times of fiscal consolidation, areas of spending that often get axed include health care, education and social spending, which has significant implications for inequality and inclusive development. Some concerns have already been voiced by international organizations to resist such temptations. Consider the following, for instance:

- **Health care (Sustainable Development Goal 3):** The World Bank (2021d) noted that Governments will have to make bold choices to continue strengthening health care and avoid potential reductions in health spending. Without additional fiscal revenues, some 11 Asia-Pacific countries, 5 of them being least developed countries[2], are expected to reduce per capita government spending below pre-COVID-19 levels over the next half decade. A return to pre-COVID-19 growth rates in per capita government health spending would require the share of government spending assigned to health to rise by approximately 5-10 percentage points compared with the shares in 2019.

- **Education (Goal 4):** According to the joint Education Finance Watch of the World Bank and UNESCO (World Bank, 2021c), education budgets are not adjusting proportionately to the challenges brought about by the COVID-19 pandemic, especially in poorer countries. Despite additional pandemic-related funding needs, two thirds of low- and lower-middle-income countries have, in fact, cut their public education budgets since the onset of the pandemic. In comparison, only one third of upper-middle and high-income countries have reduced their education budgets. They acknowledge that the budget cuts so far have been relatively small, but there is a danger that future cuts will be larger, as the pandemic continues to take its economic toll and fiscal positions worsen.

- **Social spending (Goal 1):** According to ILO (2021d), as of 2020, only 47 per cent[3] of the global population were effectively

2 Least developed countries from the Asia-Pacific region are: Afghanistan, Cambodia, Lao People's Democratic Republic, Nepal and Timor-Leste. The other six countries from the region are: Fiji, Papua New Guinea, Sri Lanka, Turkey, Turkmenistan and Viet Nam. The World Bank (2021d) stated that it expects these 11 countries to have government expenditure per capita for 2021-2026 remain below 2019 levels. Globally, 52 countries are expected to have real per capita general government expenditure reduced, compared with 126 countries with expected increase.

3 Excluding health care and illness.

covered by at least one social protection benefit (Sustainable Development Goal indicator 1.3.1) (figure 3.2), while the remaining 53 per cent – as many as 4.1 billion people – were left wholly unprotected. Behind this global average, there are significant inequalities across and within regions, with the ESCAP region averaging at about 46 per cent (ESCAP and ILO, 2020a). ILO also noted that gaps in the coverage, comprehensiveness and adequacy of social protection systems are associated with significant underinvestment in social protection. Average global spending on social protection (excluding health) is 12.9 per cent of GDP, with wide variations across country income levels, ranging from just about 1 per cent of GDP among the least developed economies to 16 per cent in the most developed ones. The coverage also varies significantly across socioeconomic groups, pointing to a still long way towards achieving universal social protection.

Against this backdrop, the chapter explores the role of fiscal policy in ensuring an inclusive recovery and in supporting inclusive development. It first estimates the impact of past consolidations on inequality and finds that large consolidations during the period 1990-2019 led to both an increase in inequality and a large fall in output levels. Hence, fiscal policy will need to pull both levers – "spend smart" and improve revenue mobilization – in order to achieve an inclusive recovery and development amid a situation of limited fiscal space. Given the likelihood of the three above-mentioned expenditure areas (namely health, education and social spending) to be put under the spotlight during such times, the chapter looks at detailed analyses in country research, according to the Commitment to Equity (CEQ) and the World Bank's public expenditure reviews (PERs) to determine what aspects can be strengthened in order to improve upon inclusion.

FIGURE 3.2
Social protection in the Asia-Pacific region is below the global average

Sustainable Development Goal indicator 1.3.1: Proportion of population covered by social protection floors/systems

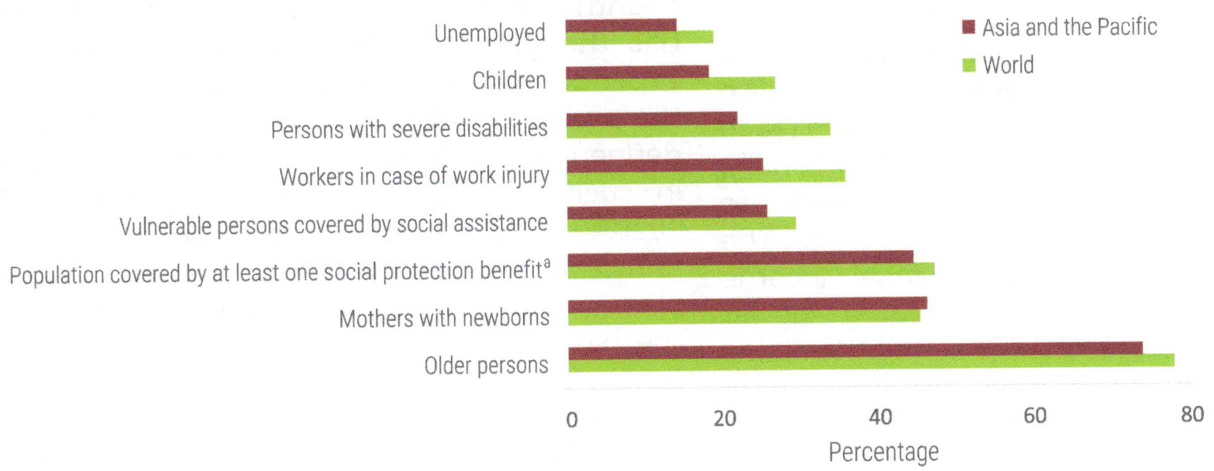

Source: ILO, 2021d.

[a] *Excluding health care and illness benefits.*

Finally, the chapter complements the discussion on fiscal space limited by the pandemic by arguing for improved revenue mobilization. This includes enhancing the efficiency of tax collection by digitalization and bringing the digital economy within the tax purview, as well as noting that it might be time to accelerate implementation of progressive personal income taxes and reform of corporate income taxation to reduce long-term inequality (ESCAP, 2018d). All these reforms require strong political will for effective implementation. However, not having been left with many additional fiscal revenue options, the pandemic has hopefully provided this window of opportunity for redesigning tax systems with overcoming inequality in mind.

In summary, the chapter argues against cutting expenditures in areas that have the potential to increase inequality – namely health, education and social protection. In this regard, prioritization of scarce resources towards basic primary health care, primary and secondary education and social protection for informal workers and vulnerable groups would be most useful in reducing inequality during the recovery. Use of technology is also recommended to increase the reach of such programmes. Additionally, it is recommended that revenues be mobilized by improving the progressivity of personal income taxes and by bringing newer revenue sources, such as the digital and the informal economy, under the tax purview.

Given the likely fiscal consolidation that will occur over the medium term (figure 3.1), the following section estimates its potential impact on inequality.

2. IMPLICATIONS OF LIKELY FISCAL CONSOLIDATION FOR INEQUALITY AND INCLUSIVE DEVELOPMENT

The fiscal consolidation that is likely to occur across Asia and the Pacific has the potential to increase inequality, with long-lasting adverse implications for inclusive development.

Empirical studies on developed economies point to the potential adverse effects of fiscal austerity on both income distribution and economic recovery. For example, Ball and others (2013) found that fiscal austerity, especially if concentrated on the expenditure side, has significant distributional effects, such as increased inequality, decreased shares in wage income and a long-term increase in unemployment for OECD countries. Similarly, Woo and others (2013) found that inequality increases more significantly through government expenditure adjustments compared with tax-based adjustments. They also found that some of the distributional impacts may be offset by progressive taxation and targeted social benefits (Rojas Cama, 2021).

Given the lack of research on developing countries in the Asia-Pacific region, this chapter fills the gap by using data on government expenditures per capita from 39 countries for the period 1990-2020. Consolidation periods are defined as the bottom 5 per cent of changes in such expenditures over the period 1990-2020.[4] This is tantamount to an annual average reduction in government expenditures of about 12 per cent. ESCAP estimates suggest that, during the past 30 years, inequality increased in Asia-Pacific countries at the time of consolidations and the impact persisted for many years (figure 3.3a). This aligns with the findings in

4 The episodes of fiscal consolidation are constructed using government expenditure contraction per capita. A preliminary range of years has been selected based on the 5th percentile (the bottom 5 per cent) of the cumulative negative change for three- and four-year periods. Finally, the fiscal episode year is defined as the second year for three-year episodes and as the third year for four-year periods (second to last).

FIGURE 3.3
Looming fiscal consolidation is expected to increase inequality and weigh down GDP growth
Impact of consolidation in government expenditure per capita on:
(a) Inequality, Gini coefficient[a]

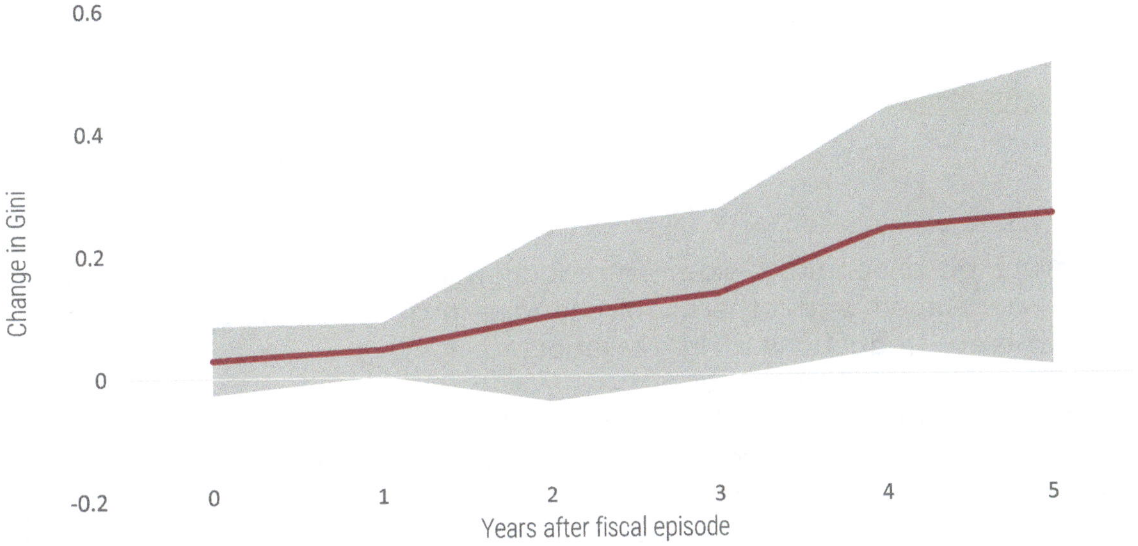

[a]*Gini scale: 0-100.*

(b) GDP per capita growth, percentage points

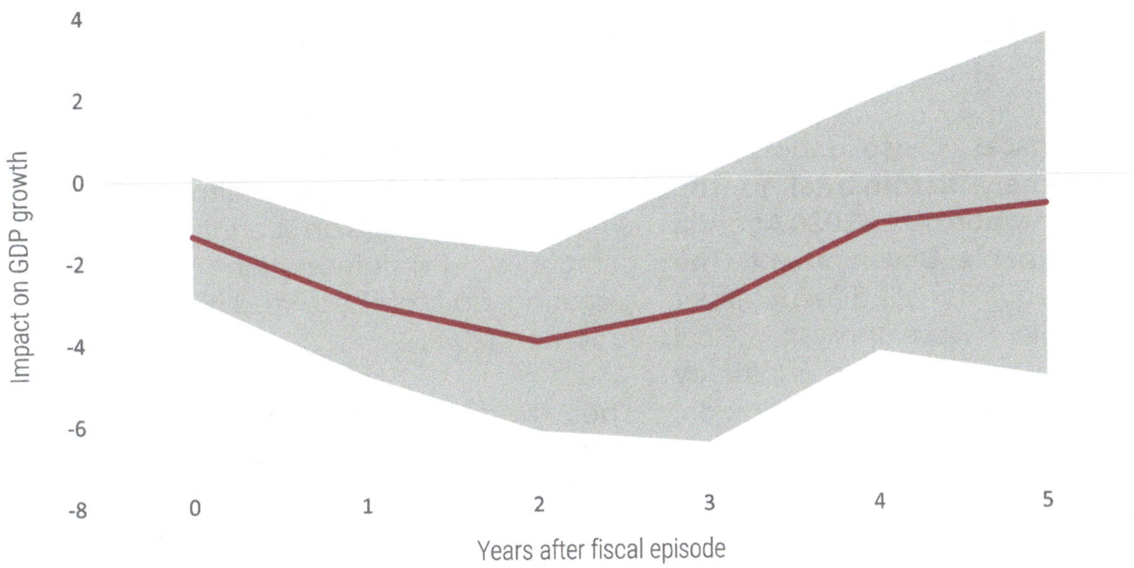

Source: ESCAP estimates based on IMF data.
Note: The dark red line indicates the estimated impact of fiscal event; the grey area represents 95 per cent confidence interval.

POLICY OPTION

Depending on the country-level economic situation, if the need to consolidate fiscal positions materializes and fiscal austerity measures must be implemented, consider prioritizing progressive tax-based adjustments over expenditure-side adjustments. Research suggests a greater adverse impact of the latter on inequality.

FIGURE 3.4

The goal on inequality reduction is behind the target to implement the 2030 Agenda

Progress in achieving the Sustainable Development Goal 10 in the Asia-Pacific region, 2020

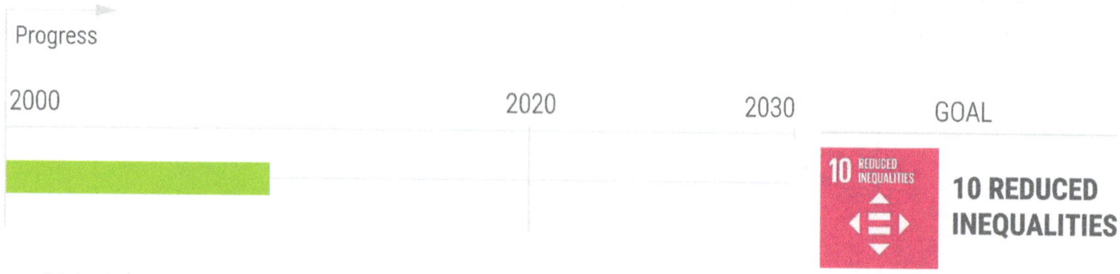

Source: ESCAP (2021c).

the literature on expenditure-side austerity (see Furceri and others, 2021), where reductions in government expenditures on assistance to vulnerable households could have driven the increase in inequality. ESCAP also found that consolidations lead to decreases in GDP (figure 3.3b), possibly due to large fiscal multiplier effects observed in recessions (Blanchard and Leigh, 2013) – an extremely important factor to consider given the need for crisis recovery.

Hence, fiscal consolidation can be extremely detrimental to the implementation of the 2030 Agenda for Sustainable Development. The rise in inequality will directly affect Sustainable Development Goal 10, for which the region is already lagging (figure 3.4). In addition, expected cuts in the usually suspected categories of health, education and social protection would make attainment of above mentioned Goals 1, 3, and 4, more difficult.

In this context of a likely increase in inequality because of consolidation, the next two sections examine ways in which fiscal policy can be redesigned and implemented with the prerogative of inequality-reduction. Policymakers need to pay more attention to the extent of reduction in inequality that occurs as a result of changes in government expenditures versus taxation.

On this topic, ESCAP examined CEQ country research based on household survey data. The CEQ research estimated the impact of fiscal policies on inequality comparing two scenarios – one based on the observed inequalities when the policies have been implemented (Gini value 1) and the other in a hypothetical scenario if fiscal policies were not implemented (Gini value 2). The difference between the two Gini values would help in understanding the impact on inequality of the specific policy intervention (CEQ, 2018). This research is complemented with findings from the World Bank's public expenditure reviews (PERs), which provide details on spending within particular categories, and information on efficiency and targeting. Both of these studies were summarized in Torbert (2021).

The findings from the above-mentioned research confirm that expenditures on education, health and direct transfers significantly reduce inequalities. They are also relatively large in terms of percentage of GDP expenditure; therefore, they deserve particular attention in terms of possible efficiency improvements (figure 3.5). Direct taxes, such as personal income tax (PIT), remain largely progressive, although they are not the most important source of government tax income in the Asia-Pacific region (figure 3.5), as will be discussed later. By contrast, indirect taxes that are a dominant source of taxes in Asia and the Pacific, such as value added tax (VAT), contribute to an increase in inequality, pointing to the potential need for redesign or extra caution in case of rate hikes.

FIGURE 3.5
The total impact of fiscal policies on inequality varies

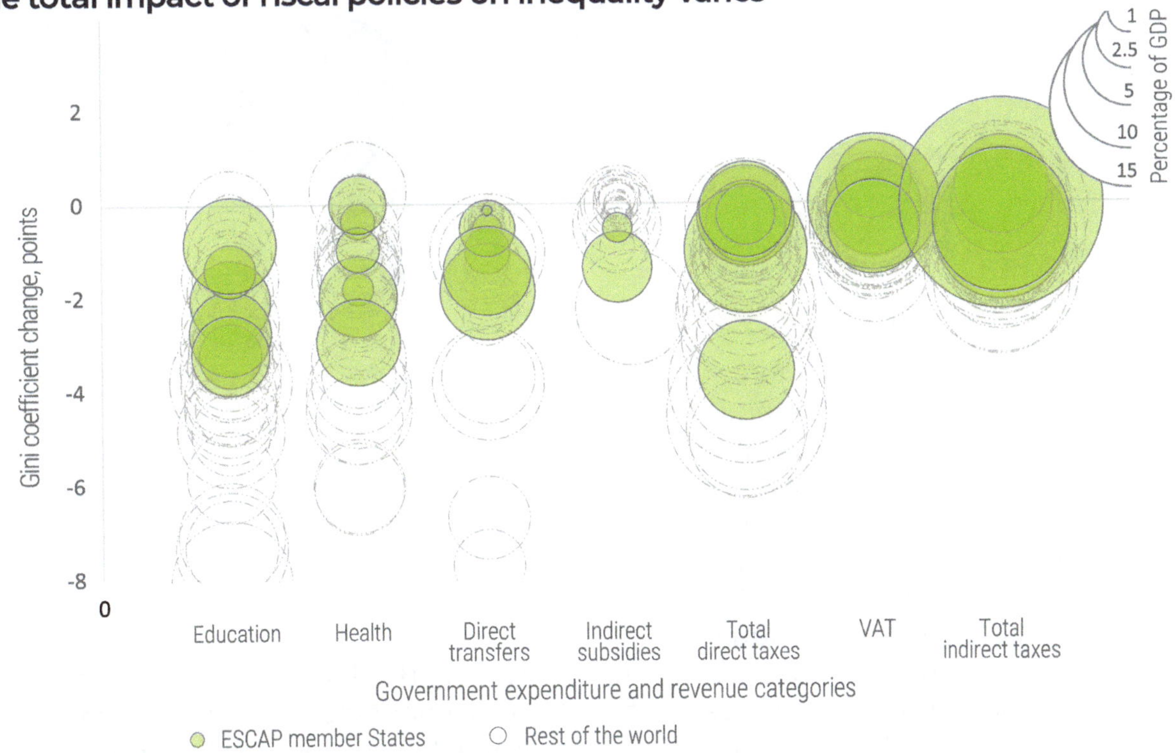

Source: ESCAP estimates based on CEQ data.
Note: The graph presents an estimate of the total inequality change with implementation of a certain policy compared with an alternative scenario where the policy would not exist. Gini coefficients are shown on a scale of 0-100 for ease of interpretation and as used in the literature. Y-axis values represent changes in Gini coefficient. The size of the circles represents total expenditure as a percentage of GDP, Asia-Pacific countries are: Armenia, China, Georgia, Indonesia, the Islamic Republic of Iran, Mongolia, the Russian Federation, Sri Lanka and Turkey.

FIGURE 3.6
Impact of seemingly same category fiscal policies varies greatly raising questions on effectiveness and targeting
Impact of fiscal policies[a] on inequality, according to 1 per cent of GDP expenditure/revenue

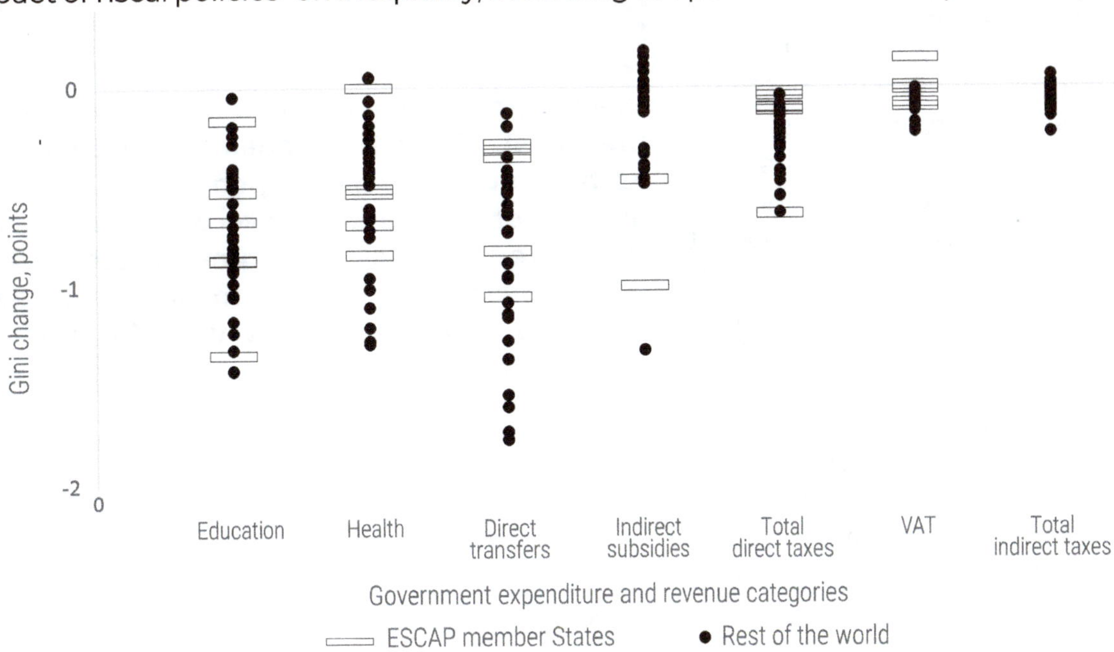

Source: ESCAP estimates based on CEQ data.
[a] Gini coefficients are shown on a scale of 0-100 for ease of interpretation.
Note: The graph presents an estimate of the total inequality change with implementation of a certain policy compared with an alternative scenario where the policy would not exist.

The impact on inequality due to expenditures in different sectors varies considerably across countries, pointing to considerable differences in implementation of spending policies.

The aggregate impact of different fiscal expenditure and revenue sources (figure 3.5) hides the highly heterogenous relative impact of respective policies on inequality. The substantial variation in the impact when looking at 1 per cent of GDP spent or collected in taxes (figure 3.6), points to the complexity of fiscal policy implementation, as well as efficiency challenges. For example, the impact of 1 per cent of GDP expenditure on education ranges from almost zero to over one-point reduction in the Gini coefficient. As discussed below, the differences may be linked to who benefits relatively more from such expenditures; for example, the relatively higher-income urban or lower-income rural populations. Similarly, the impact varies considerably for health care expenditures, which may be more beneficial to urban areas with better access to hospitals, as well as discriminate against low-income households for whom out-of-pocket expenditures limit health care accessibility (Torbert, 2021). Direct transfers may benefit only better-off communities that can register through digital means unavailable to the poorest communities. Finally, seemingly similar types of taxes, such as indirect taxes, will have different impacts on inequality depending on the baskets of products taxed and their shares in low-income household budgets.

3. FISCAL POLICY OPTIONS – "SPEND SMART"

Keeping in view the long-term determinants of inequality (see chapter 5), the ongoing pandemic and its impacts on inequality and possible expenditure cuts, this section discusses the observed and potential impact on inequality of health care, education and social spending. This *Survey* considers each expenditure area below, with an eye on what these expenditures mean for economic development and how their implementation can be improved in order to minimize inequalities.

Health care

Health expenditures should not be reduced in the midst of the fight against the pandemic. As high out-of-pocket expenditures can push millions of people into poverty, it is necessary to ensure that basic health needs are covered for all, eventually leading to universal health coverage. Inefficiencies and wasteful spending must be reduced.

Good health goes hand-in-hand with economic development and long-term wealth accumulation.

Good health supports productivity along with income and wealth accumulation. For example, good health means less absenteeism from school or work, reduced time lost in caring for dependents, or simply better performance at work. The impact of poor health on global GDP is estimated at a 15 per cent loss every year (McKinsey, 2020) – a reminder why, beyond ethical and human-centric considerations, health care must stay high on the fiscal policy agenda. As of 2021, 90 per cent of countries globally reported disruptions in essential health services due to COVID-19 (WHO, 2021b).

Despite their importance to overall economic performance, lack of sufficient investments in health care systems was noted even before the start of the COVID-19 pandemic, and universal health coverage (UHC) remained far from being widely deployed. ESCAP (2019a) estimated that an additional annual investment of $158 billion, or $38 per person, would be needed per year on average during the period 2016-2030 to ambitiously scale up health systems towards achieving the targets of Sustainable Development Goal 3. This included an additional investment of $880 million per year through 2030 in emergency preparedness, risk management and response, as part of the health system.

High out-of-pocket health expenditures are pushing millions into poverty. As a share of current health expenditures, such expenses range from 26 per cent in East Asia and the Pacific to 62 per cent in South Asia (World Bank, 2022).[5] For example, the proportion of the population pushed into extreme poverty was estimated at 6.4 per cent for Bangladesh (figure 3.7) and 3.1 per cent of the population in South Asia as a whole. On top of these old challenges, the pandemic could have pushed another 85 million people into extreme poverty in just the Asia-Pacific region alone (see chapter 1), a situation which calls for policies to shield the poor from impoverishment, including through insufficient health care protection, which has contributed to that number.

However, amid ageing societies and continuously stressed needs for broader health care coverage, the median health care expenditures in Asia and the Pacific have remained roughly constant in the last two decades, at 4.7 per cent of GDP as of 2019. This implies that growth in nominal expenditures on health care is driven mainly by GDP growth without structural changes in fiscal expenditures as a whole that would prioritize spending on health (Lee and Pongpanich, 2021).

Beyond the ongoing financing challenges, obstacles lie outside of the health care sector itself. The presence of a large informal economy makes it more difficult for health care benefits to become universal. For example, based on current legislation and available schemes, three quarters of all people in Asia and the Pacific are entitled to such services but effectively only 63 per cent of the regional population benefit from health care protection. This points to practical difficulties in access and lack of awareness of already existing health care schemes, mostly among workers in the informal economy (ILO, 2021c). Multiple countries in the Asia-Pacific region had created schemes covering informal workers even before the start of the pandemic, such as China, the Lao People's Democratic Republic and Mongolia. In these schemes informal workers may voluntarily register and, after being in the system for the required minimum contribution time, start to benefit from chosen benefits, ranging from basic health care to maternity support (ESCAP, 2017).

Furthermore, the full impact of health care in reducing inequalities in the Asia-Pacific region is less than in other parts of the world (Claus, Martinez-Vazquez and Vulovic, 2012) (see figures 3.6 and 3.7). High out-of-pocket expenditures constrain accessibility to health care services

5 Globally, some 100 million people were pushed into extreme poverty every year due to health care costs before the start of the COVID-19 pandemic (WHO and World Bank, 2017).

FIGURE 3.7
Out-of-pocket health expenditures keep pushing millions into poverty

Proportion of population pushed below the $1.90 (2011 PPP) poverty line because of out-of-pocket health care expenditures[a], 2015

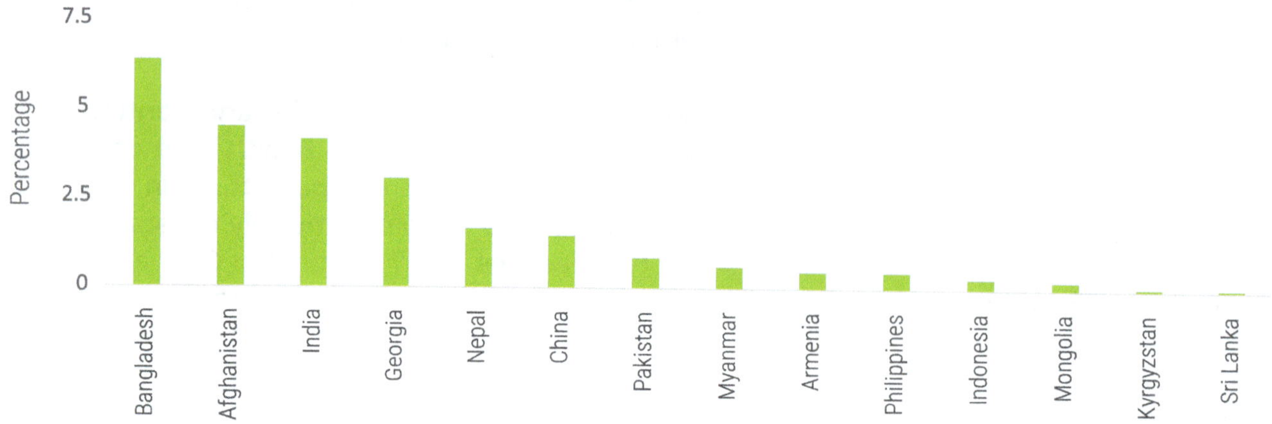

Source: ESCAP estimates based on World Development Indicators data.

[a] Fraction of a country's households experiencing impoverishing expenditures, defined as expenditures without which the household would have been above the $1.90 poverty line.

as there is a financial barrier to using physically available services; hence, there is an availability-accessibility gap which needs to be closed for achieving universality of access (Chisholm and Evans, 2010). Such financial barriers limit the inequality-reducing effects (Torbert, 2021). Therefore, policymakers need to seek locally tailored solutions, such as conditional cash transfers that might have a significant impact on accessibility to health care (see box 3.1). For example, in Cambodia in 2019, for pregnant women the Government initiated cash transfers split into a few support stages. Cash was transferred for each of up to four antenatal visits. After delivery of the child in a health facility, women would receive another transfer, which could be followed for up to 10 transfers for each post-delivery mother and child check-up. Not only does the programme improve access to health care but it also reduces poverty (WHO, 2019). Furthermore, the overall impact also differs according to the kind of support offered. For instance, primary care supports more low-income groups in contrast to specialized services that benefit higher-income groups (Abdel-Kader and Mooij, 2020), which in times of crises should not be prioritized.

There is a silver lining amid the pandemic. Evidence from 49 countries globally shows that crises tend to push countries to make advances towards universal health coverage (McDonnell and others, 2019). Although spending patterns in the last two years among low- and middle-income groups still remain unknown[6], high-income countries recorded substantial increases (WHO, 2021a). Depending on policy priorities in developing countries, such potential divergence may point to future rises in inequality between countries. Furthermore, there are countries which despite the pandemic shock continue their strong push towards implementing universal health

6 Largely through delays in standard reporting time.

BOX 3.1

China: shielding rural households from health care impoverishment

A rural-urban divide, both in poverty and inequality, remains persistent in China. In trying to reduce these discrepancies, the Government launched two medical insurance programmes which are aimed at shielding households from devastating health care expenditures which push households into poverty. The New Cooperative Medical Scheme was launched in rural China in 2003. The system covered 802 million rural residents (99 per cent of the total) by 2013, reimbursing on average up to 75 per cent of inpatient services costs. The urban system was expanded nationwide in 2010 and covers both employed and unemployed residents (Lustig and Wang, 2020).

coverage (UHC). For example, the Lao People's Democratic Republic aims to implement the UHC system by 2025, noting that for achieving this ambitious goal expenditure on human resources in health care is the priority, along with fiscal management and control (WHO, 2020) – the often-highlighted areas for inefficiency.

Given constrained fiscal space, spending on health care needs to be efficient and should leverage the potential of digital technologies.

WHO continuously highlights inefficiencies in health care spending, and the Asia-Pacific region is no exception in this regard. Even before the pandemic started, ESCAP (2019a) estimated that similar health outcomes could be achieved with 30 per cent less resources, which is in line with WHO (2010a) estimates that 20-40 per cent of health care expenditures are wasted. Therefore, in times of severe budget constraints, priority should be accorded to reducing wasteful expenditures, prioritizing cost-effective spending and increasing system-wide efficiency (Tandon and others, 2020), largely through the potential brought about by new digital technologies (WHO, 2021c).

WHO (2010b) identified health care system inefficiencies along four different sources and provided solutions to tackle them. They include:

a. **Inappropriate or costly staff mix:** Preconceived notions about doctors and nurses and what functions they can perform prevent trained nurses from performing multiple procedures. This creates a situation that currently overburdens doctors and has substantial implications for health budgets – training staff for appropriate jobs could help reduce such costs;

POLICY OPTION

Amid limited fiscal space, ensuring UHC for all could be advanced by reprioritizing expenditures in favour of health. Flexibility in budget allocations should help in this regard. Shifting available funding towards services which have the highest impact, for example primary health care, should be considered as well. Willingness to address systemic inefficiencies must be elevated.[a]

Wider deployment of digital health care technologies[b] should be considered along with continuing and learning from experiences of the accelerated digital transition initiated as a result of the COVID-19 pandemic.

[a] Due to the complex and continuously evolving nature of systemic inefficiencies, there is no standard set of guidelines which can be replicated across countries. For a broader discussion, please see "Improving health system efficiency as a means of moving towards universal coverage" (WHO, 2010b).

[b] As technologies, available health care services and demand for them change rapidly, the World Health Organization intends to provide the latest guidance. For example, see "Global strategy on digital health 2020-2025" (WHO, 2021c).

b. **Inappropriate pricing, use and standards of medicines:** It has been found that already treated patients use medicines in excess, while cheaper, generic drugs are underused[7]. Furthermore, the market is flooded with counterfeit drugs that have no healing effect.[8] Here again, establishing or strengthening prescription guidelines and improving drug regulation and quality control could go a long way;

c. **Overuse of procedures and suboptimum quality of care and medical errors:** Hospital equipment and diagnosis procedures are overused without sufficient justification or improved treatment results, either as a way to transfer the resources out of the health care system or due to fears of litigation in cases of misdiagnosis.[9] In such cases, reforming the incentive and payment structures (e.g. capitation); improving and disseminating guidelines for product use, enhancing monitoring and clinical audits; and improving hygiene standards could help reduce some of these inefficiencies;

d. **Prevalence of corruption and fraud:** These crimes generally happen due to poor accountability mechanisms. Here, governance should be improved, including through better budgetary management; undertaking expenditure surveys; and digitizing the public sector which contributes to increased transparency and accountability (Busetto and Timisina, 2020). Any lessons learned should be shared regionally.

Furthermore, more resources need to be shifted within health care spending towards preventive care and early treatment (ESCAP, 2017). Preventive care reduces long-term spending on health as fewer people suffer from long-term disease and sickness. Additionally, it can prevent long-term economic scars for workers as health challenges prevent effective labour force participation. However, such issues can be overcome at almost no cost, with already

7 There are positive action examples in the region, which may be widely deployed. Already in 2008, India launched the ***Jan Aushadhi*** campaign, promoting the sale and distribution of cheaper generic drugs in rural areas, with the aim of improving the overall health levels of the people but also cutting out-of-pocket expenditures (Joshi, Shetty, and Karande, 2019) . Promoting the use of cheaper generic drugs has also been introduced in Japan (MHLW, 2020).

8 For instance, in South-East Asia, 50 per cent of antimalaria drugs were found to contain no active ingredients (WHO, 2010a).

9 These particular actions account for 40 per cent of all wasteful spending in the United States (WHO, 2010b).

existing technologies and solutions, by focusing largely on prevention and simple medical procedures (McKinsey, 2020). Additionally, relatively little investment in health care among the poorest people would enable many of them to return to work, with direct positive implications for their incomes, poverty and inequality.

At the systemic level, financing of health expenditures also needs to be better aligned in public finance management (PFM) (Barroy and Gupta, 2021). Unlike in other fiscal expenditure areas, such as education or infrastructure, managing the revenue and expenditure sides of the health care system is highly problematic because the expenditure needs are highly unpredictable (Cashin and others, 2017). Health financing systems often do not fit overall PFM, as health spending is difficult to forecast with respect to volume, type and geographic distribution of needs, causing significant bottlenecks in health care delivery (Cashin, and others, 2017). As a result, budget allocations often exceed actual spending in many developing countries, pointing to the need for more flexible health budgets with easy-to-reallocate funds (Cho and Lee, 2021).

The challenges identified above are complex and require tailored solutions, but they have a common denominator – the need to ensure four factors: (a) access to basic health care, including for both formal and informal worker populations; (b) flexibility in budget allocations; (c) priority in devoting resources to the highest health care impact sectors – often primary care; and (d) addressing immense system-wide waste of funds.

Finally, the silver lining from the pandemic is perhaps the massive deployment of and change in human and institutional attitudes towards digital health care technologies (ITU, 2021), which brings vast benefits to health care services (WHO, 2021c). In that regard, WHO (2021c) sstressed that the shift towards digital health requires primarily decisions and commitment at the government level. With such commitment and the recently accelerated adoption of digital technology during the pandemic, digital transformation should start with the development of integrated national strategies[10], such as those listed under the ASEAN Digital Masterplan 2025. For example, with the aim of saving on medical staff capacity, telemedicine is encouraged for triage and initial health advice, e-pharmacies may facilitate delivery of medicines, which simultaneously enables controls to be placed on the unjustified prescription of drugs, while online health management systems would add to efficiency and cost reduction for circulation of medical documentation. This approach has already been implemented across the Asia-Pacific region, but needs continued strong support and encouragement to not lose its favourable momentum. For example, because of COVID-19 and related lockdown policies, electronic prescriptions became approved as being equally valid as paperwritten prescriptions in the Philippines (FDA, 2020) – a significant move towards development of a nationwide digitalized medicine prescription system. Indonesia, facing substantial challenges in terms of health care access and delivery, especially across thousands of remote islands, as well as aiming to improve overall health service delivery, launched ***Sehatpedia*** – a government-developed online platform which delivers free online health information, enables live chats with doctors or online hospital registration and integrates information under patients' medical identification details (APO, 2021).

Education

School closures and online education during the pandemic have left long-lasting scars on children, especially those who do not have access to remote learning due to the wide digital

10 WHO resolution WHA58.28 on eHealth dated 25 May 2005.

divide, and on their future earning potential when those children enter the workforce. To provide a fairer future for children, spending on early-stage education should be prioritized, while expenditures should increase accessibility and the quality of educational services.

With low investments in education even before the pandemic, the COVID-19 pandemic has taken the largest toll on children and their future.

Prior to the start of the COVID-19 pandemic, median expenditure on education across the Asia-Pacific region remained well below UNESCO guidelines of 4-6 per cent of GDP (figure 3.8) (UNICEF and UNESCO, 2021). To provide universal and good-quality pre-primary to upper-secondary education, ESCAP (2019a) estimated that the developing Asia-Pacific countries need at least an additional $138 billion on average per year. This is equivalent to 0.5 per cent of their GDP.

It is no wonder that **the pandemic was the greatest global crisis for children across the world, including those in the Asia-Pacific region (UNICEF, 2021b).** Lack of access to digital and remote learning programmes enacted to counter school closures left at least 230 million children in the Asia-Pacific region out of school (UNICEF, 2020; 2021a). These numbers translate into more visible challenges which will not only increase future inequalities, but also undermine development in all aspects. For example, in low- and middle-income countries, before the pandemic, 53 per cent of 10-year-old children were not able to read and understand age-appropriate text. The pandemic is expected to increase this share by 3-10 percentage points (World Bank, 2021b). Hence, to ensure inclusive development, it is essential to maintain investments in education in order to limit the long-term scars left by recessions and crises (Cerra, Fatas and Saxena,

FIGURE 3.8

Expenditure on education in Asia and the Pacific remains below the global target

Spending on education in the Asia-Pacific region, percentage of GDP

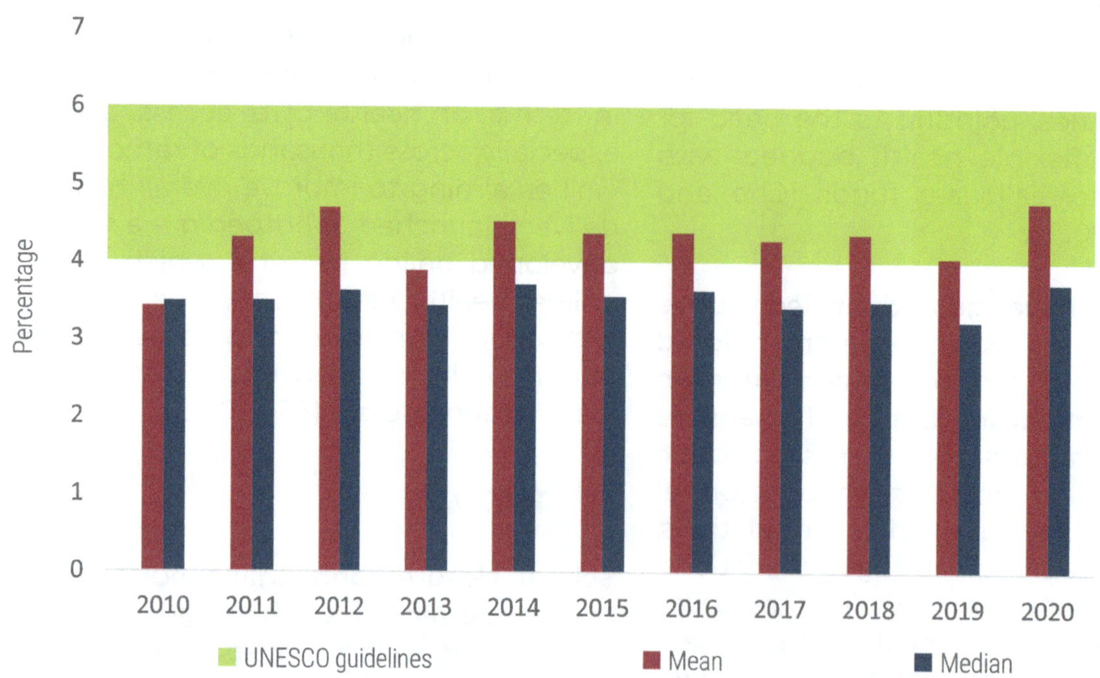

Source: ESCAP estimates based on IMF data.

2021). It is imperative that spending on education not be reduced as countries prepare for eventual fiscal consolidation. For this, they will need to prioritize spending in favour of education.

Overwhelming evidence points to the fundamental role of education in reducing inequality, especially in the early years of education.

Education lies at the foundation of socioeconomic development and is necessary for building more equitable and inclusive societies. Education leads to better individual outcomes, such as higher labour market remuneration and consequently poverty reduction, and it also fosters long-term economic growth through accumulation of human capital. Hence, Sustainable Development Goal 4 aims to "Ensure inclusive and equitable quality education and promote lifelong learning opportunities for all". Chapter 5 discusses the role of education as a long-term inequality-shaping factor.

Indeed, **the positive role of increased education attainment in reducing inequality, both in developing as well as developed countries, has been well documented** (ADBI, 2019). Cho and Lee (2021), using the most recent data on inequality and government education expenditures,[11] confirmed similar findings at the Asia-Pacific level. Furthermore, research on the region suggests that the skill premium contributes to reduction in income inequality up to three times greater when compared with other regions of the world (IMF, 2016). These general findings are confirmed at the country-level by studies[12] which found positive impacts on the reduction of inequality. By contrast, unequal access to education and, therefore, overall enrolment rates, has been singled out as fuelling growing inequalities (Claus, Martinez-Vazquez and Vulovic, 2012).

In looking at country-level experiences, a few patterns arise that point to priority areas for expenditures. For instance, ***primary and pre-primary education seems to have a particularly strong impact on reducing inequality.*** Two thirds of the reduction in inequality in Viet Nam is estimated to have been achieved through the education channel, with nearly 80 per cent of that impact attributed to primary education (World Bank, 2016a). Indeed, universality of primary education was one of the first steps in decades-long reforms of the education system, followed by a push for higher transition and retention rates in secondary education and graduation, or enhancement of teacher training. Additionally, ***making pre-school education fee-free*** resulted in a significant reduction in inequality in Georgia, Indonesia and the Philippines (Torbert, 2021).

Efficiency can also be improved with well-chosen spending targets. In their absence, spending can be drained by salaries of already employed staff instead of being invested or channelled towards system coverage (see box 3.2; World Bank, 2021b). In this vein, for example, Indonesia pushed for greater focus on improved teaching qualifications and strengthening of its national testing system, additional teacher recruitment and investment in school infrastructure – all of which translated into higher enrolment rates at all levels (World Bank, 2020b).

Synergies with other policies should also be exploited for a higher impact. For instance, in the Philippines, a social assistance programme (*Pantawid Pamilyang Pilipino Program – 4Ps*), required beneficiaries to enrol and stay in school, which resulted in an expected increase in school enrolment, especially at the secondary level (ADB, 2020), and a reduction in inequality (Torbert, 2021).

11 Classification of the Functions of Government (COFOG) data.

12 For example, studies by the Commitment to Equity (CEQ) Institute or the public expenditure reviews (PERs) of the World Bank.

BOX 3.2

Aligning education expenditure in Cambodia towards low-income households

Cambodia increased its spending on education, which was reflected in very high primary education enrolments, matching that of South-East Asian counterparts and high-income countries as of 2015 (Torbert, 2021). Nevertheless, secondary school enrolment remained at the very low level of 45 per cent (against the ASEAN average of 68 per cent), while the number of dropouts was on the rise.

Looking deeper into the education expenditures of Cambodia reveals a bias towards high-income households. ***First***, the increase in government spending on education used to be driven mostly by teachers' salaries, without addressing other systemic bottlenecks, such as the overall shortage of teachers, training and school infrastructure investment (World Bank, 2019a). Therefore, additional funds did not proportionately translate into higher enrolment rates or better teaching outcomes. ***Second***, in the past, the funds were not channelled towards the poor. For example, the top 20 per cent of households by income used to be beneficiaries of 32 per cent of all education expenditures in 2004. After reforms, this structure started to tilt towards low-income households, and the figure dropped to 22 per cent in 2014. In the same time period, the share of the funds received by the bottom 20 per cent of the households rose from 12 per cent to 17 per cent (Torbert, 2021) – an important but still insufficient shift from the perspective of reducing inequality.

POLICY OPTION

Eliminate socioeconomic barriers which lead to dropping out of school. For example, consider full coverage of education costs for those in need, especially in rural areas.

As the World Bank (2011) noted, the success story of education system reform in Viet Nam had a powerful supporter – the electrification of rural areas. While electrification is not the major challenge anymore, in looking ahead, priority should be given to ensuring that everybody has access to broadband Internet – a policy priority highlighted in the *Survey* for 2021 in the "Building forward Better" package (ESCAP, 2021a).

Furthermore, with respect to the impact of COVID-19 on education and the synergy effects of other policies with educational performance, UNICEF and UNESCO (2021) stressed the need for increased investment in children's health and well-being as pre-requisites for learning. Similarly, the WFP (2020) pointed out the need to ensure proper nutrition through school feeding programmes, especially for children in extreme poverty whose number is expected to rise because of the ongoing crisis. Such expenditures on nutrition are expected to be returned 20 times in the long run.

Special attention should be paid to gaps in access between the rural and urban populations. The higher is the access to education by wealthier households relative to poorer and often rural counterparts, the lower will be the impact of education expenditures on inequality reduction. For example, in Georgia, the already wealthier households benefit more from spending on tertiary education in contrast to their low-income counterparts (CEQ, 2017). However, as Claus, Martinez-Vazquez and Vulovic (2012) noted, even if tertiary education expenditures were channelled towards primary education, there might be little effect due to the general lack of access of the poor to education, especially in rural areas. Therefore, additional expenditure on education without appropriate channelling towards rural and low-income areas might be drained by urban schooling, which has little impact on rural education (see box 3.2). Similarly, more attention needs to be paid to the economic situation of households with children, because it has a significant impact on enrolments and graduation rates. As ESCAP (2019a) stressed, there is a need to increase support of children through non-salary recurrent spending to help marginalized children start and stay at school, which became increasingly difficult to do owing to COVID-19 impoverishment that globally pushed about 100 million children into poverty (UNICEF, 2021b).

POLICY OPTION

Ensure sufficient funding for universal education, especially in the early years, even in times of looming fiscal consolidations. These would reduce the long-lasting scarring from interruptions to formal education during the pandemic.

Address external factors which have impact on the long-term study path, such as the digital divide. Thus, ensuring access to broadband Internet access is fundamental.

Enhance inclusion in tertiary education by eliminating financial barriers, for example, via work-for-scholarship programmes and by universal young-age education.

While priority for inclusive recovery requires a laser focus on pre-primary, primary and secondary education, policymakers must also keep an eye on making tertiary education more inclusive.

For example, more has to be done for economic inclusiveness of higher education and the participation of women in science, technology, engineering and mathematics (STEM) – policy actions necessary to address changing labour market demands driven by the fourth industrial revolution (UNESCO, 2021a). Furthermore, tertiary education remains crucial for COVID-19 recovery as the pandemic depleted the existing human capital (World Bank, 2021a). Based on the regional experience, there are examples of how to move in that direction. For example, the Islamic Republic of Iran lowered financial entry barriers for tertiary education covering part of the costs in exchange for later work in the country (Enami, Lustig and Taqdiri, 2017). Similarly, support-for-work programmes, which do not impose financial debt on new graduates, can be found in Singapore (MHA, 2022).

In fact, inclusive primary education aids inclusion at the tertiary level. UNESCO (2021b) stressed that to achieve inclusive tertiary education learning must start at the primary or at even earlier levels of education. This further strengthens the call for supporting primary education, as the lack of educational opportunities in early childhood, so common during the COVID-19 pandemic, define the long-term study path. Furthermore, evidence shows that through increases in enrolment, education expenditure becomes more equitable, such as in Cambodia[13] (World Bank, 2019a).

13 Despite being more equitable, higher-income households still benefited relatively more, as they were more likely to enrol their children in school. Furthermore, scholarships were often only enhancing enrolment rates but not learning outcomes. At the same time, the major barrier to education in remote areas was lack of schooling infrastructure and teaching staff (World Bank, 2019).

BOX 3.3

China: for the poorest, in-kind subsidies are often similar to a zero-one situation – either sufficient or not at all

Compulsory education, combined with strict eradication of child labour, resulted in virtual elimination of illiteracy in urban areas of China. By contrast, in poorer rural areas even free education was not sufficient, as the cost of textbooks and other schooling-related expenditures that burdened parents remained too high. As a result, school attainment remained low and illiteracy rates high. These expenditures started to be subsidized in 2001, and by 2007 all rural households were covered, resulting in improvement in educational outcomes (Lustig and Wang, 2020).

Social protection

Two years into the pandemic, policymakers should not forget that those better-off should support the less fortunate. This includes expanding protection over informal workers and vulnerable groups, which would prevent them from being pushed into poverty and contribute to recovery from the crisis. Digital technologies can support these ambitions – efficiently.

Social protection schemes in the Asia-Pacific region are often beyond the reach of those who need them.

Social protection policies contribute significantly to reducing poverty and inequality, as well as to increasing the resilience of the socioeconomic system (ESCAP, 2018c; ESCAP, 2021d; ESCAP and ILO, 2020a). However, coverage in Asia and the Pacific remains just around the global average at 46 per cent[14] (figure 3.9), while the region spends on average one third of the global expenditure of 11.2 per cent of GDP on social protection (ESCAP, 2018c). The average numbers still mask significant variation within the region, with only 24 per cent of the population covered in South and South-West Asia to almost 80 per cent in North and Central Asia and the Pacific (figure 3.9).

In the ongoing COVID-19 pandemic, social protection has been recognized as a core enabler for socioeconomic recovery, and multiple countries have decided to scale up their social protection programmes (ESCAP and ILO, 2020a). However, the impact of seemingly similar policies is unpredictable, depending on who benefits – the rich or the poor (Torbert, 2021), or whether those in need have practical access to such policies. Hence, in focusing on the inequality angle, the impact depends on coverage, design and accessibility (Cho and Lee, 2021), as well as overall expenditure size[15] of these policies (ESCAP, 2018a). For example:

- Regarding ***design and accessibility***, about 34 per cent of social protection benefits in low-income countries go to the richest 40 per cent of households (Torbert, 2021). This sample includes 12 countries in the Asia-Pacific region. Furthermore, as almost 70 per cent of workers in the region are in the informal sector, they remain often beyond social protection schemes (ESCAP and ILO, 2020a);

- Schemes targeting the poor in the region, albeit well-intended, exclude up to 80 per cent of the poor and the best-performing poverty-targeted schemes exclude approximately half of those whom they were intended to reach (ESCAP and ILO, 2020a);

- Research on Asian countries suggests that social protection policies might be particularly misaligned compared with that of their global peers. For instance, a 1 percentage point increase in government spending on social protection in Asia increases inequality by 0.49 percentage points, compared with a 0.28 percentage point decrease for the rest of the world (Claus, Martinez-Vazquez and Vulovic, 2012). This divergence is likely to occur due to the composition of social protection expenditure in Asia where countries provide fewer services and direct transfers to people unlike what is done in the rest of the world;

- Regarding ***expenditure size***, the Asia-Pacific region spends about one third of the global average on social protection, leaving 60 per

14 Excluding health care and sickness.

15 For example, the Agricultural Card Programme in Georgia provides benefits for the purchase of certain agricultural goods based on farm size eligibility. Despite being the second most inequality-reducing programme in Georgia (high efficiency), the overall impact on inequality reduction in the country remains at a minimum due to the overall low budget of the programme (Torbert, 2021).

cent of the population without protection from illness, disability or unemployment (ESCAP, 2018c) – exacerbating all the risks which materialized in the last two years;

- Regarding ***social protection funding***, a mix of contributory and non-contributory schemes, extended towards the informal economy, are needed to ensure minimum social protection floors, including universal health coverage. However, with respect to inequality reduction and gender equality, non-contributory universal schemes allow for sufficient risk-pooling and redistribution by guaranteeing coverage of low-income groups; therefore, they remain of particular importance (ILO, 2021e).

Important reasons for these shortcomings are insufficient spending, and inefficient design and implementation. With expected fiscal consolidation in view, where available, improvements in efficiency of social protection delivery schemes should be considered, which would imply that more resources may be used for expansion of coverage and accessibility. Digital solutions play a vital role in direct transfer targeting, especially in times of crises and pandemics. New technologies contribute also to delivery of in-kind support (ESCAP and ILO, 2020a). For instance, the United Nations World Food Programme and the government of Meghalaya, India, joined forces to reform and optimize the targeted public distribution system through automation and deployment of supply chain, storage and delivery management technologies (WFP, 2021). However, the estimated savings from targeting the real beneficiaries and excluding those who can afford certain social protection schemes using private resources might be overstated, considering the rather small realized net gains from such changes

FIGURE 3.9
Social protection coverage rates vary considerably across Asia-Pacific subregions

Social protection coverage by at least one area[a] in Asia and the Pacific, latest year available

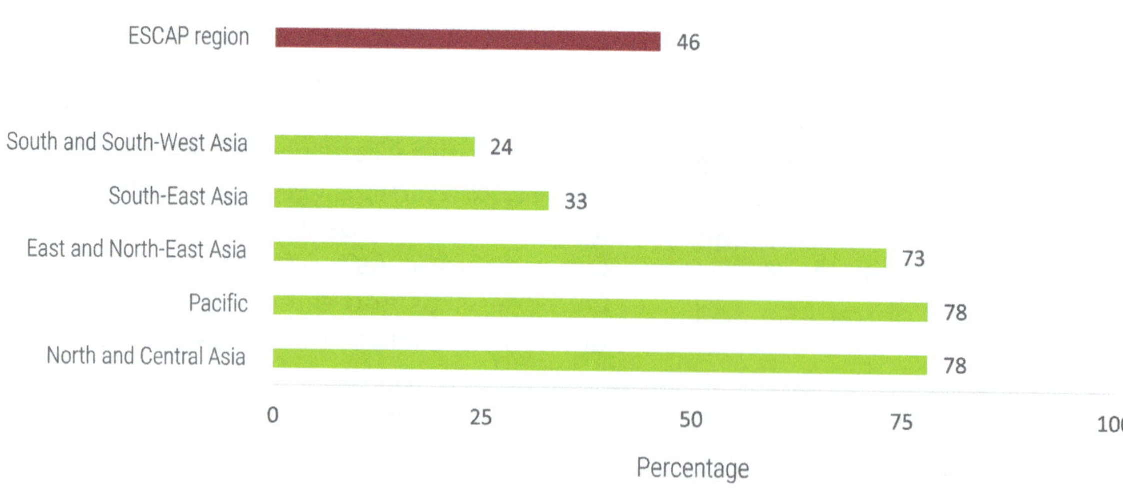

Source: ESCAP and ILO, 2020a.

[a] *Excluding health care and illness.*

(see box 3.4). At the same time, the social costs of undercoverage in the case of informal workers might also be underestimated.

Informality of employment and other economic activities or lack of registration in government income and social support databases make millions of vulnerable people "invisible" to social protection programmes (IMF, 2020). For example, 90 per cent of workers in India are in the informal economy (ILO, 2020a). Chatterjee (2020) pointed out that, although such informal workers often lack any form of social protection, they are an indispensable part of the economy, essential even in times of crisis such as the pandemic. Therefore, social protection policies must be redesigned towards greater inclusiveness extending over all, not least to cover population groups in vulnerable situations (ESCAP and ILO, 2020a; ILO, 2021c; UNDP and ILO, 2021; Torbert, 2021).

Innovations in technology can make registration and delivery more efficient and transparent. For example, thanks to the *Aadhaar* system, a verifiable 12-digit identification number issued to residents of India, social protection programmes are delivered directly to eligible and registered[16] individuals. Therefore, beyond the issue of intended support, the system addresses leakage losses, which for non-digitalized welfare programmes are estimated at 10-60 per cent (ACM, 2019). With 1 billion accounts linked to digital identities and by continuously addressing existing registration challenges or systemic bottlenecks (ESCAP, 2022), the system is proving to be a promising advance in social protection, for example, as cash transfers can be sent almost immediately at very low cost and with little fraud risk (The Economist, 2020).

16 It should be noted that eligible individuals do not fully overlap with registered individuals, for example due to the practical inability to get registered owing to the lack of a bank account, personal identification or other necessary items, which points to the social cost of such solutions and the need to expand coverage via other schemes towards those excluded.

Social protection benefits support inclusive development, but do not change inequalities overnight.

Social protection systems provide income security against normal day-to-day contingencies and needs associated with raising children, getting ill or acquiring a disability, losing a job, and growing older. They also protect people against systemic shocks that affect everyone, such as natural disasters, economic crises and pandemics. Leaving individuals and families to manage life's risks on their own breeds vulnerability. Indeed, government transfers kept millions of people out of poverty across Asia and the Pacific during the COVID-19 pandemic. For example, under the National Food Security Act, 2013, India provided 800 million people with support (NFSP, 2021). Under its digital *Aadhaar* programme, India facilitated unconditional cash transfers to 200 million women during the pandemic, while state governments disbursed the equivalent of about $762 million to 18.3 million building and construction workers (Saini and Hussain, 2021).

The COVID-19 pandemic has underscored the role of comprehensive social protection systems and their digital instruments as a key development tool to sustain economic stability for households in response to crises. Governments leveraged both contributory and non-contributory schemes to expand income and in-kind support for their citizens. Moving beyond these short-term, shock-responsive measures, a more inclusive and comprehensive social protection systems that provides predictable and stable benefits in a transparent and efficient manner can help households invest in the advancement of their health and human capital, and reduce inequalities in the long term.

BOX 3.4

Child benefits in Mongolia

Mongolia has been developing its Child Money Programme for almost two decades, with various approaches towards its coverage, universality and eligibility criteria. For example, targeted conditionality includes the following: households with three or more children, enrolment in school and having been vaccinated, among other requirements. Since 2018, 85 per cent of children receive benefits under this programme. These are children who are registered in the Programme's database and meet the eligibility criteria to receive these benefits.

The Programme has been functioning during times of expansionary fiscal policy, as well as in times of consolidation, where coverage was limited due to a lack of budgetary resources. It is aimed at shifting social support towards the bottom in terms of income distribution. Therefore, the impact of the Programme on inequality and poverty, as well as its overall efficiency, varies depending on the eligibility criteria.

However, targeting through eligibility criteria, estimated by household surveys, turned out to be inadequate, pointing to the advantages of categorical schemes having such a criterion as maximum age. For example, there was no easy way to differentiate household income based on surveys alone, while the administrative burden and administrative costs remained high. Therefore, "supporting all" might be the most efficient method in practice because available data and programme management skills and capacity might not allow pursuing the temptation for "supporting only those in need" – even if it would theoretically be the optimum approach.

Source: ESCAP (2021b); UNICEF (2019).

POLICY OPTION

Expand coverage of social protection schemes for all people, including informal workers and people in vulnerable situations, and formalize informal work to ensure access to social protection.

Accelerate deployment of digital systems and databases for better fiscal management and efficient delivery of social protection transfers.

4. FISCAL POLICY OPTIONS – TAX FAIRLY

Fiscal space redesign – untapped potential of new sources of tax revenues

Amid tighter fiscal space, additional resources must be mobilized to mitigate the negative impacts from either expenditure cuts or debt increases. With a rise in digitalization of the economy and with a large informal sector, policymakers have a lot of room to bring these two aspects under the tax purview.

As discussed above, there is a need to at least sustain expenditures on health care, education and social protection in order to pursue inclusive development pathways and counteract the negative impacts of the COVID-19 pandemic. To achieve more with the same resources, a "spend smart" approach for higher efficiency and impact would certainly help but it is unlikely to remain sufficient. For example, ESCAP (2019a) estimated that the developing countries in Asia and the Pacific need an annual average additional investment of $1.5 trillion per year to implement the 2030 Agenda, warning that this would likely increase debt to GDP ratio in the region by at least 10 percentage points over the next 20 years. Therefore, countries might need to strengthen their fiscal revenue side (ESCAP, 2021a).

"Tax fairly" – increases in tax collection efficiency and broadening of the tax base are the way forward. Similar calls to raise tax revenues have come from other international organizations in the region as well, for example, from the Asian Development Bank (ADB, 2021b; 2021c). Reforms in revenue collection would not only ease fiscal space but also minimize the adverse impact of likely fiscal consolidation on inequality. However, one might want to act with care as inequalities will depend on who gets taxed (ESCAP, 2019b).[17]

Increases in tax revenues, for example, can occur by ensuring that every individual and business entity pays its share as expected in tax regulations and by expanding the tax base into the informal economy. In this respect, loopholes should be closed, unnecessary tax incentives should be eliminated or reduced substantially while profit-shifting, illicit financial flows and informal business activities should be addressed accordingly (ADB, 2021b; ESCAP, 2018b). For example, 7.6 per cent of the tax revenue in the Asia-Pacific region was estimated to be lost due to misinvoicing in 2016 (Kravchenko, 2018). Even though progressive personal income taxes

17 Despite plentiful evidence on the various impacts of fiscal policies on inequality – both on expenditure and revenue sides – their impacts must be analysed from a holistic perspective (OECD, 2018).

(PIT) have been found to reduce inequalities over decades, their implementation and management costs may exceed the benefits, making them attractive only to more developed countries (ESCAP, 2018d). For example, the PIT system in Indonesia has been calibrated to cover only relatively high earners; thus, only 15 per cent of formal workers have to file tax returns and more than half of the total PIT income comes from just 0.5 per cent of the population (Torbert, 2021).

Tax revenues in Asia and the Pacific were relatively low even before the pandemic, while tax structures struggled to reduce inequality.

Even before the pandemic, in 2019 the 21 per cent average tax-to-GDP ratio[18] in the Asia-Pacific region was considerably below the averages in OECD and Latin America and the Caribbean countries (figure 3.10a). While that is still an improvement over the 16.4 per cent collected in 2015, it also hides substantial differences, as many countries collect only about 10 per cent of GDP via taxes (ESCAP, 2018d)

Overall, indirect taxation, which tends to increase inequalities (figures 3.5 and 3.6), was the dominant source of tax revenues at 49.8 per cent of the total, compared with the OECD average of 32.7 per cent (figure 3.10b), although the figure for the Asia-Pacific region is comparable with that of other developing economies. In comparing the total fiscal revenue mix to the OECD average, the Asia-Pacific region also collects relatively little through personal income taxes, which are administratively

18 For 24 economies with available OECD data in the Asia-Pacific region. The latest most complete IMF data on tax-to-GDP ratio for for 46 Asia-Pacific ESCAP member States indicates the average of 16.9 per cent for 2017.

FIGURE 3.10
Overall tax-to-GDP ratio in Asia-Pacific region is relatively low compared with other regions of the world

(a) Average total tax revenues as a percentage of GDP, 2019

(b) Average fiscal revenue structure, 2019

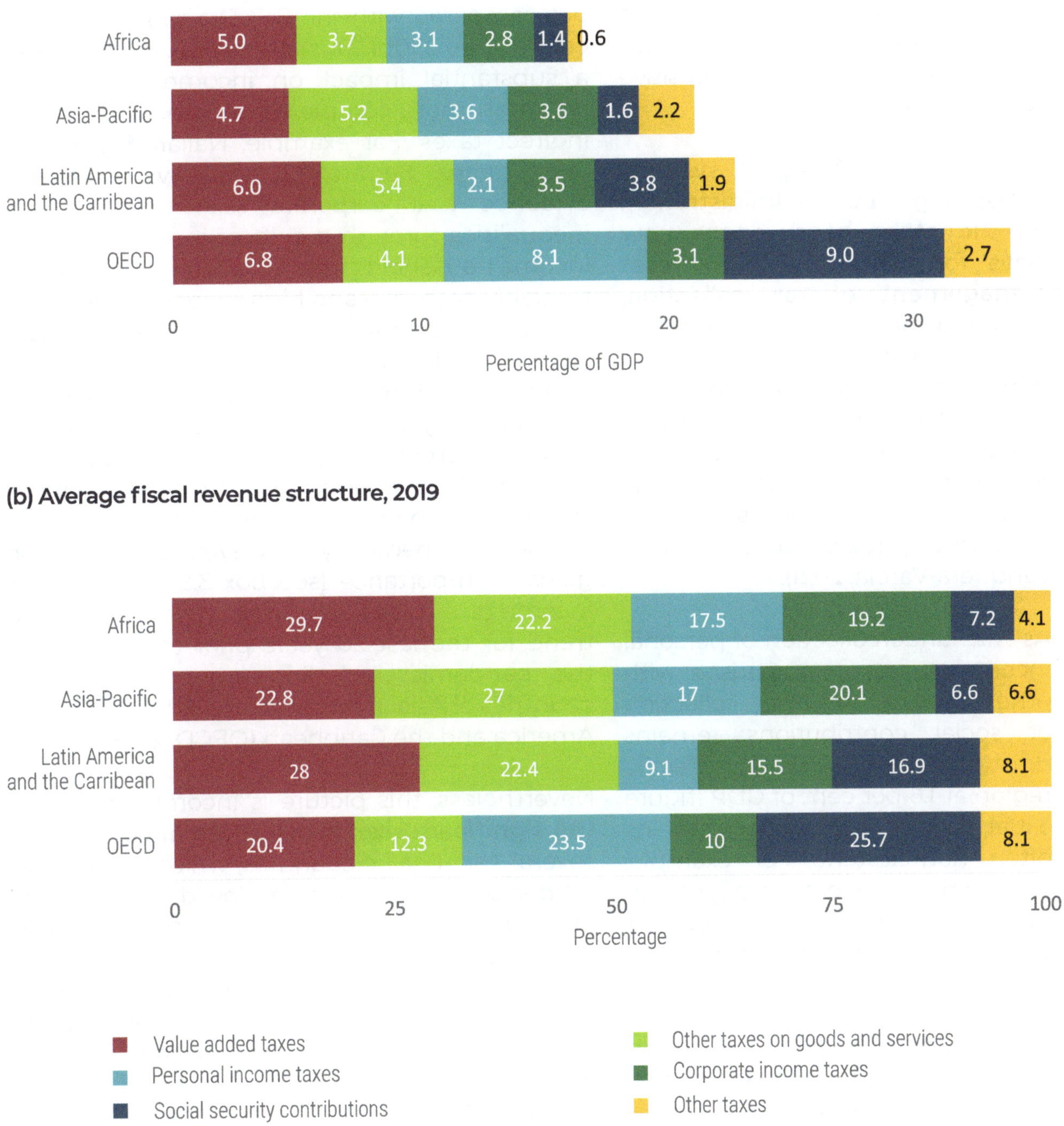

Source: OECD (2021a).

Note: 2018 data for Africa and OECD.

challenging to implement (ESCAP, 2018d), and through social security contributions (figure 3.10b).[19] The overall fiscal revenues from social security contributions stood at 1.6 per cent of GDP, well below the OECD average of 9 per cent (figure 3.10a). Because of the substantial impact of social expenditures on reducing inequality, their increase could have far-reaching positive implications.

Development of digital systems supporting tax administration, on the other hand, opens new ways for efficient and low-cost management of tax collection, including personal income taxes, which is particularly important in times of structural shifts when large shares of the economy move into a relatively easy-to-control digital environment with relatively easy-to-track digital payments (Estevão, 2021; OECD, 2021c; Lucas-Mas and Junquera-Varela, 2021).

As with undercollection of personal income taxes, in comparison with other global regions, collection of social contributions remains drastically low in the Asia-Pacific region at 1.6 per cent of GDP (figure 3.10a). This form of taxation remains often non-existent. For example, such schemes were introduced in Indonesia only in 2015, at 3 per cent and 6 per cent of contributions from employees and employers, respectively. The proceeds are intended to fund health care and pensions. This is not the general rule though. In such countries as China, the Islamic Republic of Iran, Japan and the Republic of Korea, social contributions are one of the largest tax revenue sectors (ESCAP, 2018d).

The region leads in corporate income tax (CIT) collection as a percentage of GDP. For some Asia-Pacific countries,[20] the share of CIT in all tax revenues at more than 25 per cent stands out compared with the OECD average of 10 per cent (figure 3.10b). This form of taxation also has a substantial impact on income distribution, although more complex compared with PIT or indirect taxes. For example, Nallareddy, Rouen and Suárez Serrato (2019) provided strong evidence that corporate tax cuts[21] increase inequalities through a shift of income by high-income households from labour to capital. Even if arguably both low- and high-income households benefit from an income increase, that increase would be higher for high-income households. Furthermore, Hager and Baines (2020) discussed how lowering of CIT enhances concentration of power in corporations, which amid weak labour laws, neglect workers' income and prioritize shareholder benefits, leading directly to an increase in inequality. However, CIT collection gains in importance (see box 3.5) as corporate income taxes globally have been on a downward trend for the last 20 years prior to the start of the pandemic, including among developing countries of Asia and the Pacific, Africa, and Latin America and the Caribbean (OECD, 2020).

Nevertheless, this picture is incomplete due to **the significant size of the informal economy** in several Asia-Pacific countries, which account for 68 per cent of persons employed in the region (ILO, 2018a). This means that a considerably large proportion of the regional population remains outside the tax purview. Therefore, **formalization of business activities and, consequently, taxing related personal and corporate incomes might be the largest untapped fiscal revenue resource.**[22] Taxing the informal sector through business registration and formalization would not only generate additional fiscal resources but

19 The overall impact of the most common direct taxes, PIT and social security contributions varies significantly among countries largely due to coverage differences. Evidence suggests that, among these two, PIT has greater potential for reducing inequality (Torbert, 2021).

20 Kazakhstan, Malaysia, Papua New Guinea and Singapore (OECD, 2021a).

21 Either through changes in nominal or effective tax rates.

22 For a detailed discussion on tax revenue increases, especially PIT, see ESCAP (2018d, chapter 4).

CALL FOR ACTION – muster the political will

Increase tax revenues through the "pay fair share" approach, namely closing loopholes, cutting unnecessary tax incentives, fighting profit-shifting, illicit financial flows and formalizing business activities.

Tilt the overall taxation weight towards the top of the income distribution, including but not only, through changes in PIT and CIT, tax compliance and indirect taxation. As indirect taxes are the dominant source of taxes in the Asia-Pacific region, extra caution is needed in case of potential rate hikes.

BOX 3.5

Challenges of the digital economy – outdated tax systems and agreements do not fit today's increasingly digital and globalized world

Calls for fair taxation of international corporations have been heard for decades. In the last 20 years, they have been joined by calls to tax "Internet companies". The chorus was recently strengthened by the call for taxation of e-commerce and the broader "digital economy" (United Nations, 2022). Everything points in the same direction – corporations hiding behind increasingly complex networks of transborder business operations set up for the same goal – to limit the amount of taxes they pay.

Even before the pandemic, UNCTAD (2015) pointed out that developing economies suffer relatively more from tax evasion and avoidance owing to their weaker potential for imposing countermeasures. At the same time, given the scarcity of domestic resources, tax avoidance losses have a larger impact. More recently, OECD (2021a) pointed out that the Asia-Pacific region needs to strengthen its mobilization of domestic resources – possibly through greater efforts to prevent erosion of the domestic tax base and profit shifting.

The year 2021 might have sparked a process that will change this "hide and seek" game, which in the end undermines all global efforts to achieve a fairer and more sustainable future. As was stated in OECD (2021b), the current goal is to "ensure that multinational enterprises pay a fair share of tax wherever they operate". In signing the OECD/G20 Framework of Base Erosion and Profit Shifting (BEPS), 130 countries and jurisdictions pledged to reform the century-old global tax system, which does not fit current needs.

The OECD reform intends to ensure that (a) corporations pay taxes where they operate, even without their physical presence being necessary, which should reallocate up to $100 billion annually; and (b) CIT may be voluntarily set, either by the host country or other country concerned through additional taxation, at the minimum of 15 per cent globally from 2023. This scheme should generate up to $150 billion in additional tax revenues annually. Point (a) targets in particular digital business operations as goods and, increasingly, services are sold online across borders without the payment of the taxes due (OECD, 2021b).

For such initiatives to fully succeed, however, multilateral support is crucial. For example, in December 2021, the European Commission pledged to counter shell companies across the European Union (European Commission, 2021), which often serve as tax avoidance vehicles also in the Asia-Pacific region (UNCTAD, 2015).

All developed economies in Asia and the Pacific joined the OECD framework, as well as multiple developing economies, including the largest ones, such as China, India, Indonesia, and the Russian Federation – in total, 26 member States, and 3 associate members of ESCAP. On the other hand, the benefits of the new agreement do not seem to be equal for all, as multiple low-income or least developed countries broadly refused to join the agreement. The key flaws they underlined include costs that are too high for them to implement necessary tax system changes amid doubtful net gains.[a]

[a]Multiple solutions and improvements in the field of international tax cooperation are provided by the United Nations Committee of Experts on International Cooperation in Tax Matters.

would also increase transparency and fair competition in the business environment, thus encouraging the growth of businesses and help build a culture of tax compliance (Rao, 2014; Joshi, Prichard and Heady, 2014). Formalization should also bring clear benefits to informal workers, for example through the introduction of contributory social security systems, which collect exceedingly little revenues in the Asia-Pacific region (figure 3.10a and b), thus offering transparent social security and health care benefits to those covered. As ILO (2022) noted, such schemes should be based on compulsory rather than voluntary affiliation, as the latter remains usually ineffective.[23] By contrast, increased compliance may be also achieved linking access to government services and subsidies with a proof of formalization. Depending on the current coverage, such systems may need to be introduced gradually, for example first for salaried workers then the self-employed. For instance, when the Republic of Korea pushed towards the adoption of compulsory health insurance in the 1970s, the scheme first covered companies with more than 500 employees, moving gradually towards encompassing smaller enterprises (ILO, 2008).

Last but not least, with digitalization of services, the role of which will only grow in the post-pandemic period, it is about time to tax the digital economy (see box 3.5).

23 Compulsory formalization does not imply compulsory contributions irrespective of income level, especially given volatile and often low earnings in the informal economy. In a broader context, compulsory formalization allows for extension of social security benefits over currently informal workers, the benefits of which would have to be covered under non-contributory schemes (ILO, 2022), but also would allow for future taxation in cases of sufficient income increase.

5. POLICY CONSIDERATIONS

While the vastly diverse regional economies do not allow for a "one-suit-fits-all" policy recommendation, a similar set of challenges during the COVID-19 pandemic has helped to uncover some commonalities. Therefore, the following guidelines should be helpful in choosing the right direction for fiscal policies as countries recover from the pandemic and use this opportunity to build fairer, more inclusive and equal economies, which will also be more resilient to future shocks.

Fiscal space in 2022 and beyond – move with caution

Depending on the country-level economic situation, if the need to consolidate fiscal positions materializes and fiscal austerity measures must be implemented, prioritizing progressive tax-based adjustments should be considered over expenditure-side adjustments. Research suggests that there would be a larger adverse impact on inequality in case of expenditure-side adjustments.

Fiscal expenditures – sectors to defend at all costs from fiscal cuts

Health care – as the pandemic took a heavy toll on people's health, expenditures on health remain necessary for a better quality of life, stronger economic performance, faster recovery from the crisis and building of more resilient, equal economies. It is necessary to ensure at least that basic universal health coverage is prioritized within health expenditures, as shortcomings at that level have a decisive impact on labour force participation, income generation and overall quality of life. Therefore, the following policies are recommended:

a. Amid limited fiscal space, ensure universal health coverage for all by ***reprioritizing expenditures in favour of health. Flexibility in budget allocations*** should help in this regard. Shifting available funding towards services which have the highest impact, for example primary health care, should be considered as well. Willingness to address systemic inefficiencies must be elevated;

b. Consider ***wider deployment of digital health care technologies*** and continue learning from the experiences of the accelerated digital transition initiated as a result of the COVID-19 pandemic.

Education – as the COVID-19 pandemic has already had an unprecedented impact on children due to school closures and deterioration of their economic environment, failing on education would mean preparing fertile ground for inequality to increase in the future - a trend unlikely to be reversed easily. Therefore, policymakers should maintain education expenditures and ensure that the available resources support coverage, universal access and good-quality teaching, aligning their policies with the following guidelines:

a. Ensure ***sufficient funding for universal education, especially in the early years,*** even in times of looming fiscal consolidation. This would reduce the long-lasting scarring from interruptions to formal education that have occurred during the pandemic;

b. Address ***external factors which have adverse impacts on the long-term study path.*** For example, close the digital divide by ensuring access to broadband Internet;

c. ***Enhance inclusion in tertiary education*** by eliminating financial barriers, for example via work-for-scholarship programmes and by universal young age education;

d. ***Eliminate socioeconomic barriers which lead to dropping out from school.*** For example, consider full coverage of education costs for those in need, especially in rural areas.

Social protection – which has already protected millions from falling into poverty - remains far from universal, leaving large numbers of informal workers and vulnerable groups with no support. Therefore, fiscal priorities should be aligned with the need for universality of access. Here, digital technologies offer support in the management and efficient delivery of social protection schemes, thus they should be implemented on a larger scale. In aiming to achieve these goals, the following policy options are recommended:

a. Expand ***coverage of social protection schemes to all people,*** including for informal workers and people in vulnerable situations, and formalize informal work to ensure access to social protection;

b. Accelerate ***deployment of digital systems and databases*** for better fiscal management and efficient delivery of social protection transfers.

> ***Fiscal revenues – there is an urgent need for increasing revenues, being mindful of their impacts on inequality***

Paying a fair share of taxes: Ensure that all individuals and companies pay their "fair share of taxes" under already existing tax regimes. Existing tax systems must be changed to eliminate tax avoidance and increase tax collection efficiency. For instance, digitalization of tax reporting not only lowers administrative costs but also allows for better control and management of the tax systems. In particular, policymakers can:

Increase tax revenues through a "pay one's fair share" approach, namely closing loopholes, cutting unnecessary tax incentives, fighting profit-shifting and illicit financial flows and formalizing business activities.

Shifting the burden towards high-income households: When tax rate increases are inevitable, the aim should be to shift the overall tax burden towards the top of the income distribution, for example through PIT, CIT, or social contributions, which support reduction in inequality, instead of through indirect tax channels.

As indirect taxes are the dominant source of taxes in the Asia-Pacific region, extra caution is needed in the case of potential rate hikes.

> *Fiscal management – having less to spend and aiming to achieve more requires "spending smart"*

Big bang for the buck: Reassess spending patterns for inefficiently spent resources and identify potential savings, such as those previously illustrated for the education and health care sectors. Increase impacts by redirecting part of fiscal expenditures towards vulnerable and currently excluded groups, where significant change can be achieved at relatively low cost, such as through basic health care procedures. Increase the impact

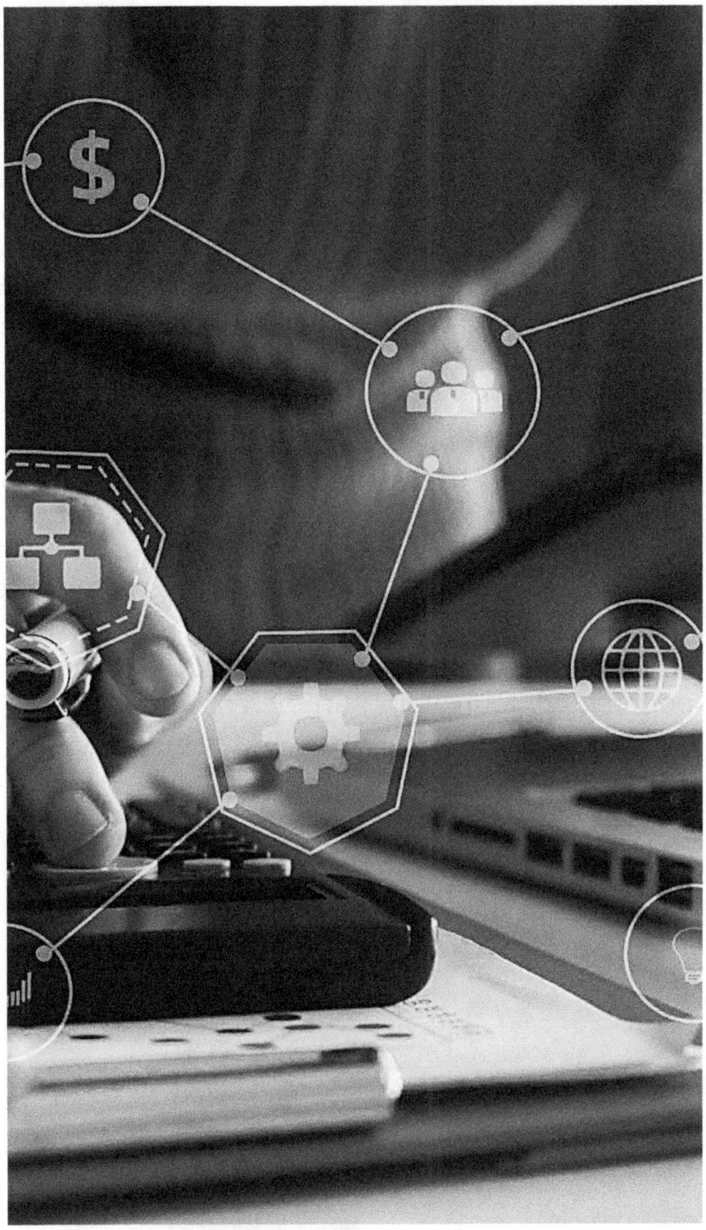

through synergies with other programmes, such as social protection programmes enabling children to access schooling system despite the current financial barriers.

Digitalization: The pandemic has opened the window of opportunity for further deployment of digital technologies, which should be broadly implemented to facilitate lowering of the administrative costs of fiscal policies. For instance, digital identities linked to the banking system facilitate formalization of economic activities, access to those in need of social support and also allow for low-cost transfers of necessary support.

6. CONCLUSIONS

After two years of the pandemic and the concurrent economic crisis, fiscal spending needs remain elevated amid a situation where fiscal revenues are very limited. Fiscal consolidations, with an expected negative impact on inequality, are on the horizon; without substantial tax revenue increases, the inequality increasing impact seems to be inevitable. With the aim to "build forward fairer" and to mitigate the negative impacts of necessary changes in fiscal policy on the poorest, while avoiding an increase in already elevated inequalities, Governments should prioritize spending on health care, education and social protection.

With the above priority spending areas and goals fully aligned with the 2030 Agenda, and with limited fiscal space, this chapter argued for a major shift in fiscal management – ***spend smart***. This means improving the efficiency of spending to obtain a so-called ***big bang for the buck*** in areas which have the potential for providing the largest beneficial impacts, such as basic health care, education and social protection coverage.

Finally, not all fiscal constraints will be put right with improved efficiency or savings alone. Hence, to mitigate the impact of inequality increasing fiscal consolidation or further debt distress, it is essential to mobilize additional domestic revenues.

CENTRAL BANKING FOR INCLUSIVE DEVELOPMENT: THROUGH A NEW LENS

CHAPTER 04

1. INTRODUCTION

Compared with fiscal policy, the role of central banking in supporting inclusive development is less frequently discussed in general as well as in the context of the COVID-19 pandemic. Until the 1980s, many central banks worldwide had developmental mandates, such as using credit allocation and special financing schemes, to promote such priority economic sectors as manufacturing activities and exports (Dafe and Volz, 2015). Since then, the spread of neoliberal economic policies[1] and the perceived failure of developmental central banking prompted many central banks in developing countries to abandon such policies and adopt an inflation-targeting approach. Such an approach primarily narrows the core mandate of central banks to maintaining price stability, which supports inclusiveness only implicitly. More recently, many central banks, particularly of advanced economies, have been criticized for launching unconventional monetary policy measures in response to the 2007-2008 global financial and economic crisis (Volz, 2017). Examples of unconventional measures include purchase of toxic assets of the corporate sector and injection of substantial liquidly into the system to support banks and spur economic activity. Such experiences have led central banks to become extra cautious or discouraged when exploring any potential additional role that may be deemed non-traditional.

Yet, given the unprecedented shocks brought about by the COVID-19 pandemic, central banks can and have played an important, complementary role in building forward fairer. As noted in chapter 1, the pandemic is estimated to have pushed back an additional 85 million people into extreme poverty in Asia and the Pacific. At the same time, sizeable fiscal stimulus and falling government revenues mean that public debt sustainability is at risk for some economies. In response to these factors, Asia-Pacific central banks have launched various somewhat unconventional measures to support financial access and liquidity of households, small and

1 Such policies favour lightly regulated, unfettered, free market capitalism and market-oriented reforms, such as deregulation, balanced fiscal budgets and small size of the Government.

medium-sized enterprises (SMEs) and Governments.[2] Amid tighter fiscal space, securing a country's inclusive development requires greater contributions by other public and private entities, including central banks. As more inclusive societies benefit people at large, inclusive central banking is at least distinct from the previous episode of developmental central banking which benefited only a small number of interest groups.

There are traditional ways how central banks contribute to inclusive development and societal welfare, but new areas of inclusive central banking are also emerging. Through their conduct of traditional monetary policy, central banks indirectly support economic equality by maintaining low inflation, and macroeconomic and financial stability. High and volatile inflation adversely affects the lower-income groups the most and thus exacerbates existing inequalities. Similarly, unstable macroeconomic performance and frequent economic downturns negatively affect the poor more, as their capacity to absorb such shocks is minimal. Thus, the contribution of central banks in maintaining low inflation and supporting macroeconomic stability should not be underestimated from the perspective of their contribution to inclusive development and societal welfare. Similarly, effective regulation of the financial sector by central banks delivers robust and competitive financial sectors, resulting in greater safety for consumer deposits and lower transaction fees, which again benefit the poor to a greater extent than others. Moreover, in some instances central banks directly promote economic equality by enhancing financial access, literacy and consumer protection. Beyond these areas, other central bank functions also have linkages with inclusive development which are less obvious and not widely discussed, such as management of official reserves and issuance of currency. Yet, these are areas which have the potential to directly aid inclusive development.

This chapter highlights four relatively new and additional aspects of central banking that can promote more inclusive development in Asia and the Pacific (figure 4.1). First, as policymakers, central banks can consider concrete actions that help make the conduct of monetary policy more mindful of inequality. Second, as investors, central banks can examine how to make the management of official reserves more socially oriented. Third, as issuers of currency, central banks can explore central bank digital currencies as an innovative approach to foster financial inclusion. Fourth, as regulators of the financial sector, central banks can encourage the issuance of innovative financial instruments for social purposes.

It is worth highlighting upfront that **these additional considerations should not come at the expense of core responsibilities of central banks**, that is, delivering low inflation and macroeconomic and financial stability. In other words, delivering these core mandates on a sustained basis must remain a top priority, and unless and until these are fulfilled, additional considerations to promote inclusive development should remain on the back burner.

This chapter contains several policy messages. *First*, central banks in Asia and the Pacific can enhance their commitment to promote inclusive finance. Only half of them currently refer to financial access, financial literacy or consumer protection in their objectives and strategies. This is a missed opportunity, given that inclusive finance is an area where central banks can contribute directly to more inclusive societies.

2 As such, central banks also support the ambition of the 2030 Agenda for Sustainable Development. This is because interrupted access to finance would limit people's access to education and health care services. Continued financial access also reduces the risk of closure of SMEs and subsequent job losses, especially among workers with lower skills.

FIGURE 4.1
Selected areas of inclusive central banking covered in this chapter

CENTRAL BANGKING AREA	CURRENT OBJECTIVE		ADDITIONAL SOCIAL CONSIDERATION
Monetary policy conduct	Price stability	+	Income and wealth distribution
Official reserve management	Safety and liquidity	+	Investment with positive social impact
Currency issuance	Adequate cash in circulation	+	Digital currency for financial inclusion
Financial regulation	Robust financial sector	+	Socially oriented financial instruments

Source: ESCAP.

Second, central banks should take deliberate actions to make the conduct of monetary policy more mindful of inequality, not least because high and persistent inequality can reduce the effectiveness of monetary policy. At a basic level, more effort can be made to better understand and communicate the distributional impacts of monetary policy, including through changes in inflation. A more ambitious approach could be to introduce economic equality as a distinct secondary objective of central banks, especially where the core mandate of inflation stability has been achieved.

Third, with certain amendments in a central bank's law and investment strategies, part of sizeable official reserves in Asia and the Pacific can be invested in socially oriented financial instruments. For instance, to directly benefit inclusive development at home, a portion of excess reserves may be deployed as seed capital to kick-start local social development projects.

Fourth, to realize the considerable potential of central bank digital currencies (CBDC) for enhancing financial inclusion, getting the design attributes right and having in place enabling digital infrastructure are critical. To avoid unintended, adverse impacts on financial stability and the central bank's credibility, central banks should clearly identify policy and operational risks arising from the issuance of CBDC, together with respective mitigation measures.

Fifth, to mobilize more financial resources for social purposes, Asia-Pacific countries should explore innovative instruments, such as social impact bonds and sustainability-linked bonds, which offer some distinct advantages over traditional instruments. Harmonized social investment taxonomies and financial assistance would help move these instruments beyond the infancy stage.

This chapter is organized as follows. Section 2 first contains a review of actions taken by Asia-Pacific central banks to ensure financial access and liquidity during the COVID-19 pandemic, then analyses the extent to which central banks in the region are promoting inclusive finance through their mission statements, strategies and membership in global initiatives. Section 3 reviews interactions between monetary policy and inequality and highlights how the conduct of monetary policy can be made more mindful of inequality. Section 4 examines factors that have constrained reserve allocation into non-traditional financial instruments and highlights how central banks could reorient part of their official reserves towards social bonds. Section 5 first reviews the concept of CBDC, then provides a snapshot of its latest development in Asia-Pacific economies and ends with a discussion of policy actions that would help CBDC work for financial inclusion. Section 6 contains a discussion of how central banks can promote the issuance of social impact bonds and sustainability-linked bonds as innovative financial instruments for social purposes. Section 7 concludes with broad policy remarks.

2. STARTING WITH THE BASICS: ASIA-PACIFIC CENTRAL BANKS CAN DO MORE TO PROMOTE INCLUSIVE FINANCE

This section highlights that, in response to the COVID-19 pandemic, many central banks in the region have actively adopted measures to support financial access (section 2.1). Yet, from a longer-term perspective, the extent to which Asia-Pacific central banks are committed to promote inclusive finance for people can be enhanced (section 2.2), especially in countries where financial access and literacy remain limited (see online annex 1). More broadly, Asia-Pacific central banks as public policy organizations can implement internal corporate actions to support inclusive development (for some examples, see online annex 2).

2.1 Policy responses to ensure financial access and liquidity: extending the lifeline

Asia-Pacific central banks launched various schemes to support financial access and liquidity amid the pandemic. Beyond reducing the policy interest rates, a step which has economy-wide impacts, there are also policy initiatives that are designed specifically to support access to finance by households, SMEs and Governments.

For households, the aim is to promote mobile money and digital financial services as access to bank branches is limited during public health lockdowns. To this end, several Asia-Pacific central banks reduced transaction fees and increased the limits on transactions and balances of mobile banking services (figure 4.2). For example, the Brunei Darussalam Central Bank waived for all customers the online local interbank transfer fees for a period of six months, while the Bangladesh Bank increased the daily transaction limit on contactless debit and credit cards from about \$35 to \$60. The use of other options to support digital financial services, such as making *know-your-customer* onboarding more flexible and simplifying transaction processes, appears to be less common in the region.

For SMEs, the focus is on ensuring adequate financial liquidity to maintain business operations. Among others, Asia-Pacific central banks adopted measures relating to debt moratorium, loan guarantees, financial assistance and lower interest rates to support SMEs (figure 4.2). On debt relief, Sri Lanka provided a six-month moratorium on bank loans for SMEs, while Malaysia allowed

FIGURE 4.2
Many Asia-Pacific central banks launched measures to support small and medium-sized enterprises and digital finances amid the pandemic

	Digital financial services		Small and medium-sized enterprises			
	Reduced transaction fees	Increased balance and transaction limits	Debt suspension	Loan guarantees	Financial assistance	Lower interest rates
Australia				*	*	
Bangladesh	*	*		*		
Brunei Darussalam	*					
China		*	*	*	*	*
Fiji				*		*
Georgia					*	
Hong Kong, China			*	*		
India				*	*	
Indonesia	*		*		*	*
Lao People's Democratic Republic						*
Malaysia			*		*	
Myanmar		*				
Nepal					*	*
New Zealand			*	*	*	
Philippines					*	
Republic of Korea					*	*
Russian Federation			*	*	*	*
Singapore			*		*	*
Sri Lanka			*	*		*
Timor-Leste		*				
Thailand			*		*	*

Source: ESCAP, based on IMF Financial Access COVID-19 Policy Tracker, as of February 2022.

Note: This figure is not exhaustive. In some countries, similar programmes were carried out by Governments and are not covered here.

temporary interest-only payments and extended the repayment period for SMEs. On loan guarantees, the existing scheme for State-guaranteed bank loans to SMEs in the Russian Federation had been expanded by €500 million. Fiji's SME Credit Guarantee Scheme was also expanded. Regarding financial assistance, the Philippines allowed SME loans to be counted as part of banks' reserve requirements and temporarily reduced their credit risk weights to 50 per cent. Finally, on lower interest rates, the Bank of the Lao People's Democratic Republic has created a 200-billion-kip fund (about $17.7 million) for low-interest rate SME loans through commercial banks.

To support fiscal space, Asia-Pacific central banks have provided loans to Governments and purchased sovereign bonds. In response to shrinking fiscal space in most Asia-Pacific economies, several central banks engaged in asset purchase schemes for the first time in 2020. The main aim was to maintain government bond yields and restore market sentiments.[3] While most of these bond purchases took place in secondary markets, central banks in Fiji, Indonesia, Papua New Guinea and Sri Lanka made the purchases in primary markets as well (figure 4.3). Central banks in Papua New Guinea and the Philippines also provided direct lending to their respective Governments. In terms of size, the value of announced measures in Fiji and the Philippines stood at close to 8 per cent of GDP, about 4 per cent of GDP in Indonesia and between 1 and 2 per cent of GDP in other developing economies (Agur and others, 2022).

3 Central banks in Japan, the Republic of Korea and Thailand also purchased corporate bonds and/or commercial papers.

2.2 Commitments to promote inclusive finance: room to step up

More central banks in Asia and the Pacific can have mission statements or strategies that refer to inclusive development and/or finance. Such references in official policy statements would facilitate the allocation of central banks' human and financial resources to foster inclusive finance. Based on a review of annual reports and websites,[4] about 20 or close to half of central banks in the region have references to inclusive finance in their vision and mission statements, strategic plans, objectives or priorities (table 4.1). The aims, among others, are to achieve an inclusive financial system and enhance financial inclusion, financial education and financial consumer protection. In addition, central banks in several countries feature a broader objective of supporting a country's inclusive economic growth or development agenda in their vision or mission statements, such as Bangladesh, Bhutan, Fiji, Pakistan, the Philippines and Thailand. In contrast, in countries such as Cambodia and Kyrgyzstan, the levels of financial access and financial literacy remain below the region's average values but there appears to be no clear central bank mandate on inclusive finance. Overall, there remains room for more central banks in Asia and the Pacific to engage with inclusive finance as this is an area where they can contribute directly to inclusive development.

Asia-Pacific central banks have established dedicated units to implement strategies and plans on inclusive finance. Examples include central banks' departments and divisions promoting financial inclusion (such

4 There are at least three caveats here. First, the amount and type of information reported on the websites and in the annual reports vary notably. While most annual reports are focused on central banks' recent activities, some are focused on macroeconomic updates. Second, this analysis reviews references to aspects of inclusive finance in central banks' official documents, but this does not indicate the actual level of engagement by central banks. Third, this review does not cover initiatives by financial supervisory agencies which may have played a role in promoting inclusive financial policy.

FIGURE 4.3
Asia-Pacific central banks supported fiscal space through loans and bond buying

	Loans to Governments and drawdown of reserves	Government bond purchases	
		Primary market	Secondary market
Australia			*
Fiji		*	*
India			*
Indonesia		*	*
Japan			*
Malaysia			*
New Zealand			*
Papua New Guinea	*	*	
Philippines	*		*
Republic of Korea			*
Russian Federation	*		
Singapore			*
Solomon Islands			*
Sri Lanka		*	
Thailand			*
Turkey			*

Source: ESCAP, based on ADB COVID-19 Policy Database (as of February 2022) and Agur and others (2022).

FIGURE 4.4
Most Asia-Pacific central banks are members of global initiatives on financial inclusion and education

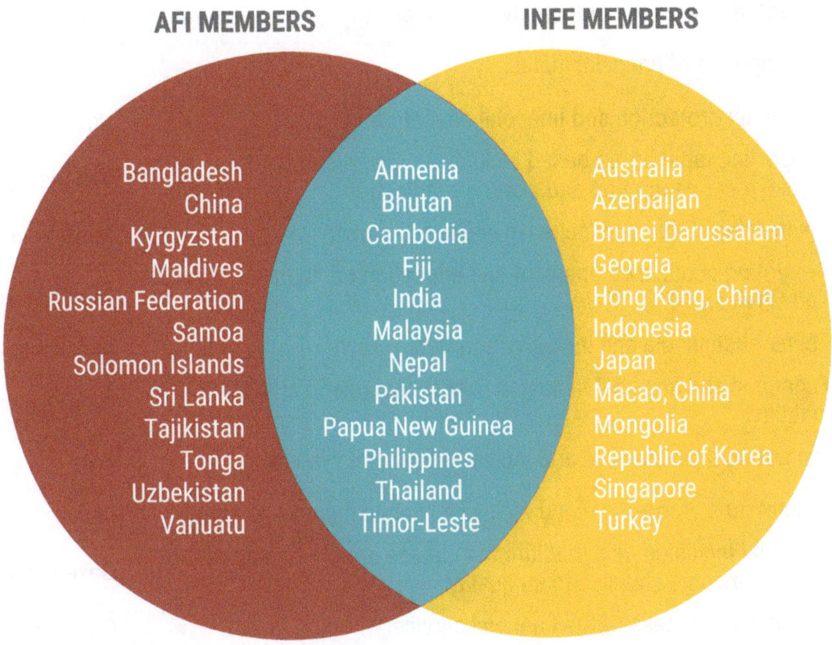

Source: ESCAP, based on data from the Alliance for Financial Inclusion (www.afi-global.org/members/) and the list of members of the OECD International Network on Financial Education (www.oecd.org/financial/education/INFE-member-lists.pdf).

as in Afghanistan, Samoa and Tonga), strengthening financial consumer protection (such as in China, Kyrgyzstan and Tajikistan) and enhancing financial literacy (such as in India and Thailand). In such countries as Bangladesh, Indonesia and Pakistan, central banks also have dedicated units to support development of SMEs. Beyond these, central banks in such countries as India and Papua New Guinea also play an important role in setting up national centres on financial inclusion, while those in Samoa and Solomon Islands engage with task forces on national financial inclusion.

Many Asia-Pacific central banks are members of the Alliance for Financial Inclusion (AFI). Established in 2008, AFI intends to make financial services more accessible to the world's unbanked people. Among others, the Alliance has working groups on consumer empowerment, digital financial services and financial inclusion strategy. To achieve its mandate, AFI works with regulatory authorities, international organizations and the business sector through peer learning and knowledge exchange. As of September 2021, 101 institutions in 89 developing countries and areas have joined the Alliance, including 24 central banks from Asia and the Pacific (figure 4.4).

Many Asia-Pacific central banks are also engaging with the OECD International Network on Financial Education (INFE). Also established in 2008, INFE intends to enhance financial education worldwide. The Network currently works on such issues as standard setting, the impact of digitalization on financial education and the needs of older consumers. For these areas of work, INFE aims to design policy instruments and share experience and good practices. As of August 2021, more than 270 public institutions in 130 countries and areas have become INFE members, including 24 Asia-Pacific central banks (figure 4.4).

TABLE 4.1
Half of the central banks in Asia and the Pacific refer to inclusive finance or development in their official documents

Country or area	Selected references to inclusive development	Source
Afghanistan	Development of financial inclusion	Strategic pillar
Armenia	Consumer protection and financial education	Strategic direction
Bangladesh	Supporting rapid broad-based inclusive economic growth, employment generation and poverty eradication	Vision statement
Bhutan	Reinforcing stable and inclusive economic growth	Mission statement
Cook Islands	Promoting public awareness of and education on financial products and services	Strategic priority
Fiji	Foster sustainable and inclusive economic growth	Mission statement
Indonesia	Economic and financial inclusion to maintain financial system stability	Strategic plan
Malaysia	Promoting a progressive and inclusive financial system	Role
	Promoting a progressive and inclusive Islamic financial system	Role
Maldives	Financial inclusion as a medium to increase prosperity and reduce regional income and wealth inequality	Governor's statement
Nepal	Increase the access of the financial service	Objective
New Zealand	Incorporating diversity, financial inclusion and sustainability into strategies	Strategy
Pakistan	Inclusive development of financial sector for the long-term benefit of the people	Vision statement
	Foster a sound and dynamic financial system to achieve sustained and equitable economic growth and prosperity	Mission statement
Papua New Guinea	Facilitating development of financial services and inclusion	Secondary function
Philippines	Promote and maintain price stability...conducive to sustainable and inclusive growth of the economy	Mission statement
	Inclusive financial system	Strategy map
Republic of Korea	Expanding financial safety nets	Strategy map
	Providing economic education	Strategic plan
Russian Federation	Expanding financial inclusion for households and businesses	Strategic goal
Solomon Islands	Include women, youth and rural families...in the national financial centre	Strategic objective
	Build financial resilience in rural households	Strategic objective
Sri Lanka	Contributing to the prosperity[a] of Sri Lanka	Vision statement
Tajikistan	Protection of benefits of consumers of banking services	Task
Thailand	Promoting a stable financial environment to achieve sustainable and inclusive economic development	Mission
Timor-Leste	Maintaining financial education of the population	Action
Tonga	Manage and promote financial inclusion initiatives	Principal function
Vanuatu	Ensure sound banking practices in order to provide protection for depositors	Mission
Viet Nam	Contributing to socioeconomic development	Major responsibility

Source: ESCAP, based on review of central banks' websites and annual reports.
[a] Here "prosperity" refers to "inclusion of all segments of the society in enjoying the benefits of development".

3. CENTRAL BANKS AS POLICYMAKERS: CONDUCT OF MONETARY POLICY

In this section it is argued that, while available evidence on the distributional impacts of monetary policy is mixed, central banks should still be concerned with economic inequality because this can undermine the effectiveness of monetary policy (section 3.1). To make the conduct of monetary policy more mindful of inequality, central banks can communicate better the distributional impacts to the public and can even consider introducing reducing inequality as their secondary goal, especially where the core objective of price stability is being met (section 3.2).

3.1 Relationship between monetary policy and inequality: going both ways

Changes in monetary policy can affect income and wealth inequality through several transmission channels (figure 4.5). The first channel is through income composition, with major income sources being labour income, government transfers and capital income. The second channel is earnings distribution, which is mainly determined by hourly wages for richer people and hours worked for low-skilled workers. The third channel is portfolio composition, which involves the type and maturity of assets and liabilities, such as financial assets, real estate and pension funds. Finally, the fourth channel is through redistribution of savings between asset holders (net savers) and debt holders (net borrowers). The effects from these transmission channels may offset or reinforce each other.

Empirical evidence on the distributional impacts of monetary policy in developed economies is mixed. Most studies have found a negligible impact of changes in monetary policy on wealth inequality, while the number of studies that report the positive and negative relationships with income inequality is comparable (Leong, 2021) (figure 4.6). Such inconclusive evidence is mainly because the overall distributional effects depend on each economy's specific conditions, such as economic and financial structure (for example,

FIGURE 4.5
Monetary policy affects income and wealth distribution through four transmission channels

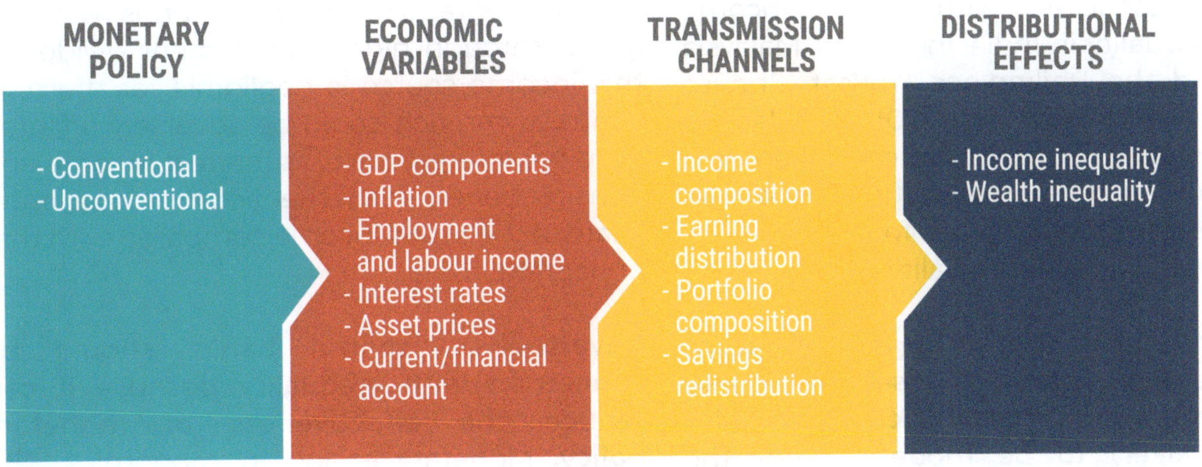

Source: ESCAP, based on Brandolini (2016), Bonifacio and others (2021) and Leong (2021).

FIGURE 4.6
Evidence on the distributional effects of monetary policy in developed countries is mixed

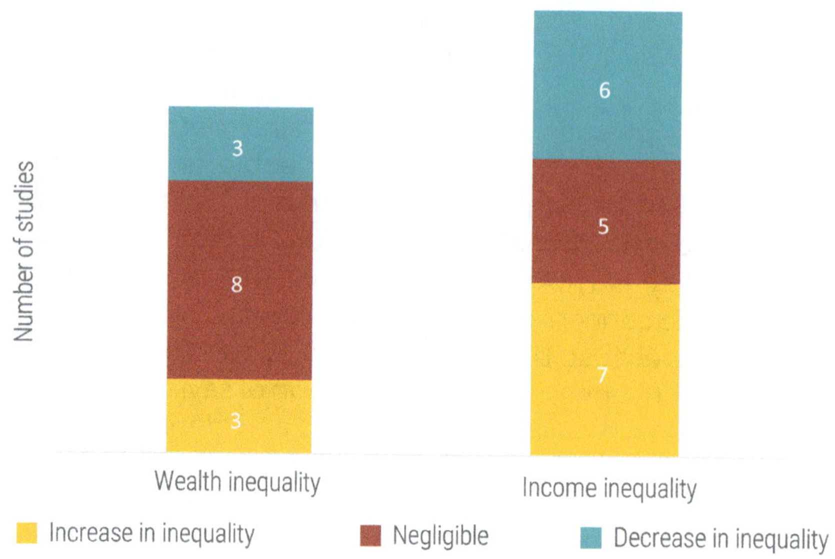

Source: ESCAP, based on Leong (2021).

dominance of banks relative to capital markets), prevailing distribution of wealth and income, and other public policies that are in place. Technical factors, such as different estimation methods and proxies of monetary policy conduct, also play a role.

Limited available evidence in Asia-Pacific economies suggests that monetary policy does have an effect on inequality. In a study that covers 10 Asia-Pacific developing countries, an increase in the real interest rates is associated with higher income inequality in India, Indonesia, Malaysia and the Philippines (Yousaf, Ghouse and Atiq-Ur-Rehman, 2018). Similarly, in a study that examines combined data from eight Asia-Pacific economies, monetary easing was found to lead to lower income inequality (Punzi, 2020).

The distributional impact of recent central banks' asset purchase programmes in Asia-Pacific economies is likely to be modest. While the size of these programmes in the region is generally small at below 2 per cent of GDP, central banks' balance sheets in major developed economies increased by 15-25 per cent of GDP during the period 2019-2020.[5] Partly driven by this modest scale, the announcement of unconventional monetary policy tools in emerging economies has not led to an increase in inflation expectations (Agur and others, 2022). Another factor at play is the composition of income and wealth. In the Philippines, the main income sources for people in the top income decile are non-agricultural salaries and personal remittances (Cabote and Fernandez, 2020). While the bond-buying programme may benefit this wealthier group through higher investment dividends, this income source is negligible for them. In contrast, the rich could be adversely affected by lower interest rates, as interest income and pension benefits together account for a larger share of their total income compared with that of poorer people.

Nevertheless, central banks should be concerned with inequality because it can reduce the effectiveness of monetary policy. Monetary easing in economies with

5 For details, see the Atlantic Council Global QE Tracker (www.atlanticcouncil.org/global-qe-tracker/).

high income inequality tends to be less effective because, despite lower borrowing costs, wealthier individuals have a lower propensity to increase their already high consumption while poor households would in any case have limited borrowing capacity. Similarly, in economies where most people are unbanked, monetary easing may not boost personal consumption because interest incomes of many households are not directly affected. More broadly, when the public believes that monetary policy plays a role in widening inequality, they may be less supportive of central banks' policy actions, which could eventually impair the effectiveness of monetary policy (BIS, 2021). Meanwhile, studies have also suggested that prevailing income inequality could affect the outcomes of monetary policy. In the United States, a large increase in savings and investments by high-income people mainly explain declining interest rate levels since the 1980s (Mian, Straub, and Sufi, 2021c).

3.2 Towards inequality-mindful conduct of monetary policy: from indirect to direct contributors

A broad view is that monetary policy tools cannot address the root causes of inequality. As economic inequality generally arises from long-term structural factors, such as automation, the digital economy and globalization, monetary policy is not an effective tool for addressing inequality (BIS, 2021; Rogoff, 2021). Moreover, having multiple objectives of price and financial stability, economic growth, employment and inclusive development, some of which may be conflicting, erodes the effectiveness of monetary policy and undermines central banks' credibility and its accountability (Budina and others, 2021). Other concerns are that central banks may need to have more policy tools at their disposal to achieve more goals and that judging central banks' performance in meeting an objective that involves other policymakers (such as fiscal policymakers for inclusive development) is difficult.

In this view, the best way that monetary policy can promote equality is by maintaining low inflation and economic stability. This is certainly true for central banks that are struggling with high inflation and volatile macroeconomic conditions. They should not try to address inequality as a separate objective through use of monetary policy instruments. Rather, their main contribution to mitigating inequalities should come from ensuring low inflation and macroeconomic stability on a sustained basis.

For economies that continue to experience high and volatile inflation, a related issue is lack of a clear definition of low and stable inflation, that is, price stability. In many countries, an announced annual inflation target keeps changing from year to year depending on actual inflation. Instead, the target should be set for 3-5 years, and central bank should be held accountable for delivering on this target. So, what should be the definition of low and stable inflation, which could serve as a target? Surprisingly, there is no firm answer in the literature, although some approaches and estimates are available. A practical approach, with a view of keeping inequality considerations in view, could be to link it with stabilizing purchasing power, which in turn can be proxied by real wages. When people are experiencing inflation, they are basically experiencing a loss in purchasing power. Some basic research at the country level can help determine the average wage growth, given labour market conditions and productivity levels. A clear definition of price stability linked with wages can strengthen the contribution of monetary policy to promoting economic equality.

There are other actions that central banks can consider. At a basic level, central banks should develop a good and deeper understanding of the distributional impacts of monetary policy. Such analysis needs to consider country-specific socioeconomic structure and conditions, with counterfactual scenarios that capture the possible rise in inequality due to persistence of high inflation and weak employment in the absence of changes in monetary policy. Currently, monetary policy statements of most central banks tend to be completely devoid of any discussion on inequality and possible linkages between inflation and inequality. Studies in the context of emerging economies should also seek to examine how domestic economic inequality is affected by the stance on monetary policy in advanced economies.

Then, central banks should publicly communicate such distributional effects. Examples are through official speeches and reports and community outreach events (Budina and others, 2021). Such communication will help people to better manage the expected impacts of changes in monetary policy. It also helps Governments and other public organizations to consider how to support adversely affected groups. For example, public pension funds could explore ways to support old-age savers amid a prolonged period of low interest rates.

Central banks should also determine the extent to which they should integrate the consideration of inequality into the conduct of monetary policy. At a basic level, when deciding on monetary policy changes, an impact assessment can also include income and wealth distribution (Prasad, 2014). Moreover, when choosing between two equally effective monetary policy strategies, central banks should adopt an option with smaller potential distributional impact (Schnabel, 2021). For example, the effect that inflation has on wealth distribution is different between inflation targeting and price-level targeting approaches (Meh, Ríos-Rull and Terajima, 2010). Meanwhile, central banks that are by and large successful in maintaining inflation at a low and stable level can include inclusive development as one of their goals. While this is sometimes perceived as a radical approach (Abu Bakar and Ho, 2018), section 2.2 notes that mission statements of several Asia-Pacific central banks already feature aspects of inclusive development.

For central banks that remain reluctant about such integration, they could prioritize objectives. Such an approach has already been used by some central banks in prioritizing the traditional objectives of monetary policy. For example, for the Maldives Monetary Authority, its second objective of maintaining financial stability is pursued only if this does not compromise the first objective on price stability. Similarly, in Solomon Islands, the central bank's additional objective of maintaining a stable financial system is subordinated to the primary objective on price stability. In a similar vein, central banks can pursue the additional objective of mitigating inequality only if the traditional objectives of monetary policy have been achieved.

Despite rising inflationary pressure in Asia and the Pacific, price stability in several economies should allow for inequality-mindful pursuit of monetary policy. The projected headline inflation rates for 2022 and 2023 in 13 out of 26 Asia-Pacific economies are below/within their respective target rates/ranges (figure 4.7). As central banks' core mandate of achieving price stability is likely to be met, consideration should be given on how to further integrate inclusive development into monetary policy formulation.

FIGURE 4.7
Around half of Asia-Pacific economies are projected to meet their inflation targets in the coming years

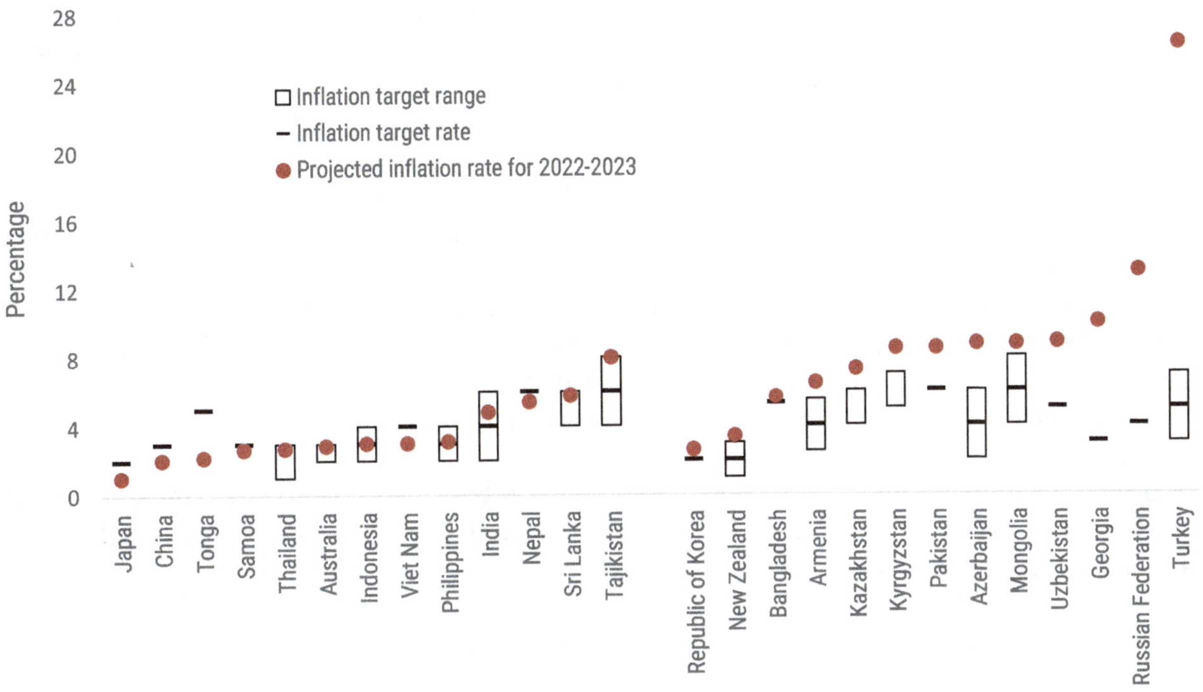

Source: ESCAP and Central Bank News (www.centralbanknews.info/p/inflation-targets.html).

As part of an unconventional monetary policy toolkit, asset purchase programmes could include support for social bonds. Central banks could allocate part of their bond-buying schemes towards social bonds locally issued by national Governments and companies. For example, in Thailand, the Bank of Ayudhya Public Company Limited (Krungsri) issued a baht-denominated social bond in January 2020 to support women who owned small enterprises and were low-income earners. In Japan, the University of Tokyo issued a yen-denominated social bond in October 2020 to fund educational activities, while the Tokyo Metropolitan Government's social bond issued in June 2021 is aimed at making the city safer.

4. CENTRAL BANKS AS INVESTORS: MANAGEMENT OF OFFICIAL RESERVES

This section notes that central banks' strategies to manage official reserves are centred around liquidity and safety considerations, thus limiting how foreign exchange reserves can be used to benefit inclusive development (section 4.1). Certain changes in the governance and objective of reserve management and adoption of responsible investment strategies can make reserve management more socially oriented (section 4.2).

4.1 Managing official reserves: currently safety comes first

The management of official reserves typically follows a risk-averse approach with the core focus being on liquidity and safety. Among others, reserve management is aimed at backstopping the value of domestic currency with external assets, assisting a Government in meeting external obligations and maintaining a reserve for emergencies (IMF, 2003). As a result, reserve management tends to be risk-averse by nature, with priority for ample liquidity and acceptable risks over financial returns. For example, close to 40 per cent of surveyed central banks worldwide are allowed only to invest in government, supranational and agency bonds with a credit rating of A+, A or A- (World Bank, 2020c). For official reserves that are invested as deposits with commercial banks, the same rating is required in almost two thirds of the respondents.

Central banks' investments in unconventional asset classes remain small. Central banks around the world hold about 82 per cent of their reserves in conventional instruments, such as high-grade bonds, deposits and gold (Hentov and others, 2019). Another 15 per cent of the portfolios is invested in less traditional instruments, such as equities and return-enhancing bonds. In Asia and the Pacific, where central banks' assets amounted to more than $9.1 trillion at end-2020 (OMFIF, 2021), a large part of these assets is invested in bank deposits, followed by money market instruments and government bonds (figure 4.8) (World Bank, 2020c). This contrasts with the dominance of government bonds in other regions of the world.

Several factors are holding back central banks' investment in non-traditional asset classes:

- *First*, many central banks are not allowed to invest in unconventional asset classes. Less than half of surveyed central banks in Asia and the Pacific are permitted to invest in emerging market bonds and investment-grade corporate bonds (figure 4.9) (World Bank, 2020c). Only a quarter of them are allowed to invest in equities in developed and developing markets, while none can invest in high-yield corporate bonds.

- *Second*, official reserves in some Asia-Pacific economies are deemed inadequate for meeting their fundamental objectives. This tends to constrain central banks' ability to fully explore how to make the management of reserves more socially oriented. According to IMF Assessing Reserve Adequacy,[6] such countries as Armenia, Pakistan and Turkey may not have adequate reserves, whereas such countries as the Philippines and Thailand are estimated to have some excess reserves.

6 This useful website contains links to numerous IMF papers, data and tools to aid in the assessment of reserve adequacy. It is available at www.imf.org/external/np/spr/ara/.

FIGURE 4.8
Much of official reserves in Asia and the Pacific are invested in bank deposits and money market instruments

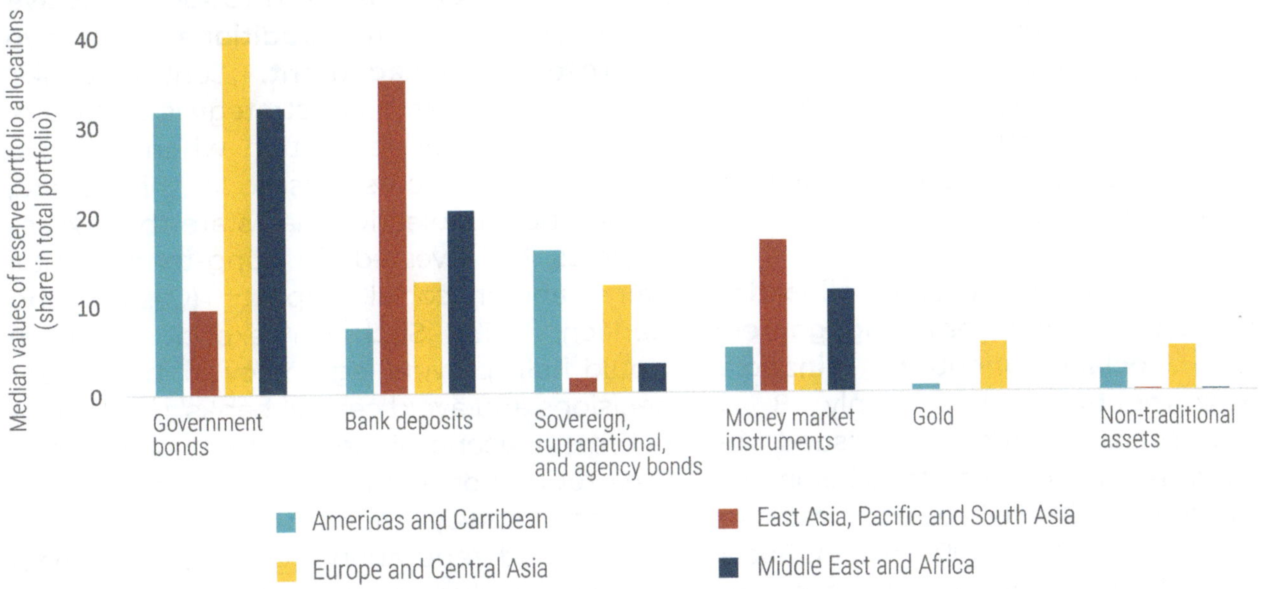

Source: ESCAP, based on World Bank (2020c).

FIGURE 4.9
Most Asia-Pacific central banks are not allowed to invest in unconventional asset classes

Source: ESCAP, based on World Bank (2020c).
Note: Asset classes highlighted in turquoise are considered as traditional, while the remainder in red are unconventional instruments.

- *Third*, most central banks have not integrated environmental, social and governance (ESG) factors into their investment frameworks. In a global survey of central banks, only 11 per cent of them have explicitly incorporated the ESG factors into investment processes (World Bank, 2019b). This could be due to concerns over portfolio performance (Fender and others, 2020).

A conservative reserve allocation strategy means less engagement with socially oriented financial instruments. Globally, only 8 of 108 social bonds are issued by supranational bodies,[7] thus belonging to the traditional asset class. An example is the $500 million Social Bond Programme introduced by the International Financial Corporation in 2017 to support smallholder farmers and women-owned enterprises (IFC, 2017). Most other social bonds are issued by non-sovereign entities, mostly in developed countries, so they are classified as unconventional assets.

4.2 Towards pro-social reserve management: changing the mindset

Central banks can take basic actions to integrate inclusive development into reserve management. They may begin by holding internal consultations to determine whether existing mandates and strategies allow such integration, then examining how reserve allocation into socially oriented financial instruments would affect the liquidity and risk-adjusted returns of their portfolios. Integrating inclusive development may be justified as risk management, as inequality-induced social unrest and political instability will undermine portfolio performance.

A direct approach is to introduce inclusive development as an additional objective of reserve management. Central banks' conservative investment strategy is partly due to concerns over reputation when portfolio management incurs losses. In this regard, an additional objective may state that excess reserves be invested for long-term capital gains and/or social impacts (Castelli and Gerlach, 2019). Such an explicit objective would help provide legitimacy to investment decisions and avoid central banks' investment in firms or economic sectors that could impair their reputation as public institutions. Indeed, a global survey shows that many central banks cited reputational gains as the main benefit of including sustainability into reserve management (Fender and others, 2020).

Changes in the governance of reserve allocation can be considered. One option is to set up an investment committee within a central bank to make reserve investment decisions (Castelli and Gerlach, 2019). Such an investment committee may function in the same way as a monetary policy committee which is established to make decisions on the direction of monetary policy and comprises experts outside central banks. Senior central bank managers can outline expectations on risk and financial return, while the investment committee will make decisions on, for example, the composition of asset classes.

Central banks that are willing to pursue socially tilted reserve management can adopt various investment strategies (NGFS, 2019). For negative screening, central banks can introduce an exclusion list that prohibits investments in such sectors as tobacco and weapons. Under impact investing, central banks' investment can explicitly target measurable social indicators alongside financial returns, such as allocations to supranational social bonds, social enterprises and equity impact funds. For voting and engagement, central

7 The Sustainable Bonds Database of the International Capital Market Association is available at www.icmagroup.org/sustainable-finance/green-social-and-sustainability-bonds-database/#HomeContent.

banks with exposure to equity and corporate bonds can take an active approach by ensuring that their investee companies are aligned with positive development outcomes. For example, the exercise of voting rights by the Swiss National Bank is focused on corporate governance of investee companies.

Central banks could mobilize part of excess reserves to promote inclusive development locally. Among others, a fund can be set up to build the capacity of asset managers in integrating social issues into asset management. An example in the context of green development is the Green Investment Programme introduced by the Monetary Authority of Singapore. Funded by a $2 billion allocation of official reserves, the fund seeks to enhance the climate resilience of official reserves, attract sustainability-focused asset managers to Singapore and serve as a catalyst for funding green projects globally (Menon, 2021).

In essence, different stakeholders have a role in making official reserve allocation socially oriented. From an issuer's perspective, supranational bodies could aim to issue more international social bonds. Similarly, there is room for sovereign entities and highly rated companies in Asia-Pacific countries with reserve currency status (such as Australia, China and Japan) to issue more social bonds to benefit development in poorer regional peers.[8] From an investor's perspective, Asia-Pacific economies that are deemed to have excess reserves could allocate part of their reserves for internationally and locally issued socially oriented bonds. Central banks could also use excess reserves as seed capital to support local social projects. Finally, even in countries the reserves of which are considered inadequate, central banks could review whether their reserve allocation strategies could have greater social impacts. An example is to switch existing bank deposits to banks with a more favourable ESG rating, which does not necessarily affect portfolio performance.

5. CENTRAL BANKS AS CURRENCY ISSUERS: A CENTRAL BANK DIGITAL CURRENCY

This section shows that, with large potential to enhance financial inclusion (section 5.1), half of the central banks in Asia and the Pacific are exploring the issuance of central bank digital currencies (section 5.2). To leverage such potential, central banks will need to carefully consider the design features, legal issues and operational risks and work with other policymakers to enhance digital connectivity and literacy (section 5.3).

5.1 Concepts and design features: making the right choices

A central bank digital currency (CBDC) is the digital form of a country's fiat currency. As with cash, CBDC is issued and backed by a central bank and can be used for payments, digitally. The key difference is that the CBDC monetary value is stored electronically, unlike physically as banknotes and coins. While CBDC is similar to electronic-based bank accounts and cryptocurrencies in a way that they are digital and universally accessible, CBDC is a liability of the central bank. Many central banks started exploring CBDC in response to the emergence of private digital currencies, such as Bitcoin. While these currencies may provide

8 Almost 40 per cent of surveyed central banks worldwide intend to increase exposure to assets denominated in Asia-Pacific currencies over the next 12-24 months (OMFIF, 2021).

faster, cheaper means of payments, their widespread adoption could undermine monetary sovereignty and financial stability in case of a firm's insolvency. Countries such as Sweden are exploring CBDC amid the declining use of cash in financial transactions.

CBDC design choices can have notable implications for digital payments in the economy and for financial inclusion. There are various CBDC attributes, such as whether financial intermediaries or central banks themselves will handle transactions, whether CBDC would be used for interbank transactions only or by the public, and whether users can access CBDC through an account or an electronic token (see box 4.1). For the aim of enhancing financial inclusion, a direct, token-based retail CBDC offers greater potential because consumers do not have to verify a person's identity[9] and rely on limited services provided by financial intermediaries. For households, CBDC can also increase efficiency and safety in making payments, lower the transfer fees of cross-border remittances and speed up the disbursement of the Government's emergency cash transfers.

The potential benefits of CBDC go beyond financial inclusion.[10] For central banks, CBDC could help lower the cost of cash distribution and management, maintain central banks' relevance and leadership in the monetary system and enhance monetary policy effectiveness. Central banks cannot and should not leave the creation of digital money (such as Bitcoin) entirely to the private sector. Nothing central to money's functioning in an economy can and should remain outside of public supervision and regulation. More broadly, CBDC could help broaden the tax base through reduced tax evasion, limit illicit financing due to its trackability and support national financial innovation and digitalization of an economy.

The choice of initial design can be important to reduce possible negative economic implications of CBDC adoption. For example, while interest-bearing retail CBDC could help enhance the effectiveness of monetary policy because commercial banks are more willing to adjust their deposit rates in responses to a change in the policy rate in order to retain their customers, many people may switch their savings from bank deposits to CBDC. This could lead to financial instability if such financial disintermediation is sizeable. Thus, one option is for central banks to start with wholesale CBDC; once the system matures, CBDC can then be made available to the public for retail purposes as well.

Retail CBDC would likely complement, rather than substitute for, cash. About one fifth of surveyed central banks worldwide noted that they plan to issue a CBDC in the next 1-6 years (Boar and Wehrli, 2021). Even when retail CBDC is issued, it will be unlikely to replace cash as consumers consider various factors when deciding on which forms of money to hold. For example, in Thailand interest-bearing retail CBDC is rated more favourably than cash on speed and transaction cost, but much less on anonymity (Chucherd and others, 2021)

5.2 CBDC in Asia and the Pacific: gaining interest

About half of central banks in Asia and the Pacific are exploring CBDCs with various design features. While none of the central banks have launched CBDC, at least 23 of them are at the stage of research, proof of concept or pilot (figure 4.10). In terms of purpose, 20 of

9 Only 40 per cent of adults in such countries as Armenia and the Lao People's Democratic Republic have an official identity card (Demirgüç-Kunt, and others, 2017). In this regard, India's *Aadhaar*, the world's largest biometric-based identification number system, can provide an example of how to provide official identification to residents (uidai.gov.in)

10 For elaboration on this issue, see Allen and others (2020), Shirai (2019) and Kiff and others (2020).

BOX 4.1

Selected design features of a central bank digital currency

Architecture. Under a direct architecture approach, CBDC is a direct claim on the central bank, which handles payments by retail consumers and records all real-time transactions. Under a hybrid approach, CBDC is also a direct claim on the central bank, but payments and transactions are facilitated by financial intermediaries.

Purpose. Under the retail purpose, CBDC is available to the public for all transactions. For the wholesale purpose, CBDC is used by financial institutions for interbank transactions and settlements.

Access. Under an account-based system, accounts are linked to users with a certain identity. Under a token-based system, such as banknotes in the traditional sense, CBDC tokens are electronic-based. A combination of accounts and tokens may be used.

Other design features. Examples of such features are whether CBDC is interest-bearing; is subject to a cap on its holding; supports anonymous transactions; supports integration with other digital currencies; permits offline payments; and is based on a centrally controlled database or distributed ledger technology.

Source: ESCAP, based on Allen and others (2020), Atlantic Council (2021) and Mikhalev and others (2021).

28 CBDCs under consideration would be for the retail purpose, while another 6 are for the wholesale purpose and 2 would cater to both purposes. Of 11 CBDCs with information on the access system, 9 are token-based and 2 are account-based. Finally, while plans on the architecture type are available for only six CBDCs, all of them are based on the hybrid approach. Box 4.2 features China's pilot CBDC.

Several Asia-Pacific central banks have established dedicated units on CBDC.[11] For example, the Bank of Korea recently set up a new unit to work on CBDC research and technology and a task force to review the impacts of CBDC issuance on its mandates. Bank Indonesia also formed a group to study CBDC technology. Meanwhile, CBDC work at the Monetary Authority of Singapore is supported by working groups comprising staff from different departments and representatives from the financial industry and blockchain ecosystem. Finally, the Fintech Facilitation Office within the Hong Kong Monetary Authority coordinates a joint CBDC project with the Bank of Thailand.

There are also other CBDC-related developments in the region.[12] Among others, the National Bank of Cambodia in October 2020 launched an interbank payments system based on a distributed ledger technology. Although not a CBDC, this initiative is aimed at promoting financial access by rural residents and small businesses. In the Federated States of Micronesia and Palau, there is a proposal to create a national payment platform for the issuance of CBDC to support unbanked populations.

11 For further information, see BSP (2021).

12 For more information, see the Atlantic Council's CBDC Tracker (www.atlanticcouncil.org/cbdctracker/).

FIGURE 4.10
Half of Asia-Pacific central banks are at various stages of exploring CBDC

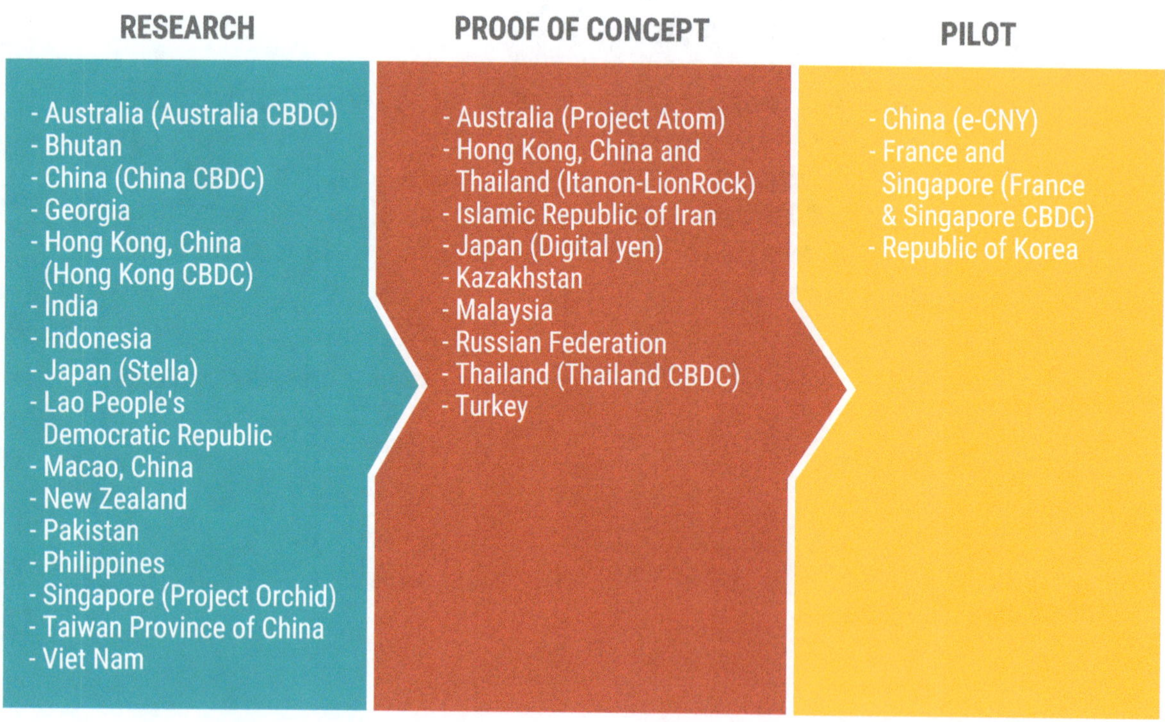

Source: ESCAP, based on the CBDC Tracker (www.cbdctracker.org), as of February 2022.
Note: For countries or areas that are exploring more than one CBDC, the names of CBDC are indicated within the parentheses.

BOX 4.2

CBDC in China: the digital yuan

The People's Bank of China began pilot testing for a retail CBDC known as the digital yuan in 11 cities in late 2019. While the launch date has not been officially announced, the digital yuan trial reached a value of 34.5 billion yuan or about $5.3 billion in transaction value as of mid-2021 (Bloomberg News, 2021). Almost 21 million people have opened a virtual wallet and made nearly 71 million transactions in total. The project's design is based on the hybrid architecture that accommodates both token- and account-based accesses (Auer, Cornelli and Frost, 2020). While onboarding and real-time payment services are operated by intermediaries, such as commercial banks and telecoms companies, the central bank provides the core infrastructure and periodically receives and stores a copy of retail transactions. Digital wallets are based on various forms of identification, which enable users to remain anonymous in daily transactions, but intermediaries are required to regularly submit transaction data to the central bank in order to ensure prudent regulation.

5.3 Making CBDC work for the poor: central banks alone are not enough

There are several steps that central banks should consider before issuing CBDC. As a first step, central banks need to be clear about their own objective(s) for issuing CBDC and whether non-CBDC options are available. After an initial decision to proceed, there are considerations on design choices and operational issues, such as legal and supervisory frameworks, risk identification and mitigation, and availability of relevant market infrastructure. These are followed by a feasibility study, further research and a pilot project.

For most central banks, enabling legal frameworks are not yet in place. Of 171 economies surveyed, only 23 per cent of them have central bank laws that allow the issuance of currency in a digital format (Bossu and others, 2020). In the Philippines, the issuance of retail CBDC is currently not possible because only the Government, commercial banks and other entities supervised by the central bank are allowed to open deposit accounts with the central bank (BSP, 2021). Amendments to anti-money-laundering and data privacy laws may also be needed.

Central banks will also need to amend governance frameworks and increase technical capacity. To issue CBDC, some central banks may need to revise their objectives, reorganize internal departments and create new regulations. Such enhanced governance frameworks would increase central banks' ability to manage reserves and deposits, protect user privacy and deal with cyberattacks, all of which functions are necessary for a smooth implementation of CBDC (Kumar and others, 2020). Moreover, while central banks will likely outsource some aspects of CBDC operations to external vendors, they still need to possess solid technical capacity to supervise these firms.

Central banks should clearly identify risks arising from the issuance of CBDC. From a policy perspective, these risks include weakened financial stability and compromised consumer protection (Kiff and others, 2020) For instance, CBDC could exaggerate systemic bank runs because a digital flight to safety could take place at a significant scale and speed, although this could be partly mitigated by a limit on withdrawal of CBDC (Mancini-Griffoli and others, 2018). From the operational perspective, examples of risks are fraud, cybersecurity and damage caused by outsourced firms.

Making retail CBDC work for financial inclusion requires broader national policy actions. Beyond having extensive networks of financial intermediaries, retail CBDC will help enhance financial access only if broad coverage of Internet networks and adequate financial literacy are in place. However, mobile-broadband subscription rates remain rather low in such countries as Afghanistan, the Lao People's Democratic Republic and Pakistan (figure 4.11). Even in countries with comparable subscription rates, the share of people who use online banking varies notably due in part to different levels of digital and financial literacy. While enhancing Internet connectivity is beyond the purview of central banks, they can still contribute by, for example, making CBDC mobile wallets easier to use in low-bandwidth rural areas.

Overall, Asia-Pacific countries should proceed with caution before issuing CBDC. As an innovative initiative that is still being studied by central banks in advanced economies, central banks in Asia-Pacific developing countries need to carefully weigh the potential benefits of issuing CBDC against their operating costs and risks, as well as considering the merits of other policy options.[13] Unless appropriate CBDC design choices are made and enabling conditions are in place, CBDC may not shift the preferences for cash among low-income consumers. Less developed or smaller countries would also benefit from multilateral cooperation, such as an agreement among central banks in Pacific island countries and areas to develop subregional payment and settlement systems (Didenko and Buckley, 2020).

6. CENTRAL BANKS AS FINANCIAL REGULATORS: INNOVATIVE SOCIALLY ORIENTED FINANCIAL INSTRUMENTS

While unconventional financial instruments for social purposes, such as social impact bonds and sustainability-linked bonds, offer some distinct advantages, their use is still very limited in Asia and the Pacific (section 6.1). To

13 Central banks could, for example, provide subsidies for commercial banks to establish more branches and offer online banking (Mancini-Griffoli and others, 2018).

FIGURE 4.11
Mobile broadband subscriptions and access to online banking remain limited in many Asia-Pacific countries

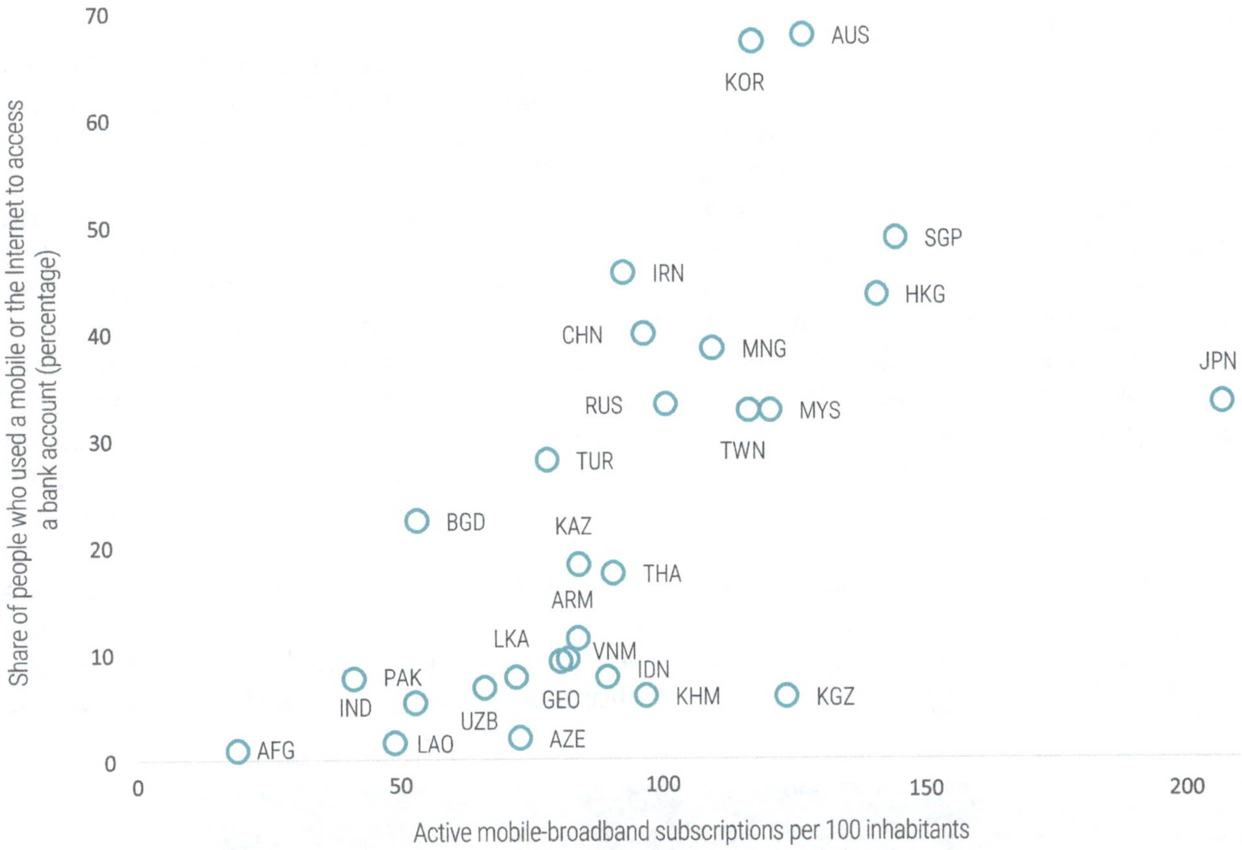

Source: ESCAP, based on the CBDC Tracker (www.cbdctracker.org), as of February 2022.

Abbreviations: Country/area codes are Afghanistan (AFG); Armenia (ARM); Australia (AUS); Azerbaijan (AZE); Bangladesh (BGD); Cambodia (KHM); China (CHN); Georgia (GEO); Hong Kong, China (HKG); India (IND); Indonesia (IDN); Islamic Republic of Iran (IRN); Japan (JPN); Kazakhstan (KAZ); Kyrgyzstan (KGZ); Lao People's Democratic Republic (LAO); Malaysia (MYS); Mongolia (MNG); Pakistan (PAK); Republic of Korea (KOR); Russian Federation (RUS); Singapore (SGP); Sri Lanka (LKA); Taiwan Province of China (TWN); Thailand (THA); Turkey (TUR); Uzbekistan (UZB); and Viet Nam (VNM).

expand the use of these modalities, central banks can work with other financial supervisory authorities to provide both technical and financial support (section 6.2).

6.1 Social impact bonds and sustainability-linked bonds: infancy stage

A social impact bond is a pay-for-success contract. Under this outcome-based modality, private investors cover the upfront capital required for service providers, usually non-government organizations or social enterprises, to set up and deliver agreed social projects. When the service provider fulfils the project's pre-defined outcomes, an outcome funder, which can be the Government, international donor or philanthropic organization, will pay the private investors the principal plus interest.[14]

14 As such, social impact bonds can be viewed as hybrid instruments with elements of debt (the payment depends on predetermined interest rate) and equity (the dividend payout is conditional on performance indicators).

Outcome funders also identify social issues to be addressed and set the project's outcome targets. Finally, external evaluators are often involved in evaluating whether the project outcomes have been met.[15]

Compared with a typical social project where the Government both funds and implements it, social impact bonds offer certain advantages. *First*, this financing modality helps ensure the effectiveness of development spending, whether by Governments or development partners, because the payment is made only when the project's positive social impact has been verified. *Second*, a project financed by social impact bond tends to exhibit greater accountability and transparency due to its impact-based nature (rather than input-based) and regular monitoring by private investors and external evaluators.

Social impact bonds have led to social gains in Asia-Pacific countries, even though there are only a few. Japan, the Republic of Korea and India are pioneers in the region; they first issued such bonds in 2009, 2014 and 2015, respectively. In India, the Educate Girls Development Impact Bond, the world's first social impact bond to support education, intended to increase enrolment for out-of-school girls and improve the literacy of both boys and girls in the northern state of Rajasthan. The three-year project targeted 166 schools with 15,000 children, 9,000 of whom were girls. The service provider (Educate Girls) trained volunteers to make door-to-door visits to beneficiary families. As the project exceeded both its enrolment and literacy targets, the Children's Investment Fund Foundation, as

15 In some cases, another stakeholder is included among intermediaries, which help mediate and form a mutual agreement on the terms and conditions of the bond. For more details, see Galitopoulou and Noya (2016).

outcome funder, paid the principal plus a 15 per cent interest rate to the investor, UBS Optimus Foundation (UBSOF, 2018).

Unlike thematic bonds the proceeds of which are earmarked for specific projects, the proceeds from sustainability-linked bonds can be used for general operations. Under this arrangement, issuers agree to meet certain sustainability performance targets and the bond coupon rate depends on whether they fully meet these predefined targets. For instance, the interest rate may be decreased by 25 basis points if the targets are met.[16] As such, issuers of this innovative bond can be more diverse, as organizations that are keen to improve their overall sustainability profiles but cannot find suitable social or green projects to implement are also allowed to participate. This possible diversification of the issuers would also help attract new investors.

While sustainability-linked bonds offer a new way for how companies can contribute to inclusive development, their use in Asia and the Pacific has been focused on environmental protection. For example, in India, UltraTech Cement raised $400 million through a bond that is aimed at reducing the company's carbon emission by 22.2 per cent for every metric ton of cementitious material it produces by end-March 2030 (UltraTech Cement, 2021). Globally, the first sustainability-linked bond that features social targets was issued by Luxembourg Novartis for €1.85 billion in 2017. During the period 2017-2028, the proceeds are and will be used to improve access to medicines in poorer countries. In France, Schneider Electric raised €650 million in 2020 from a sustainability-linked bond that targets seven socially and environmentally oriented Sustainable Development Goals, including good-quality education, gender equality and reduced inequality.

16 While investors receive lower interest income in such cases, they may still benefit from a higher price of debt because the issuer's sustainable practices could result in a narrower credit spread.

6.2 Widening the use of innovative instruments: technical and financial supports

Campaigns to enhance the understanding of innovative socially oriented financial instruments are useful. For example, when green bonds were less widely understood, financial regulators in Indonesia issued policy guidance to non-sovereign issuers on international issuance of green bonds and expanded learning networks on sustainable finance (Climate Bonds Initiative, 2018). China has also set up a knowledge platform on best practices for scaling up sustainable finance.

Central banks in the Asia-Pacific region and beyond can work together to develop and/or harmonize taxonomies for socially oriented financial instruments. Such a common framework would enhance clarity and confidence among potential investors. A recent effort on this front is the Sustainability-linked Bond Principles of the International Capital Market Association, which outline five components on selection of key performance indicators, calibration of sustainability performance targets, bond characteristics, reporting and verification (ICMA, 2020). In the area of financing green development, the Association of Southeast Asian Nations (ASEAN) introduced the Green Bond Standards in 2017, while the People's Bank of China is working with the European Union to create a green investment taxonomy across the two markets. Similar multilateral partnerships can be considered for socially oriented instruments.

TABLE 4.2
Summary of possible corporate and policy actions on inclusive central banking

Central banking area	Corporate and policy actions	
	Fundamental	More ambitious
Conduct of inequality-mindful monetary policy	Conduct research to better understand the distributional effects of monetary policy	Between two equally effective monetary policy strategies, choose an option that promotes economic equality
	Step up communication to the public about the distributional impacts of changes in monetary policy	Incorporate inclusive development into the central bank's objective, possibly as a secondary additional goal
		Allocate part of asset purchase programmes to social bonds
Management of socially oriented official reserves	Assess how socially oriented reserve management would affect the liquidity and risk-adjusted returns of portfolios	Set up an investment committee to make decisions on reserve allocation
		Adopt sustainable and responsible investment strategies
		Use excess reserves as seed capital to support domestic social projects
Central bank digital currencies	Examine various design features of issuing a CBDC and whether non-CBDC options are available	Conduct a feasibility study and further research, followed by a pilot project, if relevant
		Amend relevant laws to allow currency issuance in digital format
		Adopt CBDC design features that suit a coun-try's context and objectives
Innovative socially tilted financial instruments	Launch schemes to enhance awareness and understanding among market participants	Develop and/or harmonize taxonomies for socially oriented financial instruments
		Provide financial assistance to meet the high cost of the verification process

Source: ESCAP.

Financial incentives can be provided to increase the feasibility of innovative socially oriented financial instruments. One specific area is to provide financial assistance to meet the high cost of the external verification process, which is an integral feature of social impact bonds and sustainability-linked bonds. For example, under the Sustainable Bond Grant Scheme, the Monetary Authority of Singapore offers funds to cover expenses relating to independent review or rating of green, social, sustainability or sustainability-linked bonds that are issued and listed in Singapore.

7. CONCLUSIONS

This chapter examined how central banking can further promote inclusive development in Asia and the Pacific. It focused on central banks' roles as policymakers, investors, currency issuers and regulators. Specifically, the chapter explored how to incorporate considerations of economic inequality into the conduct of conventional and unconventional monetary policy, make management of official reserves more socially oriented, leverage the potential of central bank digital currencies for financial inclusion, and support the development of innovative socially tilted financial instruments. Table 4.2 provides a snapshot of corporate and policy actions that central banks can consider in pursuing inclusive central banking.

Beyond these specific actions, there are four broad policy issues to consider. *First*, while being pragmatic about their capacity to pursue inclusive central banking, central banks should not shy away from what they themselves can do. At a basic level, various Asia-Pacific central banks have led by example by ensuring their own inclusive staffing and procurement practices. Similarly, promoting inclusive finance is an area to which central banks can contribute directly in order to support inclusive development but many central banks in the region still do not have this as their objective. Also, central banks, even in countries which are deemed to have inadequate reserves, can consider portfolio reallocation to financial instruments that would have positive social impacts, as this does not necessarily affect the liquidity and risk of their portfolios.

Second, a shift towards inclusive central banking requires legal amendments and enhancement of technical capacity by central banks. For example, changes in central bank and other laws are required to allow central banks in many countries to invest official reserves

in unconventional asset classes and issue CBDC. Similarly, strong technical capacity helps central banks to assess the distributional impacts of monetary policy, the implications of socially oriented reserve management on portfolio performance and the feasibility of issuing CBDC.

Third, central banks cannot act alone. Central banks should work closely with fiscal and other policymakers to address economic inequality. For example, when lower interest rates help reduce expenditures on debt servicing, freed up fiscal space can be channelled to government projects that target poor households. Socially tilted management of reserves relies on larger social bond markets, thus calling for action by sovereign and corporate issuers and financial supervisory agencies. These supervisory agencies also play an instrumental role in promoting innovative socially oriented financial instruments. To realize the potential of CBDC, central banks can partner with public agencies in charge of digital connectivity and official documentation. Finally, central banks with less capacity would benefit from technical assistance by international development partners.

Fourth, while pursuing inclusive central banking, central banks should be mindful of associated risks to their operations and financial systems. For example, investing official reserves in domestic social bonds may limit central banks' ability to raise liquidity during emergency situations. Similarly, CBDC can undermine central banks' reputation in the event of fraud and cybersecurity breaches, while interest-bearing retail CBDC can lead to financial disintermediation or even bank runs.

GEARING STRUCTURAL TRANSFORMATION FOR INCLUSIVE DEVELOPMENT

CHAPTER 05

1. INTRODUCTION

Rapid economic growth in Asia and the Pacific in the last three decades "lifted many boats", with consequent remarkable reductions in poverty rates. Structural transition from low-productivity agriculture to high-productivity manufacturing and modern services[1] has been at the centre of this success, contributing to the historical income convergence between developing Asia-Pacific countries and the developed world, and to an overall reduction in between-country inequality worldwide (Chancel and others, 2022; Gradín, 2021).

However, as noted in chapter 1, this success has not lifted *all* boats. Some 85 per cent of the population in the Asia-Pacific region have experienced increases in inequality in their countries since the 1990s. A closer examination (figure 5.1) reveals that this rise in inequality in Asia-Pacific countries was primarily driven by changes in predistribution (see box 5.1 for its definition), while redistribution through taxes and transfers played only a smaller role.

In East, South-East and South Asian developing countries, which were in the middle of rapid structural transformation out of agriculture, redistribution had little impact and, in some cases, even aggravated the rise in income gaps. In industrialized economies in the region, redistribution did increase uniformly, yet it was not enough to offset surges in their predistribution inequality. In North and Central Asian countries, which suffered deeply from the economic turmoil and deindustrialization in the 1990s, both predistribution and redistribution worsened. The role of redistribution was found to be important only in Kyrgyzstan and Tajikistan.[2]

This observation suggests strongly that the strategy for inclusive development should devote more attention to predistribution policies, rather than leaving all the burdens to ex post redistributive measures (box 5.2).

1 Modern services are defined as comprising business services and finance. Business services include economic activities of information and communications services, professional, scientific and technical services, as well as administrative and support services as listed in the International Standard Industrial Classification of All Economic Activities (ISIC). The finance sector includes financial and insurance activities as listed in ISIC.

2 In both cases, changes in redistribution increased inequality between 1990 and 2018.

BOX 5.1

Is prevention better than cure? Predistribution vs. redistribution

The distribution of disposable income can be decomposed into two distinctive components:

- **Predistribution** refers to the market outcome of income distribution before taxes and cash transfers kick in
- **Redistribution** refers to ex post adjustments in income distribution through taxes and cash transfers and is measured as the difference between predistribution inequality (or inequality of market income) and the inequality of disposable income

In general parlance, the former term implies direct interventions to reduce income inequality, while the latter means redistribution of incomes after taxes have been levied. Hence, predistribution can be viewed as preventing inequalities from arising in the first place, while redistribution is a cure once inequality has arisen.

The COVID-19 pandemic has added another layer of urgency to this shift, as the fiscal space for expanding cash transfers is likely to become increasingly squeezed in most Asia-Pacific developing countries (chapter 3).

Economic structural transformation, in particular, has extensive linkages with the dynamics of predistribution inequality. For example, rapid industrialization and urbanization in developing countries in East, South-East and South Asia enlarged rural-urban income gaps and wage inequalities between different groups, when well-paid job opportunities were available for only a part of the population, while in North and Central Asia deindustrialization and economic liberalization destroyed formal industrial jobs and reversed artificial wage compression in the previous era of the command economy.[3] In industrialized economies in the region, further economic upgrading to technology-driven manufacturing[4] and modern services also resulted in the triple-challenge of skill-biased technological progress, automation and

3 In this system, economic activities and prices are controlled by a central authority, which also assigns quantitative production goals and allots raw materials to productive enterprises.

4 The contrast between a substantial decrease in manufacturing's share in total employment and the largely stable manufacturing's share in value addition clearly indicates the change.

offshoring of middle-class industrial jobs and an increase in top pay in the emerging technology and finance sectors.

In coming years, novel changes in economic structure driven by the digital-robotic-Artificial Intelligence revolution[5] are expected to affect the availability of jobs, change the labour market structure and alter predistribution outcomes as well. In particular, economic digitalization has been visibly accelerated by the COVID-19 pandemic, as remote work is becoming a norm and the consumption of digital products and services has experienced a boom. Meanwhile, worries about an accelerated transition towards automated production continue when using labour becomes more risky and costly in a lasting pandemic. These shifts may reinforce the challenges posed by the digital-robotic-AI revolution in the near future.

This chapter argues that the trajectory of inequality during structural transformation does not follow a deterministic path, leaving ample space for policies to have an impact on this process. The experience of the Asia-Pacific region suggests that "growing with equity" is possible, if supported by correct sectoral strategies and other conducive policies. However, these past lessons may not be adequate to prepare countries for the upcoming disruptions brought about by the digital-robotic-AI revolution. More proactive policy efforts would be needed to guide technological upgrading and innovations towards a labour-friendly path, to leverage the visible hand in shaping the market distribution of economic rewards and to better manage the turbulence created by more frequent and severe labour market shocks.

The chapter is organized as follows. In section 2, stock is taken of the contemporary economic understanding on the interactions between structural transformation and predistribution inequality and on the underlying structural drivers of long-term inequality trends. Section 3 provides a snapshot of the latest structural transformation experiences in Asia-Pacific developing economies and draws policy lessons on inclusive structural transformation using selected country cases. Section 4 discusses the outlook for structural transformation in the Asia-Pacific region in view of the digital-robotic-AI revolution. Section 5 discusses potential policy options to better guide, shape and manage future structural transformation for inclusive development. Section 6 provides concluding remarks.

For the purpose of this chapter, the focus will be primarily on changes and dynamics in predistribution. Thus, when the word "inequality" is used alone in the subsequent discussion, it will be referring to predistribution inequality by default, unless specifically mentioned otherwise.

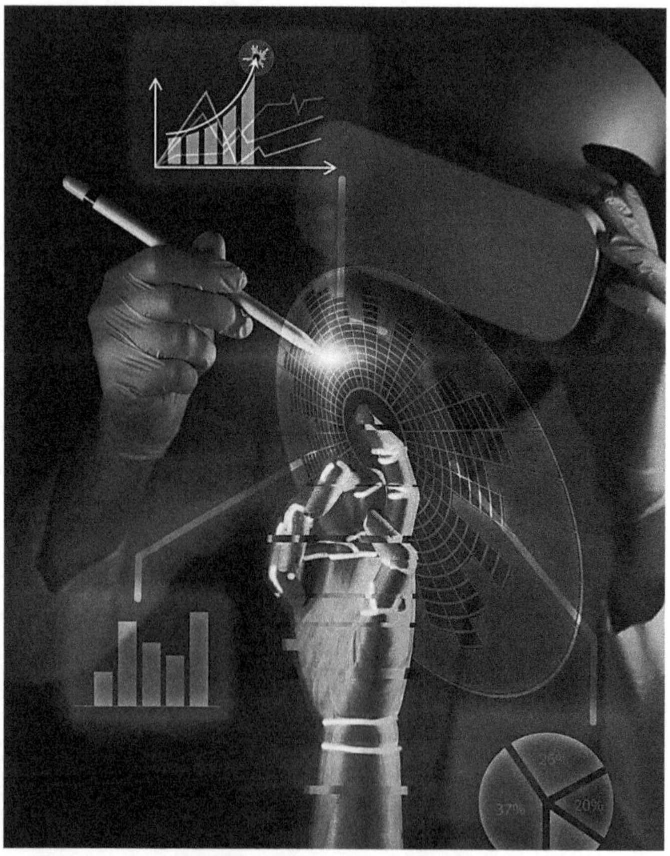

5 Which comprises disruptions to both industries and services.

FIGURE 5.1
Predistribution is the dominating factor behind inequality trends over time, 1990-2019

Source: ESCAP, based on the Standardized World Income Inequality Database (SWIID) 9.1 (accessed on 26 November 2021).
Note: Change in predistribution is measured as the change in income Gini before taxes and transfers between 1990 and 2019. Change in redistribution is measured as the change in income Gini reduction due to redistribution during the same period.

BOX 5.2

Why does predistribution matter?

In the debate on rising economic inequality, redistribution policies often receive far more attention than policies that address predistribution. Two factors may have contributed to this bias. One, the effect of policies concerning predistribution, such as education and market regulation, is much more difficult to evaluate, which means it gets less attention. Two, predistribution policies that are aimed at directly changing market outcomes can appear more distortive and inefficient than restoring equity afterwards through redistribution. Indeed, if progressive taxes and transfers are able to bring income Gini down from above 50 to a lower level of 30-35 in many European countries, why not concentrate on redistribution while leaving the market free and efficient?

As income inequality in developing countries is predominantly shaped by predistribution, it can be argued that policies should be focused on "treat(ing) the root causes of inequality, rather than attending only to the symptoms" (O'Neill and Williamson, 2012). Market distortions and failures, rather than effective market competition, can be the root cause of predistribution inequality. One can easily find pertinent examples in bargaining power imbalances in wage negotiations and in impoverished victims of pollution or climate change, which are not priced in by the market. If excessive predistribution inequality is left unchecked, it may also result in an increasingly daunting task for redistribution to correct it with potentially even greater economic distortions.

In addition, inclusive development is not simply about outcomes measured in income or consumption. It is also about self-fulfilment and social dignity earned by being a productive member of society and being rewarded fairly according to one's contributions. Such contributive justice can be served only through fairer predistribution.

Figure
Reduction in income Gini through taxes and transfers remains highly limited in Asia-Pacific developing countries (2019 or the latest year)

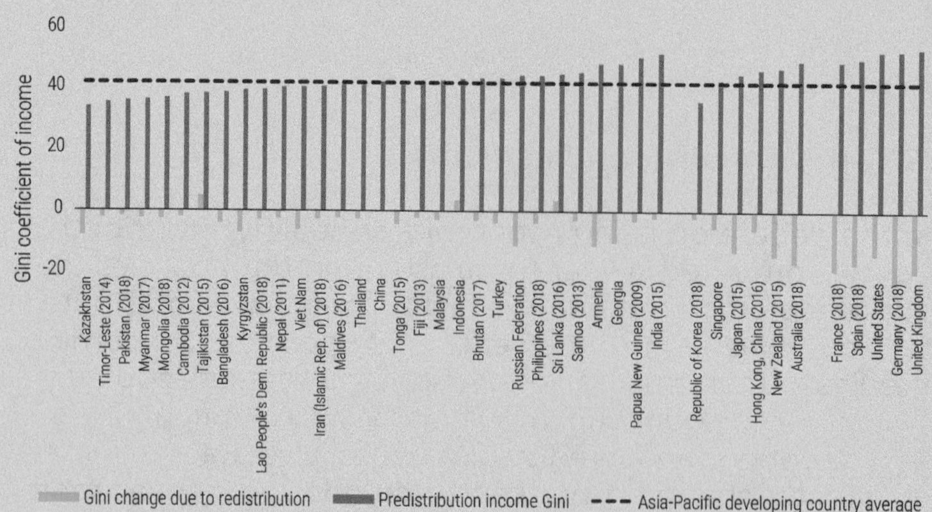

Source: ESCAP, based on the Standardized World Income Inequality Database (SWIID) 9.1 (accessed on 26 November 2021).

2. INTERACTIONS BETWEEN STRUCTURAL TRANSFORMATION AND INEQUALITY: WHAT DO WE KNOW?

2.1 Kuznets' intuition and the inverted U-shaped curve

Undoubtedly, the interactions between structural transformation and inequality can be extremely complex. In 1955, Simon Kuznets provided a simple thinking framework for understanding these interactions in the long run. He speculated that the observed income inequality trend in industrialized countries, based on the highly limited empirical evidence available at the time, could be driven primarily by labour reallocation from a low-productivity rural sector to a high-productivity urban sector in a simplistic "dual-economy" model (Kuznets, 1955).

The evolution of inequality during structural transformation follows an inverted U-shape (figure 5.2), according to this hypothesis. In the initial stage, most of the economic gains are reaped by investors, entrepreneurs and the better-paid workers in high-productivity urban sectors, while surplus labour in the rural sector keeps rural productivity and wages low. This phenomenon would result in an increase in overall predistribution inequality, creating a dilemma for policymakers – a tradeoff between structural transformation and equality/inclusion, which is also known as the Kuznets' tension. Later on, as structural transformation deepens, the surplus labour is gradually absorbed into high-productivity sectors, restoring labour-capital balance, reducing cross-sector wage gaps and eventually causing a decline in inequality.

2.2 Limitations of Kuznets' thinking framework and other important factors

Despite the usefulness of this thinking framework, especially for developing countries going through rapid rural-urban transformation, Kuznets' hypothesis is an oversimplification of a complex phenomenon. The pathways between structural transformation and inequality are not only determined by the labour reallocation between the two hypothetical sectors, but are also influenced by at least four additional factors.

First is the leading sector of structural transformation. For example, Baymul and Sen (2020) noted that the tension between structural transformation and equality happens when labour is reallocated from agriculture to services. On the other hand, labour reallocation to manufacturing could reduce such tension as it would be beneficial in both increasing economic growth and reducing inequality. Certain urban subsectors, in particular financial services, may also have unique implications for long-term predistribution inequality trends (Davis and Kim, 2015).

Second are new channels for structural transformation created during globalization. The hyperglobalization spanning the period since the 1980s to date, in particular, has provided unprecedented job opportunities and access to know-how for low-wage workers in developing countries (Baldwin, 2016), enabling and accelerating structural transformation into manufacturing through global value chains (GVCs).[6] Globally, between-country inequality reduced significantly as a result, while within-country inequality generally increased (Chancel and others, 2022; Gradín, 2021). In particular, the global top 1 per cent reaped a disproportionate share of the economic gains from globalization, while the poorest 10 per cent and the majority of the working class in developed countries saw stagnation in their income (Bourguignon, 2016; Milanovic, 2016).

Third is access to opportunities. In the developing country context, the severity and duration of the Kuznets' tension depends largely on how quickly surplus labour in agriculture can be absorbed by high-productivity sectors. This in turn is determined by two key factors: first, the speed in the creation of productive non-agricultural jobs and second, the level of equality in access to these employment opportunities.

Policies that promote greater equity in people's ability to explore economic opportunities often kill multiple birds with one stone. In taking the example of education, literacy and primary education are often a minimum requirement for even low-skill manufacturing jobs. Ensuring equal access to basic education is thus essential for containing inequality during the process of structural transformation (see chapter 3). A significant increase in skill supply through the expansion of education coverage also helps reduce education premium and wage inequality (Piketty, 2006; Goldin and Katz, 2008). Moreover, an abundance of skilled labour changes the relative cost of labour and capital in production as well, tilting technological choices in structural transformation in favour of more labour-intensive production.

Fourth is the impact of technological innovations on the demand for labour. Historically, all technological revolutions have

6 The commodity boom fuelled by fast-expanding global trade also changed inequality dynamics among resource and raw material exporters (Galbraith, 2011).

FIGURE 5.2
Kuznets' inverted U-shaped curve and its extension

Source: ESCAP.

resulted in an increase in aggregate labour demand in the long term. This makes temporary disruptions and an increase in inequality in technology-driven structural transformation less worrisome, as everyone eventually benefits from the change through employment. However, a strong concern over the aggregate employment effect of the latest digital-robotic-AI revolution has emerged in recent years, when labour displacement due to automation can potentially far outpace the creation of new jobs and when major structural shocks to the labour market could significantly aggravate inequality (see section 5.4 for a more detailed discussion).

This pessimistic prediction has not yet been borne out by empirical facts, and great uncertainties remain (Autor, 2015; Arntz, Gregory and Zierahn, 2016; The Economist, 2022). However, policy prudence is still advised, even in the absence of firm evidence. This includes taking proactive measures to catalyse a more job-rich structural transformation as technological choices can be influenced by policies. It also requires better management of socioeconomic disruptions to ensure a smooth transition.

The trajectory of inequality is neither a deterministic path nor a universal law... and policy does matter

These contemporary insights suggest that inequality trajectories are far from following a deterministic path during structural transformation as envisioned by Kuznets (figure 5.3). In fact, structural transformations in developing countries are taking many different forms, such as "unequalizing

FIGURE 5.3
Significant diversity in inequality pathways exists in Asia-Pacific countries

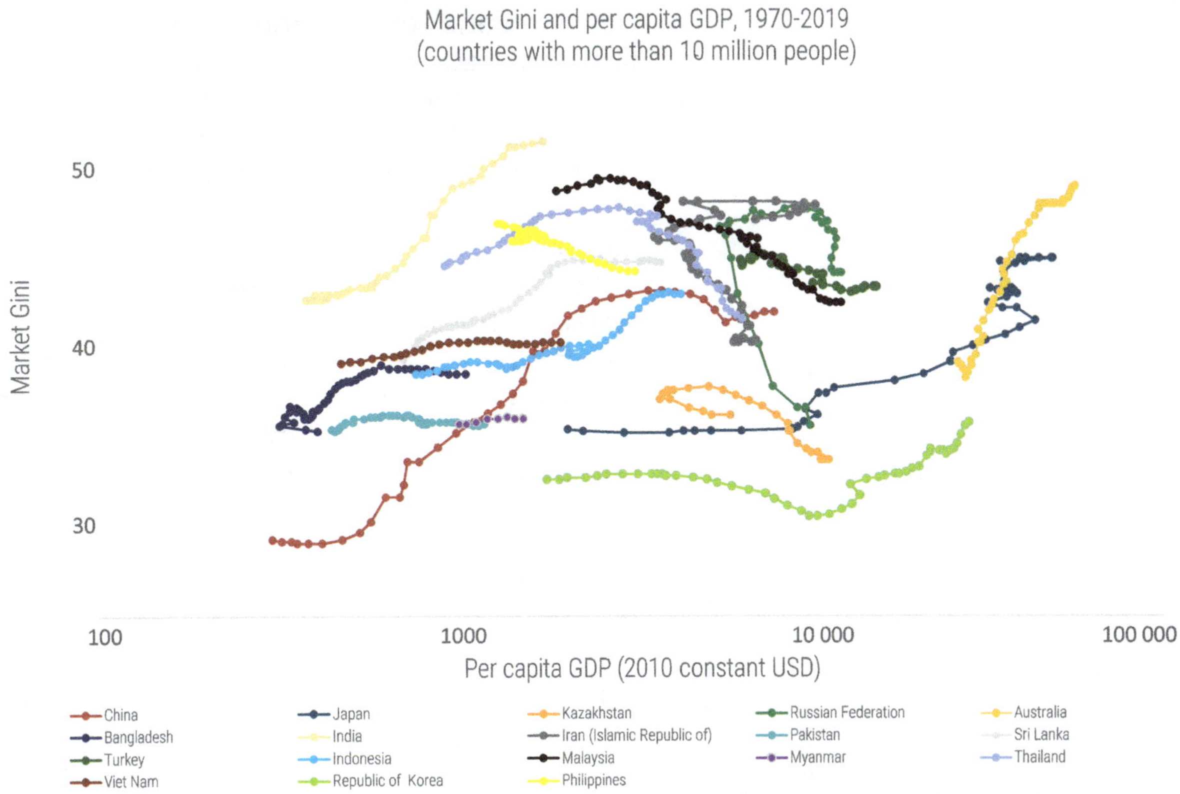

Source: ESCAP, based on the Standardized World Income Inequality Database (SWIID) 9.1 and World Development Indicators (accessed on 26 November 2021).

tertiarization",[7] urbanization without growth, or expansion of modern sectors without job creation, in addition to traditional industrialization (Sen, Sumner and Yusuf, 2020). While in developed countries, the long-term decline in inequality also reversed from the 1970s, turning Kuznets' inverted-U into a de facto-N (figure 5.2). There is now a broad consensus that the Kuznets curve is unlikely to be a universal law nor a stable pattern that can adequately guide policymaking, and significant heterogeneity exists in national experiences (Alisjahbana and others, 2020).

This national heterogeneity means that there is ample space for policies to have an impact on inequality outcomes during structural transformation. As section 3 will demonstrate, it is possible to avoid the curse of the Kuznets' tension and achieve inclusive development with a wise choice of sectoral strategies and conducive policy combinations.

3. INCLUSIVE STRUCTURAL TRANSFORMATION IN ASIA AND THE PACIFIC: RECENT EXPERIENCE AND PAST LESSONS

Asia and the Pacific is known for "defying" the Kuznets' inverted-U. Early examples are Japan, the Republic of Korea and Singapore, all of which succeeded in "growing with equity" for different periods, achieving rapid industrialization and economic growth and at the same time maintaining low and stable inequality. Such dual success was also seen later in the cases of Indonesia and Malaysia during their rapid industrialization process. However, since the 1990s, this trend has been somewhat reversed in the majority of Asia-Pacific economies, with income gaps between the rich and the poor widening while high economic growth continued. Encouragingly, episodes of "growing with equity" seem to be coming back again since the 2007/08 global financial crisis.

3.1 A snapshot of structural transformation and inequality dynamics in the period 1990-2018

The three decades between 1990 and 2018 can be loosely divided into two major periods. The first period of 1990 to 2007 is characterized by wide-ranging market-oriented economic transition and reforms and by the opening up to global trade and foreign investment in the majority of developing economies in the region. This resulted in a period of rapid structural transformation and high economic growth.[8] However, it was also accompanied by rising inequality gaps. The second period of 2007-2018 saw economic systems becoming more stable with less disruptive reforms. Structural transformation decelerated in the more developed economies in the region but kept a high pace in such countries as Bangladesh, Cambodia and Viet Nam.

Manufacturing continued to lead structural transformation and productivity growth in these three decades. Its median contribution to GDP growth was 21.5 per cent, and it accommodated 16.8 per cent of the total increase in non-agricultural employment. Although the speed of job

7 Tertiarization refers to structural transformation that is predominantly led by the expansion of the services section in employment and value addition.

8 Except for North and Central Asia, which suffered immensely from the economic recession and turmoil in the 1990s.

creation slowed after 2007 (figure 5.4a), partly due to the growing capital intensity in manufacturing production, its contribution to GDP growth has remained largely stable. The productivity advantage of manufacturing over agriculture and the traditional services sector[9] was further enhanced (figure 5.4b).

Apart from manufacturing, the modern services sector also began to play a more prominent role in leading structural transformation and economic development. Its median contribution to the increase in non-agricultural employment almost doubled between the period 1990-2007 and that of 2007-2018; it now creates more new non-agricultural jobs than manufacturing does (figure 5.4a). The modern services sector shares several desirable features of manufacturing, such as high productivity (figure 5.4b), productivity spillovers to other economic sectors, and tradability. It has the potential to become the main pillar of economic growth and job creation in more developed economies in the region and to provide a second engine of structural transformation in Asia-Pacific developing countries.

Four general observations can be highlighted for this period (figure 5.5).

1. Between the 1990 and 2007, there were mixed results for manufacturing-led structural transformation. It was associated with rising inequality in the Lao People's Democratic Republic, Sri Lanka and, to a less extent, Viet Nam, but was associated with decreasing inequality in Thailand and Turkey.

2. In contrast, manufacturing-led structural transformation seemed to be uniformly associated with "growing with equity" between 2007 and 2018, as in Bangladesh, Cambodia, Pakistan and Viet Nam.

3. Between 1990 and 2007, increased inequality in developed economies in the region accompanied rapid economic tertiarization led by modern services and rapid contraction in manufacturing's share in total employment. However, the transition from manufacturing to modern services is not necessarily associated with rising inequality in every case.

4. Between 1990 and 2007, large developing countries, in particular China and India, seem to have exhibited Kuznets' tension of rising inequality during fast structural transformation.

3.2 Experience of structural transformation in selected Asia-Pacific cases

The Republic of Korea: how "growing with equity" is achieved

Between 1965 and 1996, the Republic of Korea demonstrated a remarkable experience of "growing with equity", when GDP per capita increased 123-fold,[10] while predistribution income Gini declined from 32.7 to 31.3.

A number of crucial factors contributed to this development miracle at different stages. Between 1962 and 1978, the increase in demand for labour eased the downward pressure on rural and urban wages and improved labour's position in income distribution, offsetting the pressure of rising inequality during this initial phase of industrialization. Manufacturing played a central role, absorbing more than

9 Comprising trade services, transport services, government services and other services listed in the UNU-WIDER Economic Transformation Database.

10 From $108 to $13,403 in constant 2015 United States dollars.

FIGURE 5.4
Modern services are emerging as a second engine for economic and employment growth

(a) Sectoral contribution to GDP growth and non-agricultural employment growth (median of 18 Asia-Pacific economies)

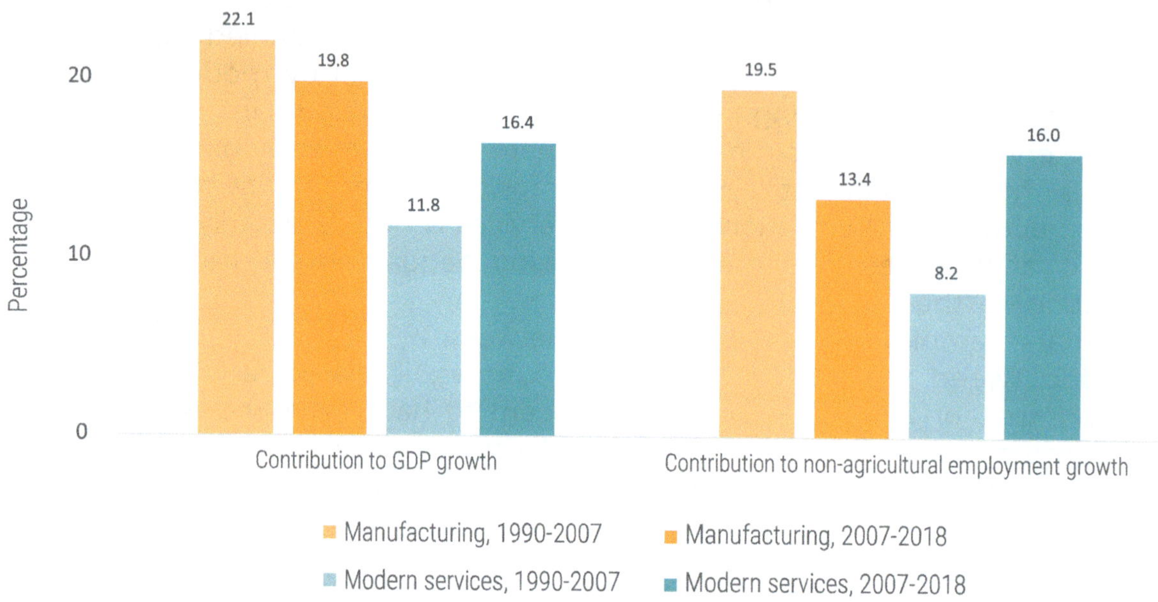

(b) Labour productivity by sector, as a percentage of all-sector average (median of 18 Asia-Pacific economies)

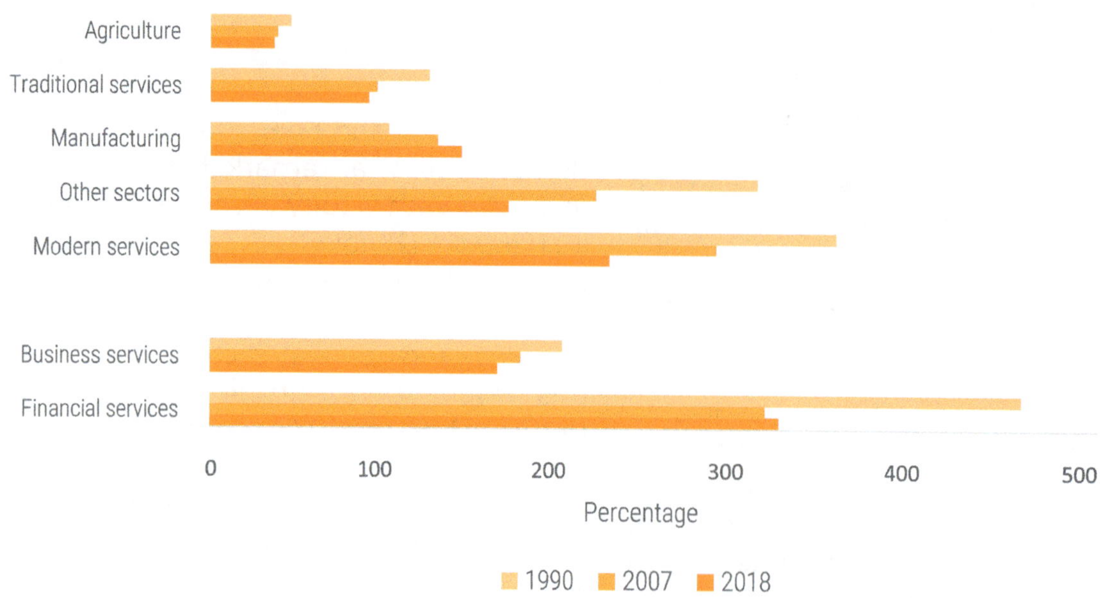

Source: ESCAP, based on the UNU-WIDER Economic Transformation Database (accessed on 26 November 2021).

FIGURE 5.5
Percentage point changes in the share of agriculture, manufacturing and modern services in total employment (left axis) and percentage point changes in predistribution income Gini (right axis)

(a) 1990-2007: tertiarization in industrialized economies uniformly led to increases in predistribution inequality; China and India also experienced significant surges in income Gini

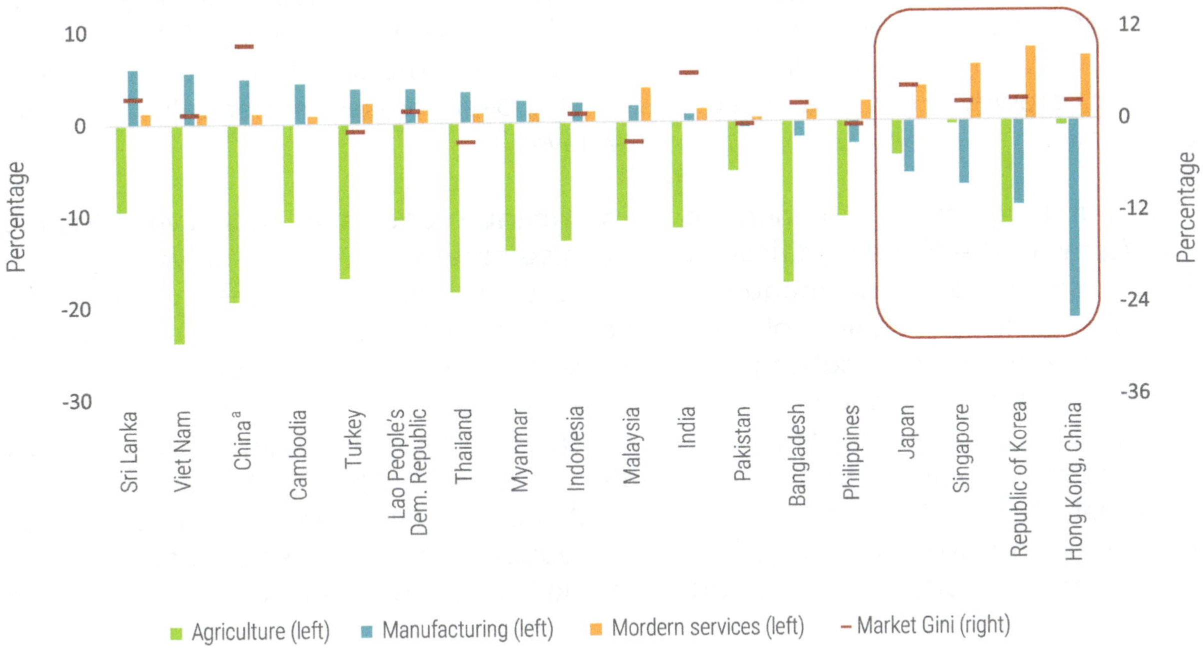

[a] *The change in manufacturing employment's share in China for the period 1990-2007 is an adjusted value which does not count in the reduction of 31 million people in manufacturing employment between 1997 and 2002 due to mass layoffs by State-owned enterprises in this short period. This adjusted value reflects more accurately the manufacturing sector's relative importance in employment during this period.*

(b) 2007-2018: new episodes of "growing with equity" began in rapidly industrializing developing countries

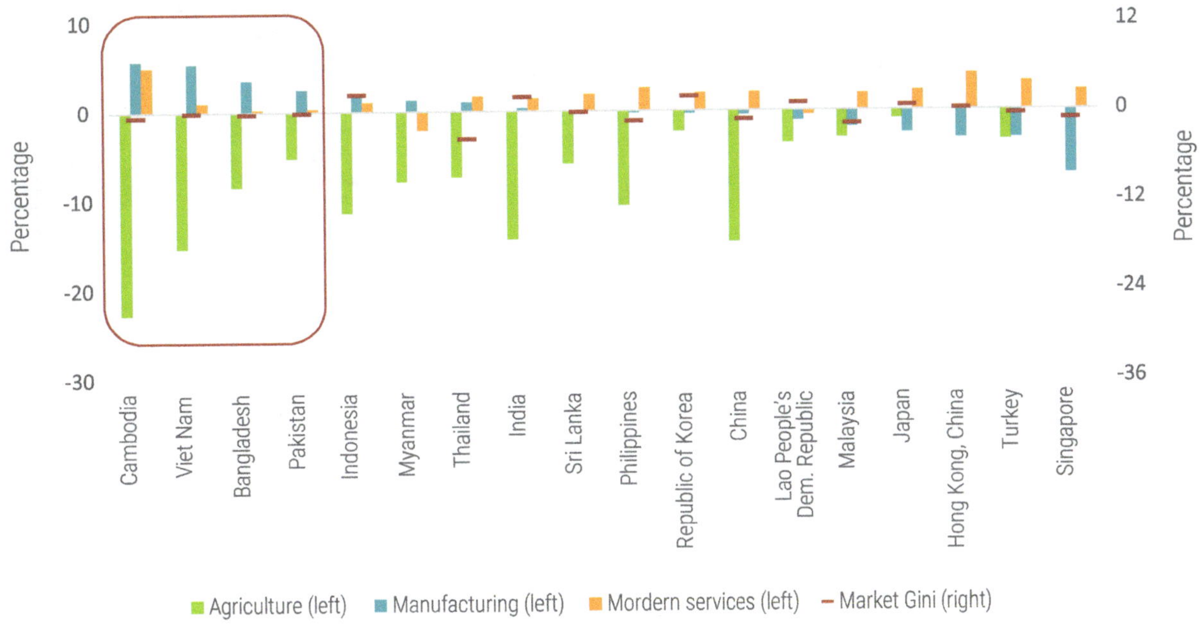

Source: ESCAP, based on the UNU-WIDER Economic Transformation Database and the Standardized World Income Inequality Database (SWIID) 9.1 (accessed on 26 November 2021).

half of the labour reallocation from agriculture. Public works programmes also expanded job availability with specific targeting on low-income populations. Between 1966 and 1976, manufacturing real wages registered an annual growth rate of 9.6 per cent (Choo, 1978) and, towards the end of the 1970s, wage growth had surpassed economic growth (Harvie and Lee, 2003).

In the rural sector, comprehensive land reforms in the 1950s significantly reduced rural poverty and inequality and helped the majority of the rural population in the subsequent structural transformation. The Seamaul Movement, a comprehensive rural development programme, was initiated in 1971, which kick-started a green revolution (Kim, 2012). Simultaneous efforts to support farmers in income generation were also made through accelerated transition from subsistence farming to commercial farming and the creation of part-time jobs under the Saemaul factory programme. The significant and broad-based agricultural productivity improvement doubled average farm household income between 1970 and 1976, outpacing income growth in the urban sector, pushing between-sector inequality down to a low level.

Significant progress in inclusive education was also essential. Close-to-universal primary education was achieved by the late 1960s, while secondary school net enrolment reached 82 per cent in 1985, more than doubling the level in the early 1970s. Tertiary education took off in the 1990s and has maintained a high growth rate since. This significant increase in skill supply not only accelerated wage growth but also reduced income gaps between skilled and less-skilled labour, with the university-high

FIGURE 5.6
Structural changes and predistribution income Gini trend in the Republic of Korea, 1971-2018

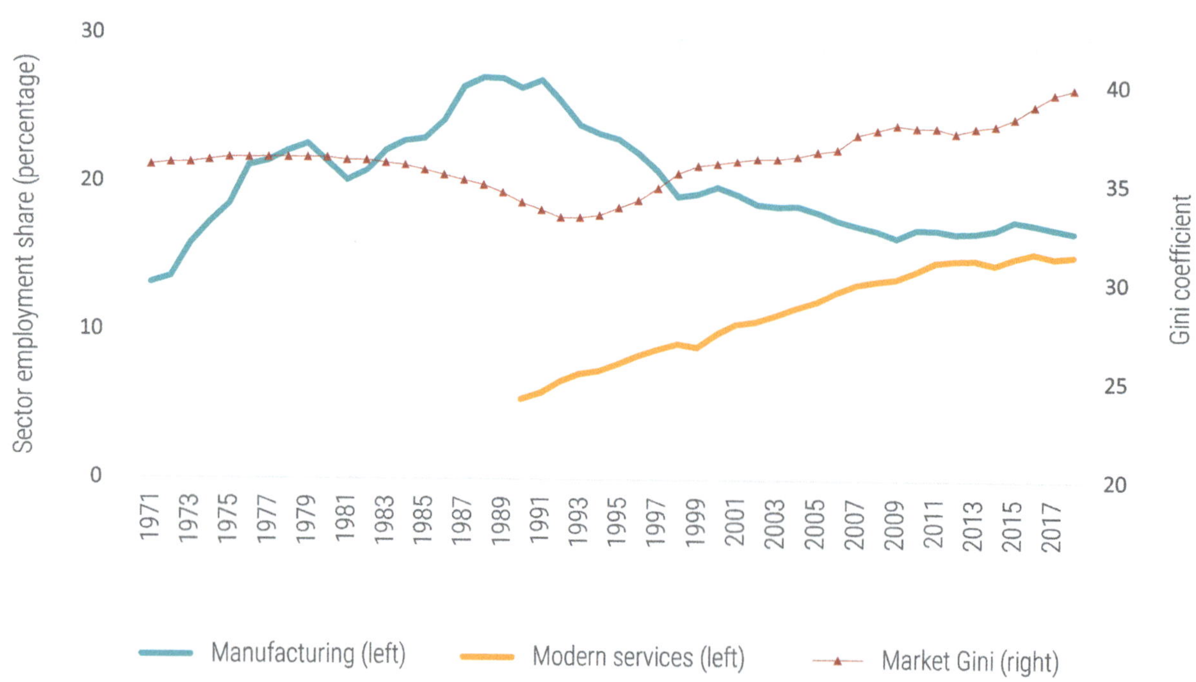

Source: ESCAP, based on the GGDC/UNU-WIDER Economic Transformation Database and 10-sector database, and the Standardized World Income Inequality Database (SWIID) 9.1 (accessed on 26 November 2021).

school wage ratio decreasing from 2.17 in the period 1975-1980 to 1.47 in the period 1990-1995 (Kang, 2001). The lasting dividend of inclusive education was a major reason why inequality remained stable in the 1980s and early 1990s.

China: experiencing the curse of the Kuznets' tension

China's export-led economic growth and its structural transformation since the late 1970s share a number of commonalities with that of the Republic of Korea, but were accompanied by a significant surge in inequality (figure 5.7).

The Kuznets' tension played a central role in China's inequality trend, when urban sectors proved unable to adequately absorb the vast pool of surplus labour in the rural sector. In particular, the share of manufacturing in total employment increased by only 4 percentage points between 1978 and its peak in 1995. In comparison, in the same 17-year timespan between 1963 and 1980, the employment share of manufacturing in the Republic of Korea grew by 14 percentage points, more than tripling the labour absorption effect. The high growth in industrial value addition pushed up urban productivity and income, while the slow pace in labour reallocation trapped surplus rural labour in agriculture. As a result, rural-urban income gaps quickly widened (table 5.1), accounting for close to half the overall inequality in the early 2000s (Luo, Li and Sicular, 2018).

The issue of rising inequality was further aggravated by the baby boom in the 1960s, the segmentation of the rural-urban labour market and the impact of the open economy. In particular, restrictions[11] on rural-urban labour mobility created additional obstacles in the rural population's access to higher-pay urban employment opportunities and further weakened their wage bargaining power. This, coupled with rural underinvestment, significantly amplified and prolonged the rural-urban income disparity. Rising inequality across geographic regions was a side effect of China's integration into the global economy. The eastern coastal provinces, where foreign investment and export-oriented manufacturing were concentrated, benefited enormously from high-productivity jobs and knowledge spillovers, while inland provinces were left behind. As a result, regional income gaps followed a similar pattern as the rural-urban income gap (table 5.1).

11 Most notably, the hukou (household registration) system, which restricted the rural population's access to urban jobs and urban public services.

TABLE 5.1
Evolution of urban-rural and between-region income ratios in China

	1988	1995	2002	2007	2013
Urban/rural	2.45	2.58	3.20	4.02	2.56
East/center	1.42	1.75	1.86	1.84	1.53
East/west	1.62	2.16	2.05	2.23	1.59

Source: Li, Sicular and Tarp (2021).

FIGURE 5.7
Structural changes and predistribution income Gini trend in China, 1971-2018

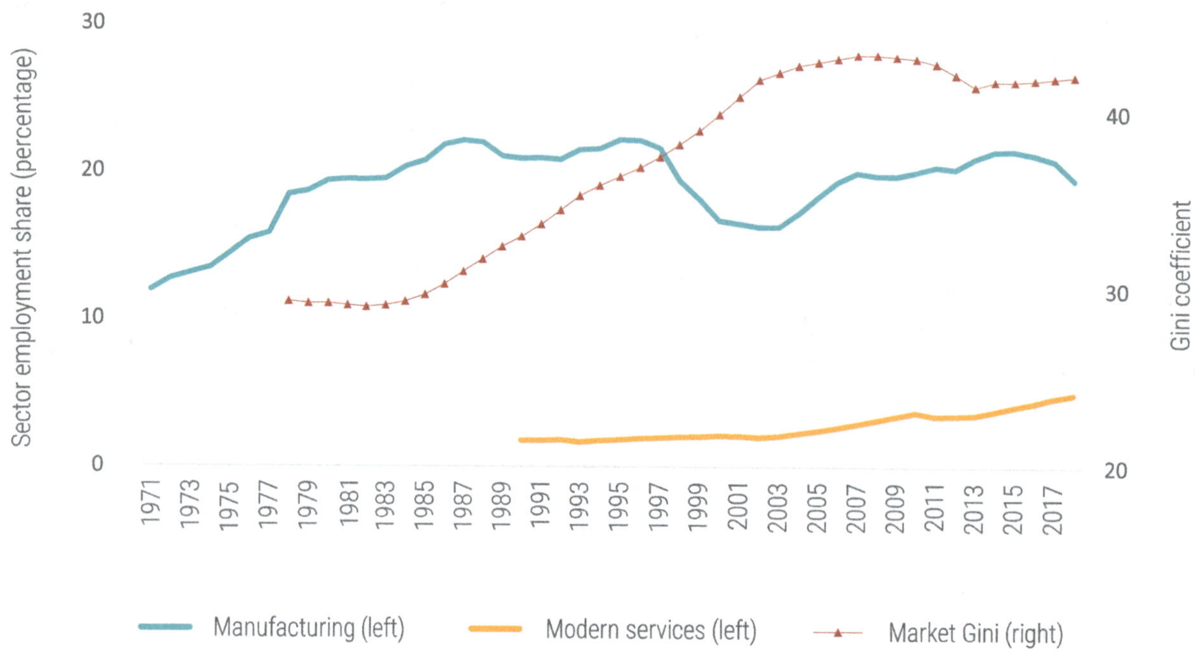

Source: ESCAP, based on the GGDC/UNU-WIDER Economic Transformation Database and 10-sector database, and the Standardized World Income Inequality Database (SWIID) 9.1 (accessed on 26 November 2021).

Economic liberalization and market-oriented reforms were another major source of rising inequality. The booming urban private sector and township and village enterprises significantly increased the income of business owners and high-pay workers, while wage growth for agricultural and low-skilled workers and workers in State-owned enterprises remained stagnant. Moreover, between 1997 and 2002, some 30 million manufacturing workers, equivalent to one fifth of the total manufacturing employment, were laid off during the privatization of such enterprises and the reform campaign, which caused another surge in urban inequality.

Three main offsetting factors helped China avoid severe disruptions to its development in this 25-year increase in inequality between 1982 and 2007. First, the poorer segments of the population also benefited substantially from the economic growth, despite receiving a much smaller share of it. In this sense, growth was "inclusive", softening public reaction to the rising inequality. Second, the very equal starting point cushioned the inequality surge and China's unique land tenure structure served as an informal social security network for the most vulnerable (Ahmad and Hussain 1991). Third, labour protection and formal social security were made available at the most critical time and mitigated the disruptions.

Inequality in China has shown signs of plateauing since the mid-2000s (figure 5.7), thanks to its transition from labour surplus to labour shortage when structural transformation continued to deepen and the demographic bulge came to an end. On the policy side, a general shift of policy focus towards "shared prosperity" since the late 2000s began to reduce rural-urban segmentation, increase public spending on agriculture, equalize access to infrastructure and basic public services and support large-scale poverty elimination initiatives. The gains from expanded education coverage also started to show in a less skewed labour market. These provided the poor with greater opportunities to improve their position in income distribution through their own efforts. However, a continued decline in inequality is not guaranteed and will be challenged by China's economic tertiarization and widening wealth gaps, if deliberate policy interventions are not maintained.

India: inequality challenges remain in a jobless structural transformation

As with China, India's economic success and structural transformation in the past three decades has been accompanied by substantial increases in inequality, but India's experience is different from that of China in two important aspects.

First, the high economic growth failed to translate into mass creation of high-productivity jobs. The phenomenon of "jobless" growth in India has been extensively discussed. For example, Bhattacharya and Sakthivel (2004) observed a collapse in aggregate employment elasticity to GDP in the 1990s, while Mehrotra and Parida (2019) noted stagnation in both total employment and real wages in the 2010s. In the context of a young and growing population, this lack of job creation led to constant pressure on the fair sharing of development dividends.

Weak labour absorption in the manufacturing sector despite decent growth in manufacturing value addition was part of the problem. The sector contributed only roughly a tenth of total non-agricultural job creation between 1990 and 2018 and accounted for 11.7 per cent of the total employment in 2018, far lower than that of East and South-East Asian economies during their economic takeoff. The modern services sector also failed to compensate for this shortfall in job creation. It accounted for an even smaller share (8.5 per cent) of the increase in non-agricultural employment in this period and is likely to have aggravated the Kuznets' tension due to its exceptionally high salaries[12] and its small share in total employment.

Instead, the construction sector absorbed most of the labour reallocation from agriculture, accounting for half of all the non-agriculture jobs created between 2007 and 2018. Yet, labour productivity of construction workers was only 49 per cent of the all-sector average in 2018, affording little advantage over agriculture (43 per cent). Meanwhile, traditional services,[13] another low-productivity sector, accounted for a third of the increase in non-agricultural jobs.

This concentration of jobs in low productivity sectors inevitably resulted in persistent economic informality and job insecurity,[14] widening income gaps between the majority of the labour force and a small group of entrepreneurs and workers in high-paying formal jobs. Chancel and Piketty (2019) estimated that, from the 1980s to the early 2010s, the top 0.1 per cent of earners captured a higher share of total growth than the bottom 50 per cent, while the top 1 per cent received a higher share of total growth than the middle 40 per cent.

Second, India's economic takeoff had a much more unequal starting point. Estimated income Gini in India already stood above

12 Call centre salaries, for example, exceeded by five times the national per capita income in India (Jiang and Schiavone 2020).

13 Comprising trade, transport, government services and other services in the UNU-WIDER Economic Transformation Database.

14 For further information, see Mehrotra and Parida (2019) and Dang and Lanjouw (2021).

FIGURE 5.8
India excels in per student spending in higher education but lags behind in education coverage

(a) Gross primary school enrolment rate (percentage)

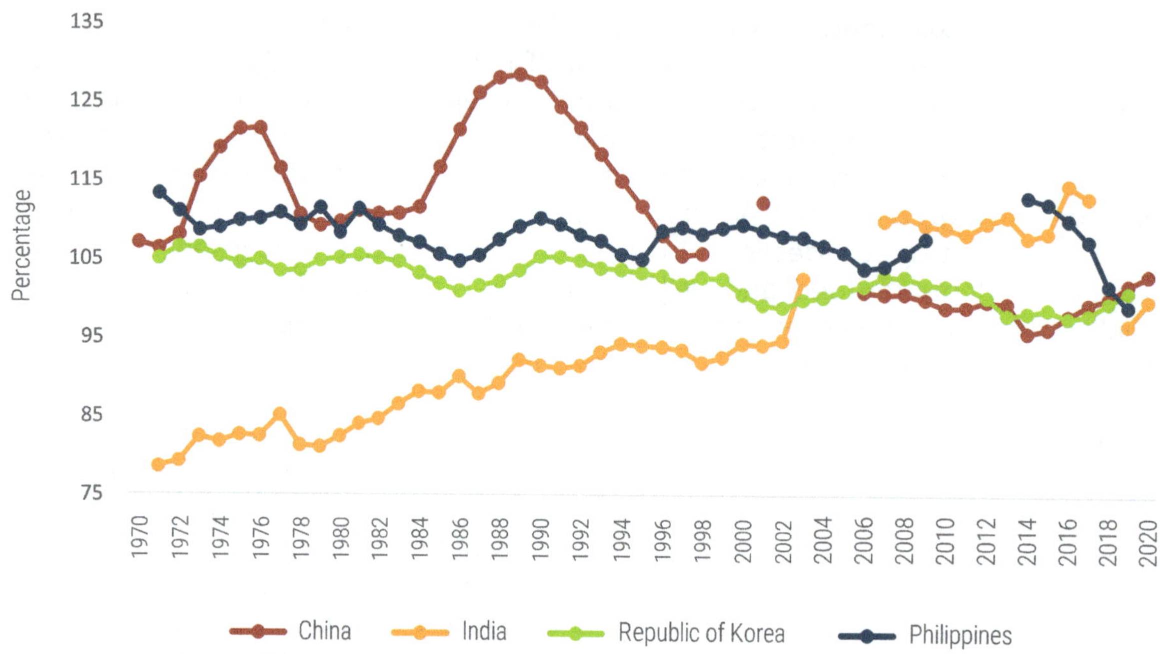

(b) Government education spending per tertiary student (percentage of GDP per capita)

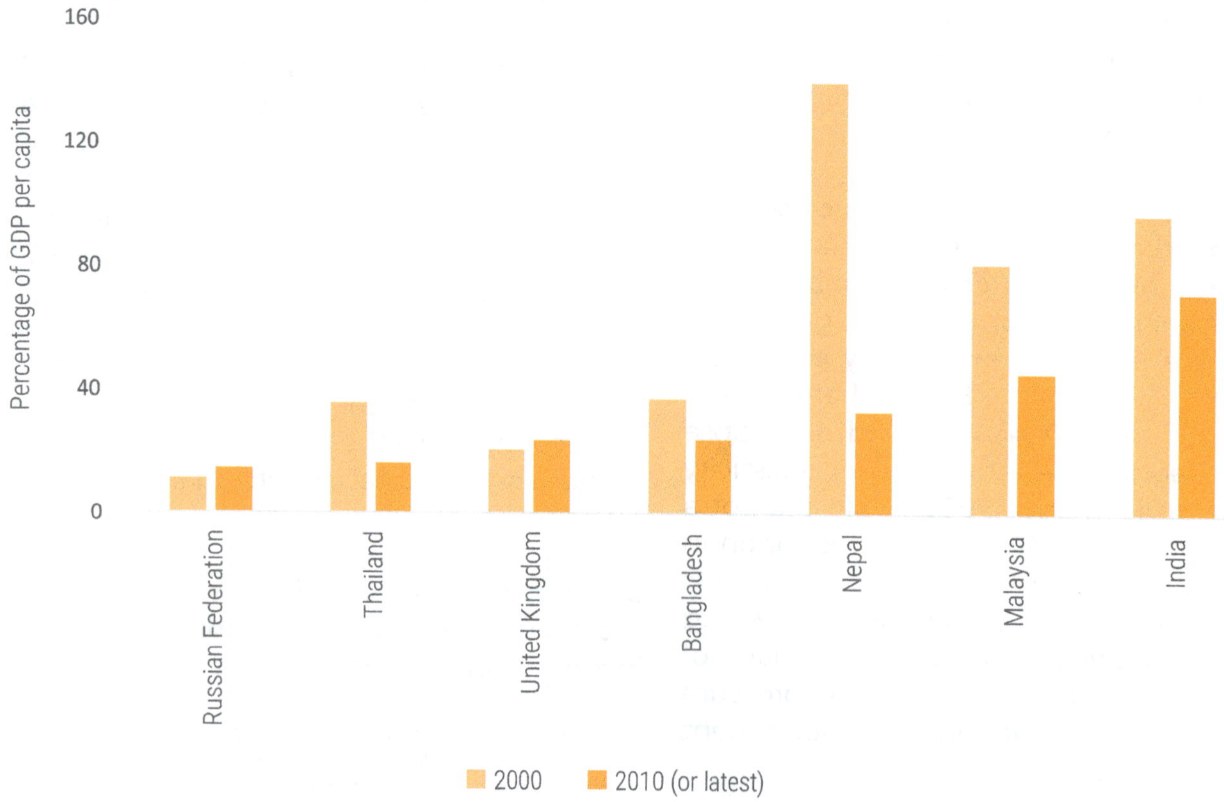

Source: ESCAP, based on World Bank and UNESCO data (accessed on 25 February 2022).

43 in 1980 and surpassed 51 in 2010, reaching a level observed only in a small group of African and Latin American developing countries.[15] This leaves little space for further inequality increase without severely jeopardizing economic development and social stability. The persistent non-monetary and horizontal inequality has been a main cause of the wide income gaps as it undermines fair access to economic opportunities. Marginalized and poorer groups,[16] for instance, persistently have worse outcomes in health and education indicators (Dang and Lanjouw, 2021) and suffer from a life-long disadvantage in productivity.

Lack of education equality remains a concern as well. India trailed far behind in primary education coverage before the 2000s while its per student spending on tertiary education was among the highest across countries (figure 5.8). This tall, rather than broad, education system succeeded in producing a small number of high-skill talent who are internationally competitive but failed in supplying qualified industrial and office workers in large quantities. The observed income polarization may well have been a result of this education polarization and a result of the sectoral polarization[17] driven by this skewed supply of skills.

Bangladesh: inclusive development built on labour-intensive manufacturing

15 It should be noted that Gini estimates are subject to data availability and quality, thus both overestimation and underestimation are possible. In addition, some developed countries also have very high predistribution inequality, but their redistributive mechanisms are much more effective.

16 Such as Scheduled Tribes and Scheduled Castes.

17 Characterized by employment concentration in low-productivity agriculture, construction and traditional services sectors, rather than sectors that offer middle-income formal jobs.

FIGURE 5.9
Structural changes and predistribution income Gini trend in Bangladesh, 1971-2018

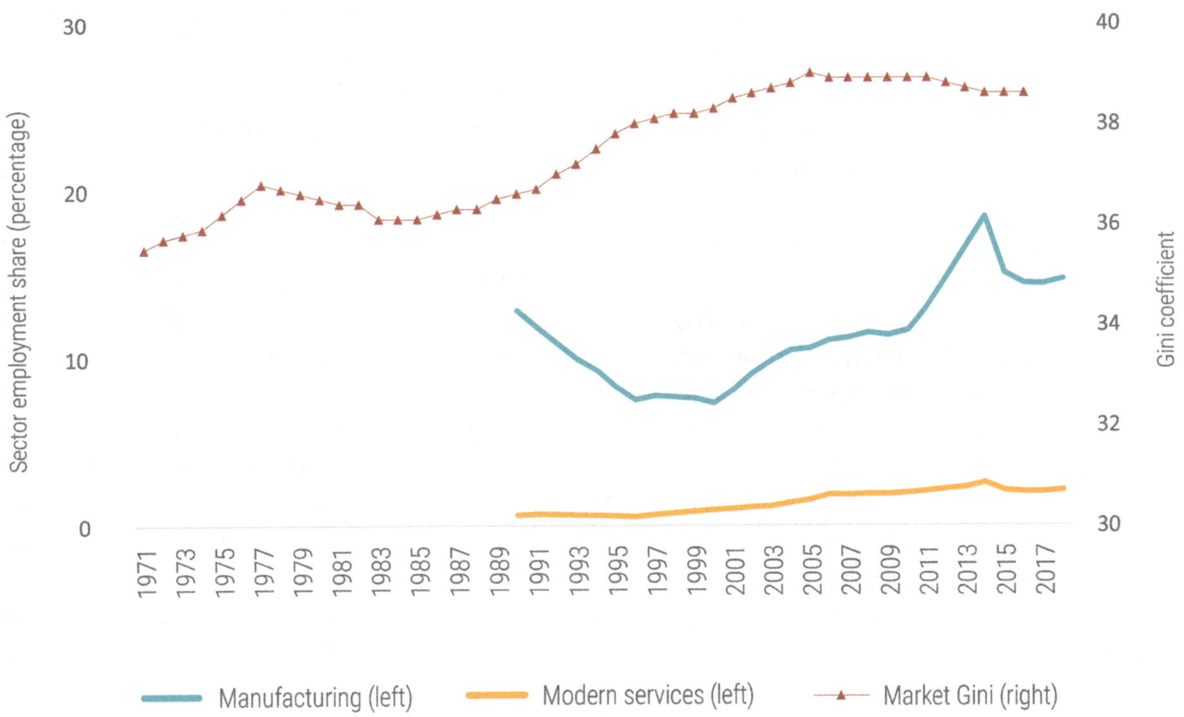

Source: ESCAP, based on the GGDC/UNU-WIDER Economic Transformation Database and 10-sector database, and the Standardized World Income Inequality Database (SWIID) 9.1 (accessed on 26 November 2021).

Bangladesh's development experience in the past three decades is broadly viewed as a remarkable success, characterized by steady and accelerating economic growth and significant improvements in social and human development across the board. This economic success is undoubtedly inclusive - the extreme poverty rate is now less than a third of the 1991 level[18] and income Gini has remained moderate and stable.[19]

Labour-intensive manufacturing has been key to this success. Between 2000 and 2018, manufacturing contributed roughly a quarter of the GDP growth and more than a quarter of the total increase in non-agricultural jobs. The ready-made garment (RMG) industry, in particular, led this transformation. It alone employed 4 million of the 9.5 million manufacturing workers in 2018 and accounted for 83 per cent of Bangladesh's total exports. Such an abundance of manufacturing jobs eased the Kuznets' tension, while the low-skill low-pay nature of these jobs also mitigated the potential widening in cross-sector income gaps. This, together with a robust improvement in agricultural productivity (World Bank, 2016c), is likely to have been a major reason for Bangladesh's success in inclusive structural transformation.

Sustaining such inclusive development in the future, however, is not without challenges. The demographic bulge in Bangladesh is expected to bring some 20 million youth into the labour force in the coming decade (World Bank, 2017). Although the RMG sector has been making progress in diversifying its customer portfolio and moving up the RMG value chain into the production of more complex products of higher value addition, the country is also being increasingly challenged by emerging competitors. Viet Nam, for instance, has overtaken Bangladesh as the second largest apparel exporter in 2020 and enjoys a logistical and geographic proximity advantage over Bangladesh as a destination of RMG value chain reallocation from China. More importantly, the overdependence on a single sector for export and economic growth erodes Bangladesh's economic resilience and confines the space for future structural transformation. Diversification into other labour-intensive manufacturing sectors, such as light engineering, plastics, leather and footwear, would be both desirable and feasible.

18 From 44 per cent in 1991 to 14 per cent in 2016/17, according to the $1.90 per day poverty threshold.

19 Estimated market Gini of income hovered between 36.7 and 39.0 during this period.

3.3 Key lessons for inclusive structural transformation

Three main lessons can be learned from the Asia-Pacific region's own past experience in inclusive structural transformation.

First, "growing with equity" is possible, but needs to be supported by job-rich development strategies and conducive policies. The creation of regular and productive jobs on a large scale is fundamental for both broad-based poverty reduction and the mitigation of the Kuznets' tension. In most cases, labour-intensive manufacturing has proven to be the most effective channel for providing surplus labour in agriculture with formal employment opportunities. Eliminating labour market segmentation and promoting more equal access to infrastructure and public services are essential for enabling fair access to these opportunities. The expansion of education coverage, in particular, not only equalizes income but also creates a conducive factor base for job-rich structural transformation by making skills more abundant and cost-efficient for production. In this sense, the implications of public spending and policies on the distribution of productive capacity[20] and access to opportunity across different population groups can be even more important than the immediate monetary effect of redistribution.

20 As reflected in, for instance, human capital (skills as one component of it), work-related networks and job experience.

CONDUCTIVE FACTORS for inclusive structural transformation	HARMFUL FACTORS for inclusive structural transformation
- Rapid and sustained creation of regular and productive jobs to ease the Kuznets' tension	- Employment concentration in informal and low-productivity sectors
- Broadened access to education and vocational training to increase the skill supply	- A youth bulge in the demographic structure, which amplifies the challenge of surplus labour
- A fairer starting point as reflected in relatively low predistribution inequality levels	- Job market segmentation and geographic fragmentation that widen and prolong income gaps
- Equalized access to infrastructure and essential public services	- Concentration of resources among the minority elite rather than the majority with regard to the education system and infrastructure delivery
- Enhanced social security and labour support to mitigate the shocks of reforms and structural changes	

BOX 5.3

Agriculture and inclusive structural transformation

Agricultural development is essential for ensuring that the poor are not left behind in structural transformation. Stagnation in agricultural productivity and wages, in particular, is the main source of inequality in developing countries with a sizeable agricultural population. On one hand, it sustains and widens the rural-urban income gap, resulting in higher Kuznets' tension during structural transformation. On the other, it also contributes to growing urban poverty and inequality when poor farmers are forced to enter low-productivity urban sectors to make a living. The bargaining power of urban workers in compensation negotiations is eroded as well, as employers have plenty of alternative labour from the agricultural sector willing to work for subsistence wages.

The Asia-Pacific experience between 1990 and 2007 affirms the importance of agricultural productivity growth for inclusive structural transformation. As shown in the figure below, a decrease in agricultural labour productivity relative to all-sector average is highly correlated with rising inequality. This phenomenon is especially clear in the case of China and India, where the gaps between agricultural labour productivity and all-sector average labour productivity widened significantly during this period while inequality surged.

Figure
Changes in agricultural labour productivity (relative to the all-sector average) were closely related to changes in predistribution inequality between 1990 and 2007

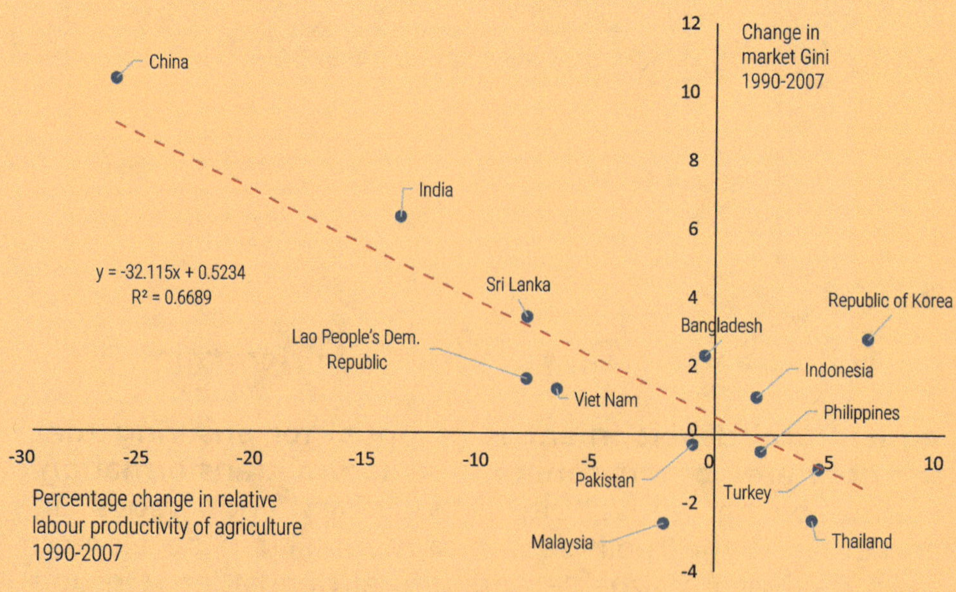

Source: ESCAP, based on the UNU-WIDER Economic Transformation Database and the Standardized World Income Inequality Database (SWIID) 9.1 (accessed on 26 November 2021).
Note: "Relative labour productivity of agriculture" of a particular year is calculated as agricultural labour productivity as a percentage of the all-sector average.

Second, investing in rural development (box 5.3) and strengthening social security help to lift up the poorest in income and ensure smooth transitions. Improvements in agricultural productivity, for instance, raise the average income of the poorest segments of the population and narrow the rural-urban divide. This benefit would be greater if the land tenure structure is also inclusive. Deliberate policy interventions to protect the most vulnerable, including through social security and labour policy measures, also play a key role in reducing the shocks of economic reforms and structural disruptions and in promoting a more inclusive sharing of the dividends from development.

Lastly, structural transformation is a continuing long-term process. Initial success in "growing with equity" is no reason for complacency. The Asia-Pacific region's early examples of "growing with equity", such as Japan, the Republic of Korea and Singapore, had all experienced substantial increases in inequality as they began to structurally shift from manufacturing to modern services.[21] Such experiences should not be overlooked as many more developing countries in the region are at an early stage of this process. Even in countries which managed to consistently reduce inequality over the past two or three decades, most notably Malaysia, the Philippines and Thailand, the public perception of inequality can be less positive. Structural factors, where specific groups are left behind despite an improvement in overall equality, can be one reason behind this contradiction.[22]

21 As measured by employment. In terms of value addition, manufacturing's share continued to grow until the early 2010s in the Republic of Korea and remained stable in Japan and Singapore.

22 Alternative explanations include the greater visibility of inequality and a stronger demand for equity and fairness among the better educated and the younger generation.

4. THE DIGITAL-ROBOTIC-AI REVOLUTION AND THE FUTURE OF STRUCTURAL TRANSFORMATION

4.1 Technology and employment: a jobless future or a false alarm?

An enormous body of literature in recent years has sounded alarm bells regarding the potential disruptive employment shocks due to the ongoing digital-robotic-AI revolution. Various studies have estimated that between 45 and 57 per cent of jobs in developed economies could be lost to automation in the coming decades (McKinsey, 2015; World Bank, 2016b; Frey and Osborne, 2017). The disruptions and long-term implications of the COVID-19 pandemic further add to this concern because accelerated digitalization and automation of the economy may lead to accelerated displacement of workers in vulnerable occupations.

Although these arguments are understandable, the doomsday predictions on aggregate labour demand have not yet been substantiated by empirical facts. Concerns over automation are often based on a narrow emphasis on the labour displacement effect of technological innovations, while in practice, technologies can also increase employment through two main channels. First, the introduction of new technologies also improves productivity, thus reducing the production or delivery cost of goods and services and boosting overall demand. If this expansion in demand for goods and services is large enough, total employment can increase despite rapid automation. Second, technologies also create new economic sectors and tasks, where labour has a competitive advantage. For example, Acemoglu and Restrepo (2018) found that about half of employment growth between 1980 and 2015 in the United States involved new job titles or tasks, while Krzywdzinski (2020) reported that the decline in manufacturing jobs in Germany was compensated by the increase in positions for engineers, technicians and data scientists.

The potential labour-displacement shock of emerging technologies seems to have been exaggerated, while the labour-complementing effect is underestimated. Arntz, Gregory and Zierahn (2016) argued that, even in occupations significantly affected by automation, there are still many tasks that cannot be automated easily. If these tasks are excluded, only 9 per cent of jobs in OECD countries are actually at risk of being automated. De Mattos and others (2020) also noted that automation is confronted with multiple bottlenecks and substantial limitations in developing countries despite theoretical potentials.

Moreover, technological feasibility doesn't equate to economic viability and the relative cost of different production methods matters in automation choices. Case studies of the apparel, footwear and electronics industries in Asia-Pacific developing countries suggest that the comparative advantage of low-cost labour seems to persist in key labour-intensive manufacturing sectors despite ongoing automation (De Mattos and others, 2020). Automation also seems to have less negative side effects on jobs and equality and strong productivity gains in ageing economies, where labour costs are high and increasing (Acemoglu and Restrepo, 2022). This may be an underlying driver behind the very high ranking of Asian economies in robot density (figure 5.10).

Although the pessimistic predictions about the "future of work" have not yet materialized, it also remains too early to call them a false alarm. In this regard, policy attention and prudence are advised. First, technological breakthroughs are not linear, and automation can accelerate significantly due to new innovations and deepening penetration of technology in economies and societies. Second, job losses due to automation may not be adequately offset if the pace of productivity improvement and creation of new jobs decelerates (Acemoglu and Restrepo, 2019). Third, even if substantial labour-displacing automation materializes only in developed countries while labour-intensive sectors are preserved in developing countries due to comparative cost advantages, the international division of labour can still be significantly affected.

Fourth, low-skill workers and middle-class workers in routine jobs are likely to bear the brunt of the adjustment costs in technological transitions, even when aggregate labour demand remains stable, with profound implications for inequality (Arntz, Gregory and Zierahn, 2016; Goos, Manning and Salomons, 2014; Acemoglu and Restrepo, 2021). Youth, who are generally less skilled and experienced and more often in vulnerable jobs, can be among the most adversely affected by automation (Nedelkoska and Quintini, 2018; ILO, 2020b), resulting in damage to both intergenerational equity and future economic growth (Sachs and Kotlikoff, 2012; Sachs, Benzell and LaGarda, 2015). The potential automation of labour-intensive manufacturing and office jobs may have a disproportionate impact on women as well (Madgavkar and others, 2019).

4.2 Manufacturing and modern services as the leading sectors in future structural transformation

FIGURE 5.10
Asia and the Pacific leads in the use of industrial robots

Source: International Federation of Robots (2021).

Manufacturing: challenges ahead but opportunities remain

Manufacturing has historically been at the centre of structural transformation and inclusive development. It provides economies of scale and functions as the leader of productivity improvement and a growth "escalator" (Kaldor, 1966; 1967; Rodrik, 2013). It is also a main provider of productive non-agricultural jobs in the early stage of structural transformation and a key ingredient in the Asia-Pacific region's "growing with equity" success stories.

Manufacturing-led structural transformation as a strategy for inclusive development, however, is increasingly being questioned in recent years (Hallward-Driemeier and Nayyar, 2017). Stiglitz (2021), for instance, discussed the "demise of a successful growth model" and advocated for a multipronged strategy for inclusive economic development in the twenty-first century, while Baldwin and Forslid (2020) went further by predicting a jobless future for manufacturing and the transition towards services as the new engine of export-led economic growth.

Indeed, manufacturing is under pressure on multiple fronts. The employment generation potential of manufacturing seems to have declined. In Asia and the Pacific, manufacturing's median contribution to the total increase in non-agricultural jobs dropped from 19.5 per cent between 1990 and 2007 to 13.4 per cent between 2007 and 2018. One factor behind this change is the increase in manufacturing's labour productivity relative to other economic sectors (figure 5.4b), resulting in fewer jobs created for each unit of growth in output. More worryingly, manufacturing's share in total employment is now plateauing at a much lower level of about 15 per cent in the region's developing countries,[23] in

23 With the exception of China, Sri Lanka and Viet Nam.

FIGURE 5.11
Global merchandise and GVC trade showed signs of plateauing before the pandemic

Source: ESCAP, based on UNCTAD and WTO data.
Note: Global intermediaries exports are used as an indicator for GVC trade.

contrast to 25-30 per cent in the earlier cases of Japan, the Republic of Korea and Singapore. This implies that the maximum employment potential of manufacturing has become much lower.

The space for manufacturing development through global value chains (GVCs) is also becoming more constrained. Both global merchandise and GVC trade[24] were showing signs of plateauing before the pandemic (figure 5.11). The slower pace in tariff reduction, surges in non-tariff barriers and ongoing trade tensions between major global economies continue to cast clouds over the global trade outlook (ESCAP, 2019c). At the same time, the position of established manufacturing centres in GVCs strengthened. Efficiency gains generated through automation and technological upgrading helped these economies to prolong their manufacturing competitiveness and maintain their share in global manufacturing output despite rising wages. The need for more nimble and resilient supply chains as well as for faster reaction to changing fashions and customer taste also strengthened GVC clustering in established manufacturing centres in order to reap the agglomeration payoffs and be closer to the end markets (Anukoonwattaka and Mikic, 2020). In this context, breaking into the global division of labour through GVC participation and moving up the existing value chains have become more difficult for smaller and latecomer developing countries, especially when restrictions imposed by international trade agreements[25] have pulled away the ladder (Chang, 2002; Stiglitz, 2021).

On the other hand, a more nuanced picture emerges when these general trends are examined in greater detail. For example, part of the observed decrease in manufacturing's share in the economy could be due to the

24 As indicated by the trade in intermediate goods.

25 Historically, industrialized countries and newly industrialized countries extensively used both tariffs and subsidies for manufacturing development, which are now heavily restricted by trade agreements. In addition, the implications of the ongoing international tax reforms on the use of tax incentives as an alternative competitive edge by developing countries also remains to be seen.

separation and outsourcing of upstream and downstream services, such as research and development (R&D), product design and after-sales services, from manufacturing processes (ECSIP Consortium, 2014). In the United States, 15 per cent of service value addition, equivalent to 11 per cent of GDP, is used directly by industry (Eichengreen and Gupta, 2011). In considering that manufacturing itself accounts for just 11 per cent of GDP in the United States, the real importance of manufacturing could actually be double that of what the statistics may suggest.

The employment impact of automation on manufacturing could also be overstated. Kucera (2020) examined the apparel and footwear industry in Asia and suggested that technology actually promoted a more collaborative engagement between workers and machines, and a semi-automated production approach, where labour works together with "cobots",[26] has delivered the greatest productivity gains. For semi-automated production, it reduces the requirement on skills and training. De Mattos (2020) also noted that in Asia's electronics industry the comparative advantage of low-cost labour persists and labour-intensive production continues. Small labour displacements due to automation are likely to be more than offset as well by the rapid growth in overall demand for electronics and expansion in productive capacity. Some evidence also suggests that automation may even generate greater demand for outsourcing and more jobs in developing countries, as in the case of the automobile industry (World Bank, 2020d).

In addition, the threat of GVC concentration could be much less for Asia-Pacific developing countries. Their geographic proximity to both world's largest manufacturing hubs and world's fastest growing consumer markets means that they are less susceptible to, in some cases can even benefit from, shortened supply chains and a shift towards nearshoring. The deepening regional economic integration[27] and booming regional value chains also give Asia-Pacific developing countries a significant competitive edge in the mass reallocation of labour-intensive manufacturing jobs out of higher-cost locations (Lin, 2011). As long as GVC opportunities remain, Asia-Pacific developing countries are arguably still in the best position to explore.

Modern services: great potential but uncertain future

The services sector was traditionally viewed as one with low productivity, limited opportunity for skill development and little economic spillover. While this perception may still be true for traditional services, such as retail, cleaning, delivery and hospitality, the more knowledge-based modern services, including information and communication services, professional services, scientific and technical services and financial services, are very different. These sectors are of high skill intensity and productivity, have broad linkages with other economic activities and have become increasingly tradable, sharing the qualities that previously were attributed mainly to manufacturing.

In developed countries, modern services have already replaced shrinking manufacturing as the main driver of economic and employment growth and have played a key role in offsetting the labour displacement shocks of manufacturing automation (Dauth and others, 2018; Krzywdzinski, 2020). **They are also starting to provide developing countries with an alternative leading sector in structural transformation and job-rich development** (Dasgupta, Kim and Pinedo

26 A computer-controlled robotic machine for assisting humans.

27 For example, the Regional Comprehensive Economic Partnership (RCEP) free trade agreement entered into force in January 2022.

Caro, 2017; Roncolato and Kucera, 2014). Between 2007 and 2018, modern services overtook manufacturing in contribution to non-agricultural job creation in more than half of Asia-Pacific developing countries (table 5.2) and had enjoyed faster growth in both value addition and employment in all these countries.

Trade played an important role behind this boom in modern services in the region. Globally, trade in all services exceeded $6 trillion in 2019, registering an average annual growth rate of 5.4 per cent in the 15 years prior to the start of the COVID-19 pandemic. Modern services[28] accounted for some 43 per cent of this total in 2017 and comprised many of the fastest-growing subsectors[29] (WTO, 2019). Asia-Pacific developing countries are pioneers in this trend. China, India, the Republic of Korea, Singapore and Thailand accounted for more than half of developing countries' total in services exports and imports in 2019 (figure 5.12), while India and the Philippines hosted about 7 in 10 call centre jobs worldwide (Jiang and Schiavone, 2020). As global value chains become increasingly knowledge-intensive and services trade costs further decrease, there is a growing potential for cross-border trade in modern services (Madgavkar and others, 2019).

28 Such as financial services, ICT services, professional services, R&D services, among other business services.

29 For example, ICT, professional services and R&D services.

TABLE 5.2
Modern services emerged as a second engine for employment and GDP growth in 2007-2018
(Percentage contributions)

	Contribution to GDP growth		Contribution to non-agricultural employment growth	
	Manufacturing	Modern services	Manufacturing	Modern services
Bangladesh	25.4	10.2	29.7	3.4
Cambodia	19.5	12.4	24.5	18.6
China	27.5	20.4	0.7	**12.9**
India	19	18.6	6.4	**9.1**
Indonesia	18.9	15	18.1	6.5
Lao People's Democratic Republic	8.2	7	-2.6	-2.1
Malaysia	20.5	18.3	13.4	**16**
Myanmar	28.5	7.5	18.7	-12.8
Pakistan	12.4	**14.4**	31.1	4.1
Philippines	19.6	19.5	6.2	**14.9**
Republic of Korea	31.8	25.4	12.7	**26.4**
Singapore	20.1	**37.4**	-8.6	**28.9**
Sri Lanka	13.2	10.9	15.2	**16.6**
Thailand	18.9	**21.9**	17.1	**18**
Turkey	19.8	16.4	11.1	**18.8**
Viet Nam	23.6	12.4	32.4	5.6

Source: ESCAP, based on the UNU-WIDER Economic Transformation Database (accessed on 26 November 2021).

The digital-robotic-AI revolution may also usher in an era of "telemigration", when a range of manual services could become tradable across borders as well (Baldwin, 2019). Remote service delivery is already common and reliable, thanks to advancements in telecommunications. Language barriers in cross-border services trade are also significantly lowered with breakthroughs in machine translation. The combination of virtual presence and robotic technology has enabled new forms of cross-border services, such as telesurgery or drone piloting. If technological innovations continue to reduce structural barriers to cross-border services trade and the cost of using robots, an expansion of large-scale services outsourcing from high-end skill-intensive services[30] to low-skill manual services, such as cleaning or gardening, is not beyond imagination (Baldwin and Forslid, 2020).

However, significant uncertainties remain for services-led globalization. AI-enabled automation has begun to threaten jobs in services, with chatbots[31] replacing humans in sales, advertising and customer services and virtual assistants taking over office work and part of routine professional tasks.[32] These changes are likely to erode the basic assumption about services jobs being outsourced to low-wage countries (Jiang and Schiavone, 2020). Meanwhile, significant policy barriers for cross-border services trade, such as occupation licensing and trade regulations, remain. In the context of growing public concerns over structural job drain caused by globalization in developed countries, the practicality of large-scale outsourcing of manual services jobs to low-wage countries would be a serious question, despite theoretical feasibility and profitability. Legal challenges concerning service provision through remotely controlled robots in another country in the "telemigration" vision may prove to be an obstacle for mass application as well.

A side effect of these challenges is that services trade could be increasingly related to growing inequality. Existing studies already support the hypothesis that the services trade benefits primarily high-skilled workers in developing countries (figure 5.13) and modern services also demonstrate a strong agglomeration tendency that favours cities and large companies (WTO, 2019). Wage gaps between skilled and unskilled workers and between rural and urban residents are enlarged in this process. This negative side effect could be further enhanced when automation pushes services outsourcing towards even more skill-intensive occupations, while policy barriers continue to restrain opportunities in manual services outsourcing that can benefit low-skill workers more.

30 Such as technician, professional or medical services.

31 A computer program designed to simulate human conversation, especially over the Internet, through voice commands or "text chats" or both.

32 Such as basic administration, accounting and data analysis.

FIGURE 5.12
Asia-Pacific developing countries lead in global services exports and imports

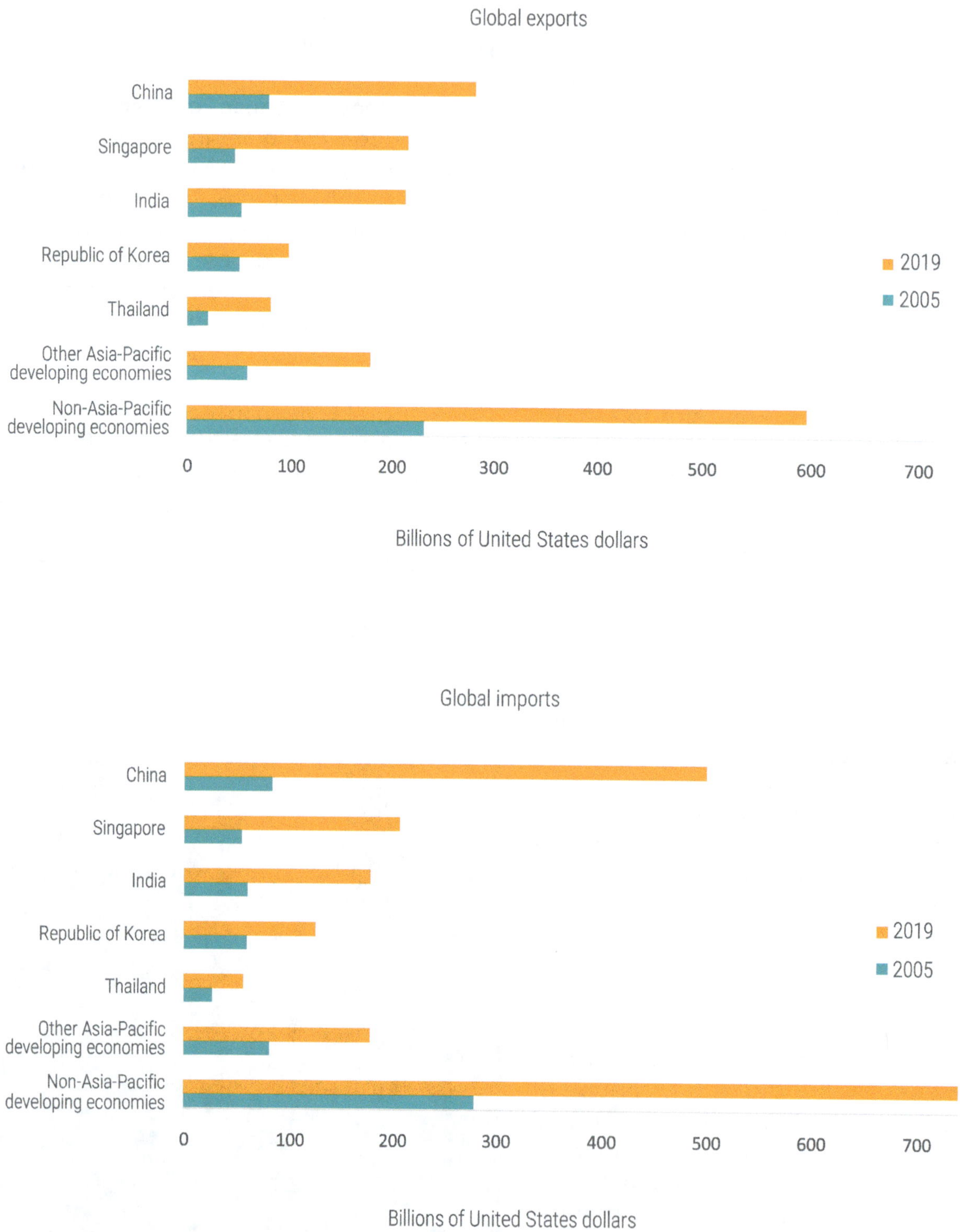

Source: ESCAP, based on UNCTAD data (accessed on 25 February 2022).

FIGURE 5.13
Call centre salaries surpass national per capita income by significant margins in India and the Philippines

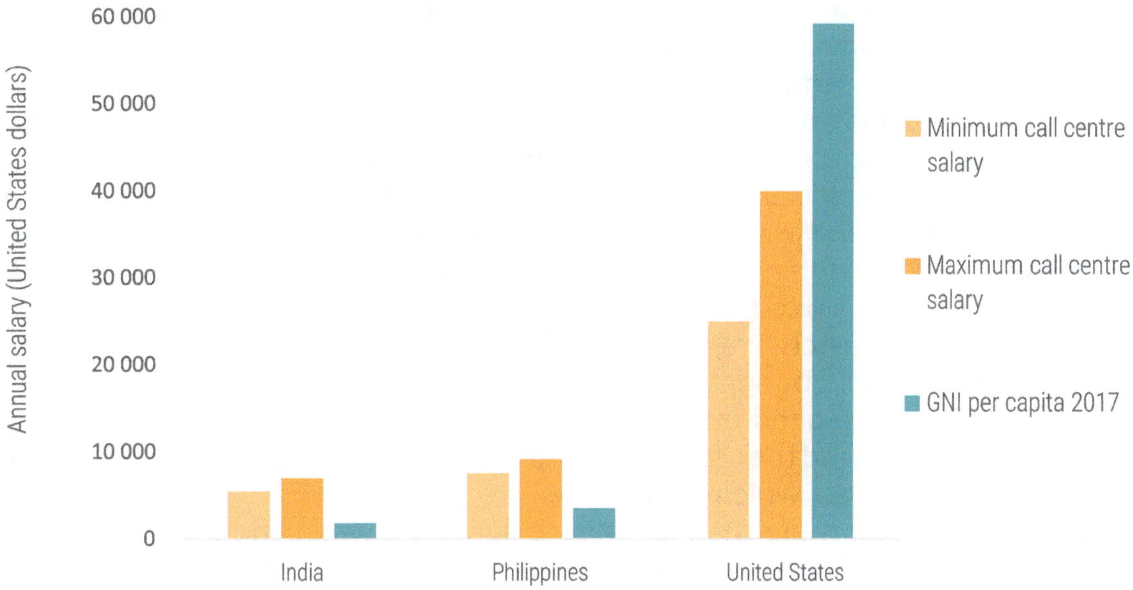

Source: Jiang and Schiavone (2020).

5. POLICY CONSIDERATIONS: GUIDE, SHAPE AND MANAGE

For most Asia-Pacific developing countries, the greatest opportunity and challenge for inclusive development lie in the process of structure transformation. The region has rich experience in "growing with equity", but these lessons would need to be adapted and updated according to the new realities in the age of the digital-robotic-AI revolution. In general, policy efforts can be made on three fronts to promote an inclusive structural transformation.

First, countries can deploy forward-looking policies to guide structural transformation towards a job-rich path. *Rapid creation of stable and productive jobs* is first and foremost a task of inclusive structural transformation, given its importance for alleviating the Kuznets' tension and ensuring opportunities for all. Strategic sectors, which have broad productivity spillovers and significant job-creation potential, remain critical in this process. Labour-intensive manufacturing used to play this role, but it is becoming increasingly important to complement manufacturing with other productive and job-rich sectors, especially modern services, as additional engines of economic and employment growth in going forward. Targeted support from industrial policies would be needed to accelerate growth in these strategic sectors and fully reap the positive social economic spillovers they generate (box 5.4).

Supporting job-friendly technological upgrading and innovation is another important policy pillar. As highlighted in section 4, the aggregate employment effect of technology depends on whether job creation through economic growth and the emergence of new sectors and occupations can outpace job displacement driven by automation. It is, therefore, essential to ensure that technological innovations can generate significant productivity gains and produce greater employment dividends. Public policies have a role in both. For example, public R&D programmes are often associated with far more fundamental and influential technological breakthroughs. In the widely cited case of the United States Defense Advanced Research Projects Agency, a tiny annual budget of 0.015 per cent of GDP resulted in the invention of the Internet and the Global Positioning System (GPS), which are estimated to account for more than 12 per cent of the United States economy in the 2020s (Liu, 2020). Prioritized support in public R&D programmes for labour-complementing technologies and incentives for job creation in frontier sectors can also be leveraged to enhance the employment impact of technological upgrading and innovations. Identifying priority sectors and technologies in national development road maps is already a common practice, and a strengthened emphasis on jobs and inclusive development should not be a challenging step in going forward.

It is also indispensable to *establish correct market signals for private sector technological choices.* For instance, if corporate or capital income is taxed at an effective rate that is substantially lower than the tax rate on payrolls or labour income, the resulting distortions would make labour-intensive production more costly and capital-intensive production more profitable. Thus, ensuring that capital is adequately and fairly taxed is important for inclusive development not only from a redistributive perspective but also in the perspective of technological choices and predistribution. Such measures can also be complemented by a broad-based change in development and business mindsets that puts greater emphasis on economic inclusiveness and prioritizes people over profits (ESCAP, 2019a).

Second, the visible hand of the Government should play a more proactive role in shaping the predistribution outcomes of structural transformation. One policy priority is to empower labour in the job market. Labour protection policies[33] and collective bargaining rights are broadly leveraged to guarantee a fairer share of labour in the predistribution of income and a more equal bargaining position between employees and employers in compensation negotiations, although a fine balance between the interest of current employees and the interest of jobseekers and those about to enter the labour market would be necessary for these policies to make a positive contribution to overall socioeconomic welfare.

Empowering labour in corporate decision-making could be as important. Circumstantial evidence from the United States suggests that monitoring boards[34] and shareholder primacy[35] have played a role in the surges of top salaries and in widening income gaps in general (Wasserman Mitchell, 2017). In contrast, codetermination[36] arrangements in Germany (box 5.5) and other European countries seem to be associated with less inequality, greater job security and faster productivity improvements (Bruegel, Berger and Vaccarino, 2016; Hayden and Bodie, 2021). In 2019, the Business Roundtable Statement on corporate purpose[37] marked a consensus on the necessity for a change in how corporates

33 Such as the mandatory use of formal employment contracts, anti-discrimination requirements, workplace safety standards, entitlement to leave days and minimum wages, among others.

34 Referring to the model in which a company is managed by executive officers, while the role of members of the board is to monitor management's performance.

35 Referring to the corporate governance philosophy that prioritizes maximization of shareholder value as its main purpose.

36 Cooperation between management and workers in corporate decision-making.

37 For additional details, see opportunity.businessroundtable.org/ourcommitment/.

BOX 5.4

Raison d'être for industrial policies

The rationale for industrial policies primarily derives from the presence of various market failures.

- **First-mover disadvantage and imperfect financial markets** Pioneers venturing into new sectors or adopting new technologies (more likely to be in the form of industrial or technological upgrading rather than innovation in the developing country context) bear the full risk while generating public information on potential economic opportunities for followers. However, they are not rewarded by the market for such externalities. Imperfect financial markets may also fail to absorb the high risks associated with innovation, resulting in less than optimum risk-taking by innovators and entrepreneurs. Therein exists a space for industrial policies to make an impact

- **Coordination challenges and information discovery** Industrial and technological upgrading often require simultaneous investments to be economically viable but the cost for individual firms to coordinate among themselves can be overwhelming. Governments can help overcome this failure by assuming the coordinator's role. Such public-private collaboration may also facilitate information discovery, when private information of different stakeholders is pooled together and disseminated

- **Positive economic spillovers** Certain industries or economic activities may have substantial economic spillovers, such as facilitating skill sharing among workers and/or promoting productivity improvements in other economic sectors. Industrial policies can help overcome market failure in recognizing these spillovers

- **Social-environmental objectives** Social-environmental objectives, such as equity and environmental sustainability, are also economic externalities that the market fails to price in. Industrial policies are already playing a central role in promoting sectoral changes to fight the deleterious effects of climate change. They can contribute to the pursuit of economic inclusiveness as well

Based on Pack and Saggi (2006), Lin and Chang (2009) and Stiglitz (2017).

are run. However, Governments' visible hand to institutionalize an inclusive corporate governance structure that involves labour and other stakeholders and to establish boundaries and socioeconomic safeguards on corporates' pursuit of profits should have a much greater role, especially when the promises of management self-discipline are falling short (Bebchuk and Tallarita, 2020).[38]

Education policy is always central in shaping predistribution outcomes. ***An inclusive education strategy that prioritizes universal access to primary and secondary schooling*** in the early stage of structural transformation has historically been a cornerstone in the Asia-Pacific region's "growing with equity" success experiences. However, the shifting technological landscape has made investment in higher education more rewarding. On one hand, middle-skill jobs are threatened by automation in both manufacturing and services and employment opportunities may become increasingly concentrated at the high-end of the skill spectrum. On the other, top talent is needed for accelerated job-friendly technological innovations to offset the labour-displacement effect of automation. This, together with potential economic competitiveness gains, would make investment in higher education more attractive to Governments.[39] This will not be a challenge for countries with ample fiscal space to pursue broader coverage of education at all levels simultaneously, but developing countries with a limited education budget would be confronted with a dilemma and thus a bigger "bang-for-the-buck" in education spending becomes crucial (chapter 3).

Nevertheless, limited access to higher education while the education premium is on the rise would further increase inequality. Access to higher education is increasingly linked to family socioeconomic status and economic inequality is being cemented through education inequality in the next generation. For instance, the fast expansion of after-school private tutoring, or "shadow education",[40] can seriously jeopardize inclusiveness by pricing out students from low-income families in the competition for access to higher education (Choi and Choi, 2016). This education "arms race" is also putting extra financial pressure on low-income families, when private tutoring alone consumes a tenth of monthly income of an average family in the case of the Republic of Korea (OECD, 2012). Evidence from OECD countries suggests that intergenerational education mobility is also stifled when offspring of university-educated parents have a 4.5 times greater chance of getting a tertiary education than offspring of those parents without a university degree (OECD, 2015). Public spending and policies would need to further prioritize education equalization to ensure an inclusive future.

Third, socioeconomic disruptions during rapid structural transformation need to be effectively managed. Social security networks offer a first line of defense. The modern concept of social security is arguably the creation of urbanization and industrialization. As structural transformation deepens, the demand for universal coverage and higher levels of protection will naturally follow. Many Asia-Pacific developing countries introduced urgent expansions in social security during the COVID-19 pandemic. Despite the increasing pressure of fiscal consolidation, it would be highly desirable to permanently preserve much of this expanded reach of social security floors (ESCAP and ILO, 2020b), not only for more robust post-pandemic recovery but also to prepare for future structural transformation.

In view of the immense uncertainties associated with the digital-robotic-AI revolution, the *importance of active labour market*

38 For further information, see fortune.com/2021/08/05/business-roundtable-letter-statement-on-the-purpose-of-a-corporation-stakeholder-capitalism-american-ceos/.

39 Of course, the leakages of brain drain will reduce the socioeconomic payoffs of government investment in higher education in developing countries and should be taken into consideration.

40 For an extensive review on private tutoring around the world, see Zhang (2021).

BOX 5.5

Codetermining inclusion: the case of Germany

Codetermination, in contrast to shareholder primacy, is the umbrella term for systems in which workers play an official role in corporate governance. In Germany, corporate governance rules require employee representation on both "works councils", which coordinate a range of matters in the workplace, and on "supervisory boards", which provide general oversight of the company.

Codetermination in Germany is marked by extensive cooperation between shareholders and employees and has generally resulted in higher productivity. Empirical evidence also suggests that codetermination is associated with higher capital investments but stable employment, suggesting that these capital investments are more likely to complement rather than replace labour. Meanwhile outsourcing is reduced.

Despite the advantages shown by the German model of codetermination during the 2007/08 global financial crisis, it remains rare due to path dependence challenges and a number of market failures that prevent transitions in corporate governance. Codetermination may also be plagued by risk aversion of employees, jeopardizing risk-taking for innovation.

Based on Hayden and Bodie (2021) and Jager, Schoefer and Heining (2021).

policies has also increased. Most of the employment shocks brought about by technological innovations would be structural in the sense that labour is constantly reallocated from automated occupations to newly created occupations rather than being permanently driven out of the labour market. Although this is not a new phenomenon, the pace of such disruptions and the skill requirement for the newly created jobs are likely to become much higher.

Public and private support for on-the-job training, lifelong learning and vocational education should be significantly strengthened to live up to this challenge. Closer collaboration between the public and private sectors would be necessary to effectively identify skills demanded by the market and remain flexible in reaction to new technological changes. Meanwhile, ICT-enhanced pedagogies can be leveraged to provide more inclusive access to reskilling opportunities (ILO, 2018b).

Labour market intermediation is essential to expedite the job-matching and re-employment process after workers are reskilled. Online registration platforms and job portals can substantially improve labour market transparency, providing broader access to information on both labour supply and demand at much lower costs.

Despite all these safeguards, structural labour market shocks of the digital-robotic-AI revolution can still exceed the absorptive capacity of the economy and threaten social stability. In such a scenario, ***government interventions to contain runaway automation and keep technological changes at a more manageable pace*** may be required. The objective here is to give more space for necessary socioeconomic adjustments to catch up in order to avoid acute disruptions and worse outcomes in the short run and ensure that no one is permanently left behind in the long run. However, such decisions would need to be based on broad consultations, given the danger that they can be highjacked by interest groups to resist changes with positive payoffs at the aggregate level but of little benefit to them.

6. CONCLUSIONS

As noted in chapter 1, reducing high levels of inequality has become not only a development objective, but also a political imperative. The COVID-19 pandemic has just added additional urgency for action. Much of the discussion so far has been focused on expanding and raising social security floors, upholding people's rights in access to equal and better public services and redistributing more by taxing the rich and providing more generous benefits to the poor.

While these measures are essential pillars of any inclusive development strategy, their overall impact in the developing country context is constrained by two challenges. First, all of them rely on higher public spending. However, in the post-COVID reality, where public debt is rising, revenues are stagnant and fiscal consolidation is highly likely, further scaling up of spending, although not impossible, appears to be a luxury for many. Second, even when redistribution can be afforded, it may still fall short in offsetting increases in predistribution inequality, as highlighted in this chapter.

"Building forward fairer", in this regard, can benefit from exploring policies that directly address the root cause of inequality by ensuring that the market would generate more equal outcomes in the first place, even before taxes and transfers. For developing countries, this requires creating both a more equal distribution of economic power among the population and, probably more importantly, economic opportunities that grow rapidly enough to leave no one behind.

Hence, to ensure a fairer future for all, structural transformations need to be inclusive. The past experience of Asia and the Pacific provides three important policy lessons to "grow with equity". These include:

- *Fast creation of regular and productive jobs* for all, which reduces the pressure for inequality to increase in the early stage of development. Labour-intensive manufacturing has historically carried the weight and continues to support inclusive structural transformation in such countries as Bangladesh and Viet Nam

- *Empowering the broad majority of the labour force* through the removal of labour market obstacles that restrict equal access to employment opportunities and through inclusive education that provides all workers with necessary skills to explore these opportunities

- *Rural development*, given rural-urban income disparity, is often a main source of inequality and agricultural workers are at high risk of being left behind during the economic takeoff

The ongoing digital-robotic-AI revolution, however, poses new policy questions. For instance, manufacturing's potential to lead an inclusive structural transformation alone is challenged. Although countries should continue to prioritize productive and job-rich sectors with extensive economic spillovers for inclusive development, ***a multipronged sectoral strategy*** becomes more desirable to diversify into new promising sectors, such as modern services.

Meanwhile, the threat of automation points to risks of shrinking labour demand, more frequent and more severe structural shocks to the labour market and intensified competition in the global division of labour. To navigate these uncertainties, ***policies should proactively promote labour-friendly technological changes and "engineer" the market for more inclusive sharing of economic rewards.*** More specifically, policies should seek to:

- **Guide** the technological upgrading and innovations through public R&D investment as a catalyst for accelerated productivity growth and the emergence of new occupations and jobs, and through targeted support and conducive market signals to encourage private sector adoption of labour-friendly technologies

- **Shape** the market distribution of income by empowering labour in compensation negotiations and in corporate decision-making processes, in addition to investment in education

- **Manage** the turbulence caused by technological shocks through significantly strengthened support for life-long learning and reskilling and for labour market facilitation in job-matching and re-employment. It would also require managing the pace of the creative destruction of new technological progress based on broad consultations with stakeholders

CHAPTER 06

TOWARDS A FAIRER FUTURE

Two years of the COVID-19 pandemic have underlined the urgency of reducing the persisting and deep-rooted socioeconomic divides across Asia and the Pacific.

Although high and sustained economic growth led to impressive reductions in poverty over the past three decades, insufficient attention to enhancing economic resilience has increased the risk of long-term scarring effects due to the COVID-19 pandemic, largely as a result of high and persistent inequalities. In simple words, those already left behind are bearing the relatively largest social and economic costs of the pandemic.

As noted in chapter 1, primary focus on rapid GDP growth over the past few decades, with insufficient attention paid to ensuring the fair sharing of its fruits, has contributed to exacerbating the region's vulnerability to shocks. The socioeconomic fallout of the pandemic, where the vulnerable groups have borne the brunt of its impacts, is the latest example. Arguably, a certain level of income inequality is inevitable and even beneficial for short-term economic growth, but its persistence at high levels can undermine the prospects for long-term economic growth. Therefore, reducing income inequality is a social, economic and political imperative – national policymaking can no longer wait to prioritize the "S" of the ESG (environmental, social and governance) aspects of an inclusive and sustainable stakeholder framework. In analysing these shortcomings, the ***Survey*** for 2022 sets out a policy blueprint for the region's inclusive recovery from the pandemic and for laying the foundations of inclusive development.

Smart spending and fair taxation in a time of fiscal constraints

The significant social and economic costs of the pandemic in the region could have been mitigated if more people-focused investments had been made, especially in health care, education and social protection. With fiscal space now dwindling in many developing countries due to the unprecedented level of public spending to help cushion the impacts of the pandemic shocks, fiscal consolidations may be expected over the medium term. These are likely to have negative long-term impacts on inequalities in the region.

Under such fiscal constraints but with ambitious spending needs and goals, chapter 3 examined how Asia-Pacific countries can enhance the efficiency of fiscal spending through "smart spending" and revenue mobilization based on the "tax fair" principle.

It is important to maintain and, where there is sufficient fiscal room, increase spending on health care, education and social protection – the three most effective, inclusiveness-enhancing fiscal expenditure areas.

Political will, good governance and digital technologies will play an important role in the effective use of the expenditure and mobilization levers of fiscal policy, especially given currently constrained fiscal positions.

People-centric central banking and financial policy

The unprecedented scale and severity of the pandemic's socioeconomic impacts afford an opportunity to put traditional monetary and financial policy tools to non-conventional use; chapter 4 made a case for widening the scope of central banking into the area of inclusive development. Central banks, even in the absence of a clear inclusive development mandate, can and should respond to inequality concerns. Only half of the central banks in the Asia-Pacific region are working on promoting inclusive finance. This is a missed opportunity because financial inclusion benefits the poor relatively more than the better off. By contrast, high levels of inequality reduce the effectiveness of monetary policy, thus adding setbacks to an already difficult recovery outlook.

To become more people-centric, central banks can orient their core roles of monetary policymaking, official reserve management and currency issuance towards promoting financial and economic inclusiveness.

Furthermore, central banks can also support mobilizing additional financial resources for social purposes by fostering social impact and sustainability-linked bonds.

Preventing inequality from taking root

In an age of technological innovation-driven economic growth, people in a socioeconomically disadvantaged situation are at increasing risk of further marginalization with the likely shrinking of labour-intensive manufacturing and services. With respect to long-term economic trends and structural transformations, chapter 5 emphasized the importance of predistributive policies in shaping inequality dynamics; it argued for Governments to proactively guide, shape and manage structural transformation to promote inclusive economic outcomes. This role would include, among others, support for development of labour-enhancing technologies and opportunities for strengthening the capacity of the labour force to negotiate fair terms of employment.

The *Survey* for 2022 complements the messages in its 2020 and 2021 editions, which were aimed at steering policymaking and public discourse towards the accelerated implementation of the 2030 Agenda for Sustainable Development, setting out action plans for strengthening the three pillars of such development.

At the core of the Agenda's Sustainable Development Goals is the acceptance of a "New Social Contract" that creates equal opportunities for all.

REFERENCES

Abdel-Kader, Khaled, and Ruud De Mooij (2020). Tax policy and inclusive growth. IMF Working Paper, No. 2020/271. Washington, D.C.: International Monetary Fund.

Abu Bakar, Zul-Fadzli, and Ho Sui-Jade (2018). Central banking and inequality – the current state of the conversation. Blog article (15 March). Available at https://tunismailalichair.my/2018/03/15/central-banking-and-inequality-the-current-state-of-the-conversation/.

Acemoglu, Daron (2021). The supply chain mess. ***Project Syndicate***, 2 December.

_____ and James A. Robinson (2006). ***Economic Origins of Dictatorship and Democracy***. New York: Cambridge University Press.

_____ and Pascual Restrepo (2018). The race between machine and man: implications of technology for growth, factor shares and employment. ***American Economic Review***, vol. 108, No. 6, pp. 1488–1542.

_____ (2019). Automation and new tasks: how technology displaces and reinstates labor. ***Journal of Economic Perspectives***, vol. 33, No. 2, pp. 3-30.

_____ (2021). Tasks, automation, and the rise in US wage inequality. NBER Working Paper, No. 28920. Cambridge, Massachusetts: National Bureau of Economic Research.

_____ (2022). Demographics and automation. ***Review of Economic Studies***, vol. 89, No. 1, pp. 1-44.

Ahmad, Ehtisham, and Athar Hussain (1991). Social security in China: a historical perspective. In ***Social Security in Developing Countries***, Ehtisham Ahmad, Jean Drèze, John Hills and Amartya Sen, eds. Oxford: Oxford Scholarship Online. E-book.

Agur, Itai, and others (2022). Monetary finance: do not touch, or handle with care? IMF Departmental Paper, No. 2022/001. Washington, D.C.: International Monetary Fund.

Aksoy, Cevat Giray, Barry Eichengreen and Orkun Saka (2020). The political scar of epidemics. EBRD Working Paper, No. 45. London: European Bank for Reconstruction and Development.

Alisjahbana, Armida, and others (2020). The developer's dilemma: a survey of structural transformation and inequality dynamics. WIDER Working Paper, No. 2020/35. Helsinki: UNU-WIDER.

Aljazeera (2022). Infographic: How much of your country's oil comes from Russia? 10 March. Available at www.aljazeera.com/news/2022/3/10/infographic-how-much-of-your-countrys-oil-comes-from-russia-interactive (accessed on 16 March 2022).

Allen, Sarah, and others (2020). Design choices for central bank digital currency: policy and technical considerations. Global Economy & Development Working Paper, No. 140. Washington, D.C.: Brookings Institute.

Anukoonwattaka, Witada, and Mia Mikic (2020). Beyond the COVID-19 pandemic: coping with the 'new normal' in supply chains. ESCAP Policy Brief. Bangkok. Available at www.unescap.org/resources/beyond-covid-19-pandemic-coping-new-normal-supply-chains.

Arntz, Melanie, Terry Gregory, and Ulrich Zierahn (2016). The risk of automation for jobs in OECD countries. OECD Social, Employment and Migration Working Papers, No. 189. Paris: Organisation for Economic Co-operation and Development.

Asian Development Bank (ADB) (2020). Impact evaluation of the Pantawid Pamilyang Pilipino Program. Manila. Available at www.adb.org/projects/documents/phi-52257-001-rrp (accessed on 15 February 2022).

_____ (2021a). Learning and earning losses from COVID-19 school closures in developing Asia: special topic of the Asian Development Outlook 2021. Manila.

_____ (2021b). 2021 ***Annual Evaluation Review: Supporting the Sustainable Development Goals***. Manila.

_____ (2021c). Collaboration on domestic resource mobilization and international tax cooperation critical to a green, inclusive, resilient Asia and the Pacific. News release, 24 November 2021. Available at www.adb.org/news/collaboration-domestic-resource-mobilization-and-international-tax-cooperation-critical-green (accessed on 27 January 2022).

Asian Development Bank Institute (ADBI) (2019). ***Demystifying Rising Inequality in Asia***. Tokyo.

Asian Productivity Organization (APO) (2021). ***Digitalization of Public Service Delivery in Asia***. Tokyo.

Association for Computing Machinery (ACM) (2019). India stack---digital infrastructure as public good. ***Communications of the ACM***, vol. 62, No. 11, pp. 76–81.

Atlantic Council (2021). Central Bank Digital Currency Tracker. Available at www.atlanticcouncil.org/cbdctracker/.

Auclert, Adrien, and others (2021). Demographics, wealth, and global imbalances in the twenty-first century. NBER Working Paper Series, No. 29161. Cambridge, Massachusetts: National Bureau of Economic Research.

Auer, Raphael, Giulio Cornelli, and Jon Frost (2020). Rise of the central bank digital currencies: drivers, approaches and technologies. BIS Working Papers, No. 880. Basel, Switzerland: Bank for International Settlements.

Autor, David H. (2015). Why are there still so many jobs? The history and future of workplace automation. ***Journal of Economic Perspectives***, vol. 29, No. 3, pp. 3-30.

Baldwin, Richard (2016). ***The Great Convergence: Information Technology and the New Globalization***. Cambridge, Massachusetts: Harvard University Press.

_____ (2019). T***he Globotics Upheaval: Globalization, Robotics, and the Future of Work.*** Oxford: Oxford University Press.

_____ and Rikard Forslid (2020). Globotics and development: when manufacturing is jobless and services are tradable. NBER Working Paper, No. 26731. Cambridge, Massachusetts: National Bureau of Economic Research.

Ball, Laurence M., and others (2013). The distributional effects of fiscal consolidation. IMF Working Papers, No. 13/151 (21 June).

Bangko Sentral ng Pilipinas (BSP) (2021). ***Central Bank Digital Currency for the BSP: Fundamentals and Strategies***. Manila. Available at www.bsp.gov.ph/Media_And_Research/Publications/CBDC_for_the_BSP_Book.pdf.

Bank for International Settlements (BIS) (2021). Annual Economic Report 2021. Basel, Switzerland: Bank for International Settlements.

Barrett, Philip, and others (2021). After-effects of the COVID-19 pandemic: prospects for medium-term economic damage. IMF Working Paper, No. 2021/203. Washington, D.C: International Monetary Fund.

Barro, Robert J., José F. Ursúa, and Joanna Weng (2020). The coronavirus and the great influenza pandemic: lessons from the "Spanish Flu" for the coronavirus's potential effects on mortality and economic activity. NBER Working Paper Series, No. 26866. Cambridge, Massachusetts: National Bureau of Economic Research.

Barroy, Hélèn, and Sanjeev Gupta (2021). Fifteen years later: moving forward Heller's heritage on fiscal space for health. ***Health Policy and Planning***, vol. 36, No. 8, pp. 1239-1245. (October).

Baymul, Çinar, and Kunal Sen (2020). Was Kuznets right? New evidence on the relationship between structural transformation and inequality. ***Journal of Development Studies***, vol. 56, No. 9, pp. 1643-1662.

Bebchuk, Lucian A., and Roberto Tallarita (2020). The illusory promise of stakeholder governance. ***Cornell Law Review***, vol. 106, pp. 91-178.

Berg, Andrew, and Jonathan D. Ostry (2011). Inequality and unsustainable growth: two sides of the same coin? IMF Staff Discussion Note, 11/08. Available at www.imf.org/external/pubs/ft/sdn/2011/sdn1108.pdf.

_____ and Jerome Zettelmeyer (2011). What makes growth sustained? IMF Working Paper, No. 08/59. Available at www.imf.org/external/pubs/ft/wp/2008/wp0859.pdf.

Bergant, Katharina, Anke Weber, and Andrea Medici (2022). Winning the war? New evidence on the measurement and the determinants of poverty in the United States. IMF Working Paper, No. 2022/004. Washington, D.C.: International Monetary Fund.

Bhattacharya, B. B., and S. Sakthivel (2004). Economic reforms and jobless growth in India in the 1990s. New Delhi: Institute of Economic Growth.

Birdsall, Nancy (2010). The (indispensable) middle class in developing countries. In ***Equity and Growth in a Globalizing World***, Ravi Kanbur and Michael Spence, eds. Washington, D.C.: World Bank on behalf of Commission on Growth and Development, p. 158.

_____ (2014). A note on the middle class in Latin America. In ***Inequality in Asia and the Pacific: Trends, Drivers and Policy Implications***, Ravi Kanbur, Changyong Rhee and Juzhong Zhuang, eds. London: Routledge, pp. 257-287.

Blanchard, Olivier, and Daniel Leigh (2013). Growth forecast errors and fiscal multipliers, IMF Working Paper, No. 13/1. Washington, D.C.: International Monetary Fund.

Bloomberg News (2021). China's digital yuan trial reaches $5.3 billion in transactions (16 July).

Boar, Codruta, and Andreas Wehrli (2021). Ready, steady, go? – Results of the third BIS survey on central bank digital currency. BIS Papers, No. 114. Basel, Switzerland: Bank for International Settlements.

Bonifacio, Valentina, and others (2021). Distributional effects of monetary policy. IMF Working Paper, No. 2021/201. Washington, D.C.: International Monetary Fund.

Bossu, Wouter, and others (2020). Legal aspects of central bank digital currency: central bank and monetary law considerations. IMF Working Paper, No. 2020/254. Washington, D.C.: International Monetary Fund.

Bourguignon, François (2016). ***The Globalization of Inequality***. Princeton, NJ, and Oxford: Princeton University Press.

Brandolini, Andrea (2016). Wealth distribution and central banks. A presentation made at the Household Finance and Consumption Survey Workshop, Vienna, 20 June.

Bruegel, Bennet Berger, and Elena Vaccarino (2016). Codetermination in Germany – a role model for the UK and the US? Bruegel blog post, available at www.bruegel.org/2016/10/codetermination-in-germany-a-role-model-for-the-uk-and-the-us/.

Budina, Nina, and others (2021). Inequality interest: central banks should better communicate monetary policy's distributional effects. Finance & Development (June). Washington, D.C.: International Monetary Fund.

Burgess, Simon, and Hans Henrik Sievertsen (2020). Schools, skills, and learning: the impact of COVID-19 on education. VOXEU Blog, 1 April. Available at https://voxeu.org/article/impact-covid-19-education.

Busetto, Bradley, and Anga Timisina (2020). The role of technology and anti-corruption measures in fighting COVID-19. United Nations Development Programme blog. (15 September). Available at www.undp.org/blog/role-technology-and-anti-corruption-measures-fighting-covid-19 (accessed on 14 February 2022).

Cabote, Nickson J., and Justin Ray Angelo Fernandez (2020). Distributional impact of monetary policy: evidence from the Philippines. BSP Working Paper Series, No. 2020-09, Manila: Bangko Sentral Ng Pilipinas.

Capital Economics (2022). Capital Economics Russia-Ukraine Global Exposures. Available at https://data.capitaleconomics.com/lfqnbec/russia-ukraine-global-exposures (accessed on 16 March 2022).

Cashin, Cheryl, and others (2017). Aligning public financial management and health financing: sustaining progress toward Universal Health Coverage. Health Financing Working Paper, No. 4. Geneva: World Health Organization.

Castelli, Massimiliano, and Stefan Gerlach (2019). Central banks are too risk averse as investors. SUERF Policy Note, No. 78. Wien, Austria: European Money and Finance Forum.

Cerra, Valerie, and Sweta C. Saxena (2005). Growth dynamics: the myth of economic recovery. IMF Working Paper, No. 05/147. Washington, D.C.: International Monetary Fund.

Cerra, Valerie, Antonio Fatas, and Sweta Saxena (2021). Fighting the scarring effects of COVID-19. ***Industrial and Corporate Change***, vol. 30, No. 2, pp. 459–466.

_____ (forthcoming). Hysteresis and business cycles. Journal of Economic Literature.

Cerra, Valerie, Ruby Lama, and Norman Loayza (2021). Links between growth, inequality, and poverty: a survey. IMF Working Paper, No. 21/68. Washington, D.C.: International Monetary Fund.

Cerra, Valerie, Ugo Panizza, and Sweta C. Saxena (2013). International evidence on recovery from recessions. ***Contemporary Economic Policy***, vol. 31, No. 2, pp. 424-439.

Chancel, Lucas, and Thomas Piketty (2019). Indian income inequality, 1922-2015: from British raj to billionaire raj? ***Review of Income and Wealth***, vol. 65, pp. S33-S62.

Chancel, Lucas, and others (2022). ***World Inequality Report*** 2022. Paris: World Inequality Lab. Available at https://wir2022.wid.world/.

Chang, Ha-Joon (2002). ***Kicking Away the Ladder: Development Strategy in Historical Perspective***. New York: Anthem Press.

Chatterjee, Arup Kumar (2020). How to insure essential yet informal workers during the pandemic. Asian Development Blog, Asian Development Bank. (October). Available at https://blogs.adb.org/blog/how-insure-essential-yet-informal-workers-during-pandemic (accessed on 4 January 2022).

Chatterjee, Shiladitya (2018). Early lessons in implementing the Sustainable Development Goals in India: the example of Assam. South and South-West Asia Development Papers, No. 1804. New Delhi: United Nations, Economic and Social Commission for Asia and the Pacific (ESCAP).

Chisholm, Dan, and David B. Evans (2010). Improving health system efficiency as a means of moving towards universal coverage. World Health Report (2010) Background Paper, No. 28. Geneva: World Health Organization.

Cho, Chloe, and Daniel Lee, 2021. Public expenditures and inequality in Asia-Pacific: A preliminary assessment. MPFD Policy Brief, unpublished. Bangkok: United Nations, Economic and Social Commission for Asia and the Pacific (ESCAP).

Choi, Hoon, and Álvaro Choi (2016). Regulating private tutoring consumption in Korea: lessons from another failure. ***International Journal of Educational Development***, vol. 49, pp. 144-156.

Choo, Hakchung (1978). Economic growth and income distribution in Korea. Working Paper, No. 7810. Sejong, Republic of Korea: Korea Development Institute.

Choudhury, Saheli Roy (2022). China's central bank cuts key lending rates, including one for the first time in nearly 2 years. CNBC, China economy. 19 January. Available at www.cnbc.com/2022/01/20/china-economy-pboc-cuts-loan-prime-rates-lpr-for-1-year-5-year.html#:~:text=China's%20central%20bank%20cut%20the,coronavirus%20pandemic%20in%20the%20country.

Chucherd, Thitima, and others (2021). Monetary and financial perspectives on retail CBDC in the Thai context. PIER Discussion Paper, No. 152. Bangkok: Puey Ungphakorn Institute for Economic Research.

Claus, Iris, Jorge Martinez-Vazquez, and Violeta Vulovic (2012). Government fiscal policies and redistribution in Asian countries. ADB Economics Working Paper Series, No. 310. (October). Manila: Asian Development Bank.

Climate Bonds Initiative (2018). ***Green Infrastructure Investment Opportunities Report, Indonesia***. London.

Commitment to Equity (CEQ) (2017). The distributional impact of fiscal policy in Georgia. CEQ Working Paper, No. 42. (May). New Orleans, Louisiana: CEQ Institute.

_____ (2018). ***Commitment to Equity Handbook: Estimating the Impact of Fiscal Policy on Inequality and Poverty***. New Orleans and Washington, D.C.: CEQ Institute and Brookings Institution Press.

Dafe, Florence, and Ulrich Volz (2015). Financing global development: the role of central banks. Briefing Paper, No. 8/2015. Bonn, Germany: German Development Institute.

Dang, Hai-Anh, and Peter Lanjouw (2021). Inequality trends and dynamics: the bird's-eye and the granular perspectives. In ***Inequality in the Developing World***, Carlos Gradín, Murray Leibbrandt, and Finn Tarp, eds. Oxford: Oxford Scholarship Online. E-book.

Dasgupta, Sukti, Kee Beom Kim, and Luis Pinedo Caro (2017). As much to be gained by merchandise as manufacture? The role of services as an engine of growth. ***Japanese Political Economy,*** vol. 43, Nos. 1–4, pp. 9–37.

Dauth, Wolfgang, and others (2018). Adjusting to robots: worker level evidence. Institute Working Paper, No. 13. Minneapolis, Minnesota: Opportunity and Inclusive Growth Institute, Federal Reserve Bank of Minneapolis.

Davis, Gerald F., and Suntae Kim (2015). Financialization of the economy. ***Annual Review of Sociology***, vol. 41, pp. 203-221.

De Mattos, Fernanda Bárcia (2020). The electronics industry. In ***Robotics and Reshoring: Employment Implications for Developing Countries***, Fernanda Bárcia de Mattos, and others, eds. Geneva: International Labour Organization.

_____ and others (2020). ***Robotics and Reshoring: Employment Implications for Developing Countries.*** Geneva: International Labour Organization.

Demirgüç-Kunt, Asli, and others (2017). ***The Global Findex Database 2017: Measuring Financial Inclusion and the Fintech Revolution***. Washington, D.C.: World Bank Group.

Didenko, Anton, and Ross Buckley (2020). Central bank digital currencies: a potential response to the financial inclusion challenges of the Pacific. Issues in Pacific Development, No. 3. Manila: Asian Development Bank.

The Economist (2020). Covid-19 spurs national plans to give citizens digital identities. (7 December). Available at www.economist.com/international/2020/12/07/covid-19-spurs-national-plans-to-give-citizens-digital-identities (accessed on 30 January 2021).

_____ (2021). A perfect storm for container shipping. 18 September. Available at www.economist.com/finance-and-economics/a-perfect-storm-for-container-shipping/21804500.

_____ (2022). Economists are revising their views on robots and jobs. 22 January.

Eichengreen, Barry, and Poonam Gupta (2011). The service sector as India's road to economic growth. NBER Working Paper, No. 16757. Cambridge, Massachusetts: National Bureau of Economic Research.

Enami, Ali, Nora Lustig, and Alireza Taqdiri (2017). Fiscal policy, inequality and poverty in Iran: assessing the impact and effectiveness of taxes and transfers. CEQ Working Paper, No. 48 (November). New Orleans, Louisiana: CEQ Institute.

Estevão, Marcello (2021). Why tax administrations are embracing digital transformation. World Bank Blogs (1 December). Available at https://blogs.worldbank.org/voices/why-tax-administrations-are-embracing-digital-transformation (accessed on 2 February 2022).

European Commission (2021). Fair Taxation: Commission proposes to end the misuse of shell entities for tax purposes within the EU. (22 December). Available at https://ec.europa.eu/commission/presscorner/detail/en/IP_21_7027 (accessed on 20 January 2022).

European Competitiveness and Sustainable Industrial Policy (ECSIP) Consortium (2014). Study on the relation between industry and services in terms of productivity and value creation: within the Framework Contract for Industrial Competitiveness and Market Performance – ENTR/90/PP/2011/FC. Rotterdam, Netherlands.

Fender, Ingo, and others (2020). Reserve management and sustainability: the case for green bonds? BIS Working Papers, No. 849. Basel, Switzerland: Bank for International Settlements.

Food and Agriculture Organization of the United Nations (FAO) (2022). The importance of Ukraine and the Russian Federation for global agricultural markets and the risks associated with the current conflict. Information Note. Available at www.fao.org/3/cb9013en/cb9013en.pdf (accessed on 16 March 2022).

Frey, Carl B., and Michael A. Osborne (2017). The future of employment: How susceptible are jobs to computerisation? ***Technological Forecasting and Social Change***, vol. 114, pp. 254-280.

Funakoshi, Minami, Hugh Lawson, and Kannaki Deka (2022). Tracking sanctions against Russia. Reuters. 9 March. Available at https://graphics.reuters.com/UKRAINE-CRISIS/SANCTIONS/byvrjenzmve/ (accessed on 16 March 2022).

Furceri, Davide, and others (2021). Will COVID-19 have long-lasting effects on inequality? Evidence from past pandemics. IMF Working Paper, No. 2021/127. Washington, D.C.: International Monetary Fund.

Galbraith, James K. (2011). Inequality and economic and political change: a comparative perspective. ***Cambridge Journal of Regions, Economy and Society***, vol. 4, No. 1, pp. 13-27.

Galitopoulou, Stellina, and Antonella Noya (2016). Understanding social impact bonds. OECD Working Papers. Paris: Organisation for Economic Co-operation and Development.

Goldin, Claudia, and Lawrence F. Katz (2008). ***The Race Between Education and Technology***. Cambridge, Massachusetts: Belknap Press for Harvard University Press.

Goos, Maarten, Alan Manning, and Anna Salomons (2014). Explaining job polarization: routine-biased technological change and offshoring. ***American Economic Review,*** vol. 104, No. 8, pp. 2509–2526.

Gradín, Carlos (2021). Trends in global inequality using a new integrated dataset. WIDER Working Paper, No. 2021/61. Helsinki: UNU-WIDER

Grömling, Michael (2021). COVID-19 and the Growth Potential. ***Intereconomics***, vol. 56, No. 1, pp. 45-49.

Hager, Sandy Brian, and Joseph Baines (2020). The tax advantage of big business: how the structure of corporate taxation fuels concentration and inequality. ***Politics and Society***, vol. 48, No. 2, pp. 275-305.

Hallward-Driemeier, Mary, and Gaurav Nayyar (2017). Trouble in the Making? ***The Future of Manufacturing-Led Development***. Washington, D.C.: World Bank.

Harvie, Charles, and H. H. Lee (2003). Export-led industrialisation and growth: Korea's economic miracle, 1962-1989. ***Australian Economic History Review***, vol. 43, No. 3, pp. 256-286.

Hayden, Grant M., and Matthew T. Bodie (2021). Codetermination in theory and practice. ***Florida Law Review***, vol. 73, No. 2, pp. 1-42.

He, Laura (2022). Another big Chinese real estate developer might need to sell off property. ***CNN Business***, 11 January. Available at www.edition.cnn.com/2022/01/11/business/china-shimao-debt-downgrade-intl-hnk/index.html.

Hentov, Elliot, and others (2019). How do central banks invest? Embracing risk in official reserves. Boston and London: State Street Global Advisors and OMFIF (Official Monetary and Financial Institutions Forum).

Hirschman, Albert O., and Michael Rothschild (1973). The changing tolerance for income inequality in the course of economic development. ***Quarterly Journal of Economics***, vol. 87, No. 4 (November), pp. 544-566.

Hsieh, Chang-Tai, and others (2019). The allocation of talent and U.S. economic growth. ***Econometrica***, vol. 87, No. 5 (September), pp. 1439-1474.

Huang, Zhenqian, and Sweta C. Saxena (2021). Will I be rich if I come from an impoverished family? Improving intergenerational mobility in Asia and the Pacific. MPFD Policy Brief, No. 122. Bangkok: United Nations, Economic and Social Commission for Asia and the Pacific (ESCAP). Available at https://hdl.handle.net/20.500.12870/3891.

International Capital Market Association (ICMA) (2020). Sustainability-linked Bond Principles: voluntary process guidelines. Paris.

International Federation of Robots (2021). ***World Robotics 2021: Industrial Robots***. Frankfurt, Germany.

International Finance Corporation (IFC) (2017). IFC launches innovative social bond program, raising $500 million through benchmark bond. Washington, D.C. Available at https://pressroom.ifc.org/all/pages/PressDetail.aspx?ID=24635.

International Labour Organization (ILO) (2008). Social health protection: an ILO strategy towards universal access to health care. Paper 1/International Labour Office, Social Security Department. Geneva.

_____ (2018a). More than 68 per cent of the employed population in Asia-Pacific are in the informal economy. Bangkok. (2 May). Available at www.ilo.org/asia/media-centre/news/WCMS_627585/lang--en/index.htm (accessed on 26 January 2022).

_____ (2018b). ***Skills and the Future of Work: Strategies for Inclusive Growth in Asia and the Pacific***. Akiko Sakamoto and Johnny Sung, eds. Geneva.

_____ (2020a). ILO Monitor: COVID-19 and the world of work. Second edition: updated estimates and analysis. Geneva. (7 April).

_____ (2020b). ***Global Employment Trends for Youth 2020: Technology and the Future of Jobs***. Geneva.

_____ (2021a). An uneven and gender-unequal COVID-19 recovery: update on gender and employment trends 2021. ILO brief, October. Available at www.ilo.org/wcmsp5/groups/public/---ed_emp/documents/publication/wcms_824865.pdf.

_____ (2021b). Building Forward Fairer: Women's rights to work and at work at the core of the COVID-19 recovery. ILO brief. July. Available at www.ilo.org/wcmsp5/groups/public/---dgreports/---gender/documents/publication/wcms_814499.pdf.

_____ (2021c). Extending social health protection: accelerating progress towards Universal Health Coverage in Asia and the Pacific. Bangkok. (7 December).

_____ (2021d). ***World Social Protection Report 2020-22: Social Protection at the Crossroads – in pursuit of a better future***. Geneva.

_____ (2021e). ***Extending Social Security to Workers in the Informal Economy: Lessons from International Experience***, 2nd ed. Geneva.

_____ (2022). Investing more in universal social protection: filling the financing gap through domestic resource mobilization and international support and coordination. ILO Working Paper, No. 44. Geneva.

International Monetary Fund (IMF) (2003). Guidelines for foreign exchange reserve management: accompanying document. Washington, D.C. Available at www.imf.org/external/np/mae/ferm/2003/eng/index.htm.

_____ (2005). Back to basics – fiscal space: what it is and how to get it. ***Finance and Development***, vol. 42, No. 2.

_____ (2016). Regional Economic Outlook: Asia and Pacific. Washington, DC: International Monetary Fund.

_____ (2020). Digital solutions for direct cash transfers in the COVID-19 crisis. International Monetary Fund Fiscal Affairs, Special Series on Fiscal Policies to Respond to COVID-19. (April). Available at https://blog-pfm.imf.org/pfmblog/2020/04/-digital-solutions-for-direct-cash-transfers-in-the-covid-19-crisis-.html (accessed on 4 January 2022).

International Telecommunication Union (ITU) (2021). How COVID-19 accelerated digital healthcare. (7 April). Available at www.itu.int/hub/2021/04/how-covid-19-accelerated-digital-healthcare/ (accessed on 30 January 2022).

ISI Emerging Markets Group (2021) ***Foresight 2022***. Available at https://info.ceicdata.com/foresight-2022-report.

Jäger, Simon, Benjamin Schoefer, and Jörg Heining (2021). Labor in the boardroom. ***Quarterly Journal of Economics,*** vol. 136, No. 2, pp. 669-725.

Japan, Ministry of Health, Labour and Welfare (MHLW) (2020). Regulatory system on generic drugs in Japan. Available at www.pmda.go.jp/files/000234055.pdf (accessed on 2 February 2022).

Jiang, Xiao, and Ansel F. Schiavone (2020). Call centres in India and the Philippines. In R***obotics and Reshoring: Employment Implications for Developing Countries***. Geneva: International Labour Organization.

Jordà, Òscar, Sanjay R. Singh, and Alan M. Taylor (2020) Long-run economic consequences of pandemics. NBER Working Paper, No. 26934. Cambridge, Massachusetts: National Bureau of Economic Research.

Joshi, Anuradha, Wilson Prichard, and Christopher Heady (2014). Taxing the informal economy: the current state of knowledge and agendas for future research, ***Journal of Development Studies***, vol. 50, No. 10, pp. 1325-1347.

Joshi, S.S., Y.C. Shetty, and S. Karande (2019). Generic drugs – the Indian scenario. ***Journal of Postgraduate Medicine***, vol. 65, No. 2, pp. 67-69.

Kaldor, Nicholas (1966). ***Causes of the Slow Rate of Economic Growth of the United Kingdom***. Cambridge: Cambridge University Press.

_____ (1967). ***Strategic Factors in Economic Development***. Ithaca, New York: ILR Press.

Kanbur, Ravi, Changyong Rhee, and Juzhong Zhuang, eds. (2014). ***Inequality in Asia and the Pacific: Trends, Drivers and Policy Implications***. New York: Asian Development Bank and Routledge.

Kang, Seoghoon (2001). Globalization and income inequality in Korea: an overview. Paper presented at a Technical Meeting on FDI, Human Capital and Education in Developing Countries, 13-14 December 2001. Paris: Organisation for Economic Co-operation and Development.

Kaplan, Greg, Benjamin Moll, and Giovanni L. Violante (2018). Monetary policy according to HANK. ***American Economic Review***, vol. 108, No. 3, pp. 697-743.

_____ (2020). The great lockdown and the big stimulus: tracing the pandemic possibility frontier for the U.S. NBER Working Paper Series, No. 27794. Cambridge, Massachusetts: National Bureau of Economic Research.

Kiff, John, and others (2020). A survey of research on retail central bank digital currency. IMF Working Paper, No. 20/104. Washington, D.C.: International Monetary Fund.

Kim, Djun Kil (2012). ***The Saemaul Undong Movement in the Republic of Korea: Sharing Knowledge on Community-driven Development.*** Mandaluyong City, Philippines: Asian Development Bank.

Klapper, Leora, Annamaria Lusardi, and Peter van Oudheusden (2014). ***Financial Literacy around the World: Insights from the Standard & Poor's Ratings Services Global Financial Literacy Survey***. Washington, D.C.: World Bank Group.

Kravchenko, Alexey (2018). Where and how to dodge taxes and shift money abroad using trade misinvoicing: a beginner's guide. TIID Working Paper, No. 01/18. Bangkok: United Nations, Economic and Social Commission for Asia and the Pacific (ESCAP).

Krzywdzinski, Martin (2020). Automation, digitalization, and changes in occupational structures in the automobile industry in Germany, Japan, and the United States: a brief history from the early 1990s until 2018. ***Industrial and Corporate Change***, vol. 30, No. 3, pp. 499-535.

Kucera, David (2020). The apparel and footwear industry. In ***Robotics and Reshoring: Employment Implications for Developing Countries***, Fernanda Bárcia de Mattos, and others, eds. Geneva: International Labour Organization.

Kumar, Aditi, and others (2020). National digital currencies: the future of money? Cambridge, Massachusetts: Belfer Center for Science and International Affairs, Harvard University.

Kuznets, Simon (1955). Economic growth and income inequality. ***American Economic Review***, vol. 45, No. 1, pp. 1–28.

Lee, Daniel, and Kiatkanid Pongpanich (2021). Advancing UHC under fiscal pressure: Lessons from Asia-Pacific's pandemic response. MPFD Policy Brief, unpublished. Bangkok: United Nations, Economic and Social Commission for Asia and the Pacific (ESCAP).

Leong, Jinny (2021). An overview of the distributional effects of monetary policy. Analytical Notes, No. AN2021/5. Wellington: Reserve Bank of New Zealand.

Li, Shi, Terry Sicular, and Finn Tarp (2021). Structural change, transition, rent-seeking and corruption, and government policy. In ***Inequality in the Developing World***, Carlos Gradín, Murray Leibbrandt and Finn Tarp, eds. Oxford: Oxford Scholarship Online. E-book.

Lin, Justin, and Ha-Joon Chang (2009). Should industrial policy in developing countries conform to comparative advantage or defy it? A debate between Justin Lin and Ha-Joon Chang. ***Development Policy Review***, vol. 27, No. 5, pp. 483-502.

Lin, Justin Yifu (2011). From flying geese to leading dragons: new opportunities and strategies for structural transformation in developing countries. Policy Research Working Paper, No. WPS 5702. Washington, D.C.: World Bank.

Liu, Shaoshan (2020). DARPA: a global innovation differentiator. ***IEEE Engineering Management Review***, vol. 48, No. 2, pp. 65-71.

Lucas-Mas, Cristian Óliver, and Raúl Félix Junquera-Varela (2021). ***Tax Theory Applied to the Digital Economy: A Proposal for a Digital Data Tax and a Global Internet Tax Agency***. Washington, D.C.: World Bank Group. Available at https://openknowledge.worldbank.org/bitstream/handle/10986/35200/9781464816543.pdf?sequence=1&isAllowed=y (accessed on 2 February 2022).

Luo, Chuliang, Li Shi, and Terry Sicular (2018). The long-term evolution of income inequality and poverty in China. WIDER Working Paper, No. 2018/153. Helsinki: UNU-WIDER.

Lustig, Nora, and Yang Wang (2020). The impact of taxes and transfers on income inequality, poverty, and the urban-rural and regional income gaps in China. ECINEQ Working Paper Series, No. 2020 556. Palma de Mallorca, Spain: Society for the Study of Economic Inequality.

Ma, Chang, John Rogers, and Sili Zhou (2020). Global economic and financial effects of 21st century pandemics and epidemics. CEPR Press COVID Economics Vetted and Real-time Papers, Issue 5, 16 April. Washington, D.C.: Centre for Economic Policy Research.

Madgavkar, Anu, and others (2019). The future of women at work: transitions in the age of automation. Washington, D.C.: McKinsey Global Institute. Available at www.mckinsey.com/featured-insights/gender-equality/the-future-of-women-at-work-transitions-in-the-age-of-automation.

Mancini-Griffoli, Tommaso, and others (2018). Casting light on central bank digital currency. IMF Staff Discussion Note, No. 18/08. Washington, D.C.: International Monetary Fund.

Mazzucato, Marianna (2021). A new global economic consensus. ***Project Syndicate Newsletter.*** Available at www. project-syndicate. org/commentary/cornwall-consensus-rebuilding-global-governance-by-mariana-mazzucato-2021-10.

McDonnell, Anthony, Ana F. Urrutia, and Emma Samman (2019). Reaching universal health coverage: a political economy review of trends across 49 countries. ODI Working Paper, No. 570. London: Overseas Development Institute.

McKinsey (2015). As the automation of physical and knowledge work advances, many jobs will be redefined rather than eliminated—at least in the short term. Available at www.mckinsey.com/business-functions/mckinsey-digital/our-insights/four-fundamentals-of-workplace-automation.

_____(2020). Prioritizing health: a prescription for prosperity. McKinsey and Company. (8 July).

Meh, Cesaire, José-Víctor Ríos-Rull, and Yaz Terajima (2010). Aggregate and welfare effects of redistribution of wealth under inflation and price-level targeting. ***Journal of Monetary Economics***, vol. 57, No. 6, pp. 637-652.

Mehrotra, Santosh, and Jajati Parida (2019). India's employment crisis: rising education levels and falling non-agricultural job growth. CSE Working Paper, No. 23. Available at https://cse.azimpremjiuniversity.edu.in/wp-content/uploads/2020/10/Mehrotra_Parida_India_s_Employment_Crisis_October_2019.pdf.

Menon, Ravi (2021). Being the change we want to see - a sustainable future. Speech given by the managing director of the Monetary Authority of Singapore, at the launch of the inaugural MAS Sustainability Report, 9 June. Available at www.bis.org/review/r210609g.pdf.

Mian, Atif, R., Ludwig Straub, and Amir Sufi (2021a). Indebted demand. ***Quarterly Journal of Economics***, vol. 136, No. 4, pp. 2243-2307.

_____ (2021b). The saving glut of the rich. NBER Working Paper, No. 26941. Cambridge, Massachusetts: National Bureau of Economic Research. Available at www.nber.org/papers/w26941

_____ (2021c). What explains the decline in r*? Rising income inequality versus demographic shifts. BFI Working Paper, No. 2021-104. Chicago: University of Chicago, Becker Friedman Institute for Economics.

Mikhalev, Igor, and others (2021). CBDC Tracker whitepaper. Available at http://cbdctracker.org.

Milanovic, Branko (2016). ***Global Inequality: A New Approach for the Age of Globalization***. Cambridge, Massachusetts: Harvard University Press.

Moll, Ben, and Natalie Rickard (2021). How are economic models adapting to rising inequality and the pandemic. ***Economics Observatory***. 9 April.

Nagumo, Jada (2019). Asia's highest paid CEOs trump US execs in pay rankings. Nikkei Asia. Available at https://asia.nikkei.com/Business/Business-trends/Asia-s-highest-paid-CEOs-trump-US-execs-in-pay-rankings.

Nallareddy, Suresh, Ethan Rouen, and Juan Carlos Suárez Serrato (2019). Do corporate tax cuts increase income inequality? NBER Working Paper, No. 24598. Cambridge Massachusetts: National Bureau of Economic Research.

National Food Security Portal (NFSP) (2021). Ration card activity summary. Available at https://nfsa.gov.in/public/nfsadashboard/PublicRCDashboard.aspx (accessed on 4 January 2022).

Nedelkoska, Ljubica, and Glenda Quintini (2018). Automation, skills use and training. OECD Social, Employment and Migration Working Papers, No. 202. Paris: Organisation for Economic Co-operation and Development.

Network for Greening the Financial System (NGFS) (2019). ***A Sustainable and Responsible Investment Guide for Central Banks' Portfolio Management.*** Technical Document. Available at www.ngfs.net/sites/default/files/medias/documents/ngfs-a-sustainable-and-responsible-investment-guide.pdf.

Nolsoe, Eir, and Valentina Pop (2022). Russia sanctions list: what the West imposed over the Ukraine invasion. ***Financial Times***. 4 March. Available at www.ft.com/content/6f3ce193-ab7d-4449-ac1b-751d49b1aaf8 (accessed on 16 March 2022).

Nunn, Nathan, Nancy Qian, and Jaya Wen (2020). Distrust and political turnover during economic crises. Harvard Working Paper, No. 24187. Cambridge, Massachusetts: Harvard University.

Official Monetary and Financial Institutions Forum (OMFIF) (2021). ***Global Public Investors*** 2021.

Okun, Arthur M. (1975). ***Equality and Efficiency: The Big Tradeoff.*** Washington, D.C.: Brookings Institution.

Organisation for Economic Co-operation and Development (OECD) (2012). OECD Economic Surveys: Korea 2012. Paris.

_____ (2015). Are young people attaining higher levels of education than their parents? Education Indicators in Focus, No. 28. Paris: OECD Publishing.

_____ (2018). Tax policies for inclusive growth in a changing world. (July). Available at www.oecd.org/g20/Tax-policies-for-inclusive-growth-in-a-changing-world-OECD.pdf (accessed on 27 January 2022).

_____ (2020). Corporate tax statistics, 2nd ed. Paris: OECD Publishing.

_____ (2021a). ***Revenue Statistics in Asia and the Pacific 2021: Emerging Challenges for the Asia-Pacific Region in the COVID-19 Era.*** Paris.

_____ (2021b). 130 countries and jurisdictions join bold new framework for international tax reform. Newsroom, 1 July. Available at www.oecd.org/newsroom/130-countries-and-jurisdictions-join-bold-new-framework-for-international-tax-reform.htm (accessed on 28 December 2021).

_____ (2021c). Digital platforms have an important role to play in value added tax policy in the sharing and gig economy. Newsroom, 1 July. Available at www.oecd.org/tax/consumption/digital-platforms-have-an-important-role-to-play-in-value-added-tax-policy-in-the-sharing-and-gig-economy.htm (accessed on 2 February 2022).

O'Neill, Martin, and Thad Williamson (2012). The promise of predistribution. Available at https://philpapers.org/rec/ONETPO-5.

Ortiz-Ospina, Esteban, and Max Roser (2016). Government spending. ***Our World in Data***.

Ostry, Jonathan D., Andrew Berg, and Charalambos G. Tsangarides (2014). Redistribution, inequality and growth. IMF Staff Discussion Note, 14/02. Washington, D.C.: International Monetary Fund. Available at www.imf.org/external/pubs/ft/sdn/2014/sdn1402.pdf.

_____ Prakash Loungani, and Davide Furceri (2020). The pandemic will leave the poor further disadvantaged. IMF Blog. Washington, D.C.: International Monetary Fund. Available at www.weforum.org/agenda/2020/05/pandemics-poor-rich-economics-coronavirus-covid19/

Pack, Howard, and Kamal Saggi (2006). The case for industrial policy: a critical survey. Policy Research Working Paper, No. 3839. Washington, D.C.: World Bank.

Philippines, Food and Drug Administration (FDA) (2020). Guidelines in the implementation of the use of electronic means of prescription for drugs for the benefit of individuals vulnerable to COVID-19. FDA Circular, No. 2020-007, Republic of the Philippines, Department of Health. Available at www.fda.gov.ph/wp-content/uploads/2020/03/FDA-Circular-No.-2020-007.pdf (accessed on 14 February 2022).

Piketty, Thomas (2006). The Kuznets curve: yesterday and tomorrow. In ***Understanding Poverty***, Abhijit Vinayak Banerjee, Roland Bénabou and Dilip Mookherjee, eds. Oxford: Oxford Scholarship Online. E-book. Available at http://digamoo.free.fr/piketty06.pdf.

Prasad, Eswar (2014). Distributional effects of macroeconomic policy choices in emerging market economies. ***IMF Economic Review***, vol. 62, No. 3, pp. 409-429.

Pritadrajati, Dyah S., Anggita C.M. Kusuma, and Sweta C. Saxena (2021). Scarred for life: lasting consequences of unemployment and informal self-employment – an empirical evidence from Indonesia. ***Economic Analysis and Policy***, vol.70, pp. 206-219. (June).

Punzi, Maria Teresa (2020). ***The Distributional Impact of Monetary Policy in SEACEN Member Economies***. Kuala Lumpur: South East Asian Central Banks (SEACEN) Research and Training Centre.

Rajan, Raghuram (2010). ***Fault Lines: How Hidden Fractures Still Threaten the World Economy***. Princeton, New Jersey: Princeton University Press.

Rao, Sujata, and Jonathan Saul (2021). Analysis: Shipping costs – another danger for inflation-watchers to navigate. Reuters, Commodities. 10 December. Available at www.reuters.com/markets/commodities/shipping-costs-another-danger-inflation-watchers-navigate-2021-12-10/.

Rao, Sumedh (2014). Tax reform: topic guide. Birmingham, United Kingdom: GSDRC, University of Birmingham. Available at https://gsdrc.org/wp-content/uploads/2015/07/GSDRC_Tax_Reform_Topic_Guide.pdf.

Ratha, Dilip, and Eung Ju Kim (2022). Russia-Ukraine conflict: implications for remittance flows to Ukraine and Central Asia. World Bank blogs. 4 March. Available at https://blogs.worldbank.org/peoplemove/russia-ukraine-conflict-implications-remittance-flows-ukraine-and-central-asia (accessed on 16 March 2022).

Rodrik, Dani (2013). Unconditional convergence in manufacturing. ***Quarterly Journal of Economics***, vol. 128, No. 1, pp. 165–204. Available at https://doi.org/10.1093/qje/qjs047.

Rogoff, Kenneth (2021). Are central banks to blame for rising inequality? Prague: Project Syndicate. (4 August).

Rojas Cama, Freddy (2021). Impact of fiscal consolidations on inequalities in developing countries of Asia-Pacific. MPFD Policy Brief, unpublished. Bangkok: United Nations, Economic and Social Commission for Asia and the Pacific (ESCAP).

Roncolato, Leanne, and David Kucera (2014). Structural drivers of productivity and employment growth: a decomposition analysis for 81 countries. ***Cambridge Journal of Economics***, vol. 38, No. 2, pp. 399–424.

Sachs, Jeffrey D., Seth G. Benzell, and Guillermo LaGarda (2015). Robots: curse or blessing? A basic framework. NBER Working Paper, No. 21091. Cambridge, Massachusetts: National Bureau of Economic Research.

Sachs, Jeffrey D., and Laurence J. Kotlikoff (2012). Smart machines and long-term misery. NBER Working Paper, No. 18629. Cambridge, Massachusetts: National Bureau of Economic Research.

Saini, Shweta, and Siraj Hussain (2021). Leveraging India's Aadhaar platform to ease COVID-19 pain. East Asia Forum. (1 October).

Sandbu, Martin (2021). The global state of inequality. ***Financial Times***, 13 October.

Sandel, Michael J. (2020). ***The Tyranny of Merit: What's Become of the Common Good?*** London: Penguin Books.

Schnabel, Isabel (2021). Monetary policy and inequality. Statement at a virtual conference on "Diversity and Inclusion in Economics, Finance, and Central Banking". 9 November, Frankfurt am Main, Germany. Available at www.ecb.europa.eu/press/key/date/2021/html/ecb.sp211109_2~cca25b0a68.en.html.

Sen, Kunal, Andy Sumner, and Arief Yusuf (2020). Double dividends and mixed blessings: structural transformation, income inequality and employment dynamics. ***Journal of Development Studies***, vol. 56, No. 1, pp. 1-5.

Sever, Can, and Emekcan Yucel (2021). Electoral cycles in inequality. Working Paper, No. 2021/01. Istanbul: Bogazici University, Department of Economics.

Shirai, Sayuri (2019). Money and central bank digital currency. In Marlene Amstad, and others (eds.), ***Central Bank Digital Currency and Fintech in Asia***. Tokyo: Asian Development Bank Institute and the Chinese University of Hong Kong, Shenzhen.

Singapore Green Plan 2030 (n.d.). Introducing the Green Plan. Available at www.greenplan.gov.sg/ (accessed on 10 October 2021).

Singapore, Ministry of Home Affairs (MHA) (2022). Singapore Government Scholarship. Available at www.mha.gov.sg/careers/scholarships/mha-scholarships/singapore-government-scholarship-(sgs) (accessed on 2 February 2022.

Solt, Frederick (2008). Economic inequality and democratic political engagement. ***American Journal of Political Science***, vol. 52, No. 1, pp. 48-60.

Stiglitz, Joseph E. (2017). Industrial policy, learning, and development. In ***The Practice of Industrial Policy***, John Page and Finn Tarp, eds. New York: Oxford University Press.

_____ (2021). From manufacturing-led export growth to a twenty-first-century inclusive growth strategy: explaining the demise of a successful growth model and what to do about it. In ***Inequality in the Developing World***, Carlos Gradín, Murray Leibbrandt and Finn Tarp, eds. Oxford: Oxford Scholarship Online. E-book.

STR (2021). Tourism after lockdown: current travel barriers. Data Insights Blog. 19 August. Available at https://str.com/data-insights-blog/tourism-after-lockdown-current-travel-barriers.

Tandon, Ajay, and others (2020). Economic impact of COVID-19: implications for health financing in Asia and Pacific. Health, Nutrition and Population Discussion Paper. Washington, D.C.: World Bank Group.

Thai PBS (2022). Prolonged Russia-Ukraine war could derail Thai economic recovery. 27 February. Available at www.thaipbsworld.com/prolonged-russia-ukraine-war-could-derail-thai-economic-recovery/ (accessed on 16 March 2022).

Torbert, Sally (2021). The impact of taxes and social spending on inequality and poverty in the Asia-Pacific region. MPFD Working Paper, unpublished. Bangkok: United Nations, Economic and Social Commission for Asia and the Pacific (ESCAP).

UBS Optimus Foundation (UBSOF) (2018). Educate Girls Development Impact Bond brochure. Available at http://instiglio.org/educategirlsdib/wp-content/uploads/2018/07/Educate-Girls-DIB_results_brochure_final-2.pdf.

Uh, SooBong (2018). Job training in Korea. Working Paper. Washington, D.C.: World Bank.

UltraTech Cement (2021). Our performance vis on vis our sustainability performance target. Available at www.ultratechcement.com/content/dam/ultratechcementwebsite/pdf/financials/financial-results/fy08/q1/SLB%20Progress%20Report_VF-combined.pdf.

United Nations (2022). ***World Economic Situation and Prospects 2022***. New York.

United Nations Children's Fund (UNICEF) (2019). Universal child benefit case studies: the experience of Mongolia. (July). Available at https://www.unicef.org/media/70471/file/MNG-case-study-2020.pdf (accessed on 5 February 2022).

_____ (2020). COVID-19: are children able to continue learning during school closures? – a global analysis of the potential reach of remote learning policies using data from 100 countries. Factsheet. Available at https://data.unicef.org/wp-content/uploads/2020/08/COVID-19-Remote-Learning-Factsheet_English_2020.pdf.

_____ (2021a). COVID-19 'biggest global crisis for children in our 75-year history' – UNICEF. Available at www.unicef.org/eap/reports/covid-19-education-situation-analysis-asia (accessed on 20 December 2021).

_____ (2021b). ***Preventing a Lost Decade: Urgent Action to Reverse the Devastating Impact of COVID-19 on Children and Young People***. New York. Available at www.unicef.org/media/112891/file/UNICEF%20 75%20report.pdf.

_____ and United Nations Educational, Scientific and Cultural Organization (UNESCO) (2021). Situation analysis on the effects of and responses to COVID-19 on the education sector in Asia: regional synthesis report. (October). Available at www.unicef.org/eap/media/9301/file/Regional%20Situation%20Analysis%20 of%20the%20Impacts%20of%20COVID-19%20on%20Education.pdf (accessed on 20 December 2021).

United Nations Conference on Trade and Development (UNCTAD) (2015). World Investment Report 2015: ***Reforming International Investment Governance.*** New York and Geneva.

United Nations Development Programme (UNDP) and International Labour Organization (ILO) (2021). ***Informality and Social Protection in African Countries: A Forward-looking Assessment of Contributory Schemes***. New York.

United Nations, Economic and Social Commission for Asia and the Pacific (ESCAP) (2017). ***Economic and Social Survey of Asia and the Pacific 2017: Governance and Fiscal Management***. Bangkok.

_____ (2018a) ***Inequality in Asia and the Pacific in the Era of the 2030 Agenda for Sustainable Development***. Available at www.unescap.org/publications/inequality-asia-and-pacific-era-2030-agenda-sustainable-development.

_____ (2018b). ***Financing for Development in Asia and the Pacific: Highlights in the Context of the Addis Ababa Action Agenda***. Bangkok.

_____ (2018c). ***Social Outlook for Asia and the Pacific 2018: Poorly Protected***. Bangkok.

_____ (2018d). Tax policy for sustainable development in Asia and the Pacific. ESCAP Financing for Development Series, No. 2. Bangkok.

_____ (2019a). ***Economic and Social Survey of Asia and the Pacific 2019: Ambitions beyond Growth.*** Bangkok.

_____ (2019b). Mainstreaming the Sustainable Development Goals into economic policymaking. ESCAP/CMPF/2019/1. Available at www.unescap.org/sites/default/files/CMPF-2019-1%20Mainstreaming%20 SDGs_0.pdf (accessed on 26 January 2022).

_____ (2019c). ***Asia-Pacific Trade and Investment Report 2019: Navigating Non-tariff Measures towards Sustainable Development***. Bangkok.

_____ (2020). ***Economic and Social Survey of Asia and the Pacific 2020: Towards sustainable economies.*** Bangkok. Available at https://www.unescap.org/publications/economic-and-social-survey-asia-and-pacific-2020.

_____ (2021a). ***Economic and Social Survey of Asia and the Pacific: Towards post-COVID-19 Resilient Economies***. Bangkok. Available at https://www.unescap.org/kp/2021/economic-and-social-survey-asia-and-pacific-2021-towards-post-covid-19-resilient-economies.

_____ (2021b). Mongolia's Child Money Programme: results from ESCAP's Social Protection Simulation Tool. Policy Paper, No. 2021/07. (July). Bangkok.

_____ (2021c). ***Asia and the Pacific SDG Progress Report 2021***. (16 March). Bangkok.

_____ (2021d). ***Why we need social protection***. Policy brief (16 March). Bangkok.

_____ (2022). Facilitating COVID-19 responses: Aadhaar. Social Protection Toolbox. Bangkok.

_____ and International Labour Organization (ILO) (2020a). ***The Protection We Want: Social Outlook for Asia and the Pacific***. Bangkok.

_____ (2020b). Social protection responses to COVID-19 in Asia and the Pacific: the story so far and future considerations. Discussion paper prepared in collaboration with the United Nations Issue-based Coalition for Inclusion and Empowerment. Bangkok.

United Nations Educational, Scientific and Cultural Organization (UNESCO) (2021a). To be smart, the digital revolution will need to be inclusive: excerpt from the UNESCO science report. Available at https://unesdoc.unesco.org/ark:/48223/pf0000375429.locale=en (accessed on 30 December 2021).

_____ (2021b). Right from the start: build inclusive societies through inclusive early childhood education. UNESCO Policy Paper, No. 46. (July). Available at https://en.unesco.org/gem-report/rightfromthestart (accessed on 31 January 2022).

Varoufakis, Yanis (2021). A progressive monetary policy is the only alternative. ***Project Syndicate Newsletter***, 28 October.

Verma, Sunny (2022). Inflation over comfort range of 6%; no need for alarm: RBI. ***The Indian Express***. 15 February. Available at www.indianexpress.com/article/business/economy/india-january-2022-cpi-consumer-price-index-retail-inflation-mospi-government-data-7773245/.

Volz, Ulrich (2017). On the role of central banks in enhancing green finance. United Nations Environment Programme Working Paper, No. 17/01. Geneva: International Environment House.

Wasserman Mitchell, Ezra (2017). Corporate governance and income inequality: the role of the monitoring board. ***Social Science Research Network Electronic Journal***. Available at https://ssrn.com/abstract=3012406.

Webb, Quentin (2022). How bad are things in China's property market? ***The Wall Street Journal***, 22 January. Available at www.wsj.com/articles/how-bad-are-things-in-chinas-property-market-11642847407.

Woo, Jaejoon, and others (2013). Distributional consequences of fiscal consolidation and the role of fiscal policy: what do the data say? IMF Working Papers, No. 13/195. Washington, D.C.: International Monetary Fund.

World Bank (2011). Vietnam: ***State and People, Central and Local, Working Together – the Vietnam rural electrification experience***. Washington, D.C.: World Bank Group.

_____ (2016a). ***Vietnam Systematic Country Diagnostic: Sustaining Success – priorities for inclusive and sustainable growth***. Washington, D.C. Available at http://documents1.worldbank.org/curated/en/334491474293198764/pdf/108348-REVISED-PUBLIC-ACS.pdf (accessed on 20 December 2021).

_____ (2016b). ***World Development Report 2016: Digital Dividends***. Washington, D.C.

_____ (2016c). Bangladesh: growing the economy through advances in agriculture. Washington, D.C.

_____ (2017). Creating jobs and diversifying exports in Bangladesh. Washington, D.C.

_____ (2018). Global Database on Intergenerational Mobility, Development Research Group. Washington, D.C.: World Bank Group.

_____ (2019a). *Improving the Effectiveness of Public Finance: Cambodia Public Expenditure Review.* Washington, D.C.

_____ (2019b). Inaugural RAMP Survey on the reserve management practices of central banks: results and observations. Available at https://openknowledge.worldbank.org/handle/10986/31461

_____ (2020a). *Poverty and Shared Prosperity 2020: Reversals of Fortune*. Washington, D.C. Available at https://openknowledge.worldbank.org/bitstream/handle/10986/34496/9781464816024.pdf?sequence=33&isAllowed=y.

_____ (2020b). *Indonesia Public Expenditure Review: Spending for Better Results.* Washington, D.C. Available at https://openknowledge.worldbank.org/bitstream/handle/10986/33954/148209.pdf?sequence=1&isAllowed=y (accessed on 15 January 2022).

_____ (2020c). *Central Bank Reserve Management Practices: Insights into Public Asset Management from the Second RAMP Survey*. Washington, D.C.: World Bank Group.

_____ (2020d). *World Development Report 2020: Trading for Development in the Age of Global Value Chains.* Washington, D.C.

_____ (2021a). World Bank: tertiary education is key to rebuilding COVID-hit economies. Press release, 25 September. Available at www.worldbank.org/en/news/press-release/2021/09/25/world-bank-tertiary-education-is-key-to-rebuilding-covid-hit-economies (accessed on 30 December 2021).

_____ (2021b). Education finance watch 2021. Available at https://documents.worldbank.org/en/publication/documents-reports/documentdetail/226481614027788096/education-finance-watch-2021 (accessed on 30 December 2021).

_____ (2021c). Two-thirds of poorer countries are cutting education budgets due to COVID-19. Press Release, 22 February. Available at www.worldbank.org/en/news/press-release/2021/02/22/two-thirds-of-poorer-countries-are-cutting-education-budgets-due-to-covid-19 (accessed on 15 December 2021).

_____ (2021d). From double shock to double recovery: implications and options for health financing in the time of COVID-19 – technical update: widening rifts. Health, Nutrition and Population Discussion Paper. Washington, D.C. Available at https://openknowledge.worldbank.org/bitstream/handle/10986/35298/From_Double_Shock_to_Double_Recovery%20Revision%2020210916.pdf?sequence=7&isAllowed=y (accessed on 12 February 2022).

_____ (2022). World Development Indicators. Washington, D.C. Available at https://data.worldbank.org/.

World Food Programme (WFP) (2020). *A Chance for Every Schoolchild: Partnering to Scale up School Health and Nutrition for Human Capital – WFP School Feeding Strategy 2020-2030*. Rome. Available at https://docs.wfp.org/api/documents/WFP-0000112101/download/?_ga=2.104255616.1856692493.1645348700-1935329892.1645348700 (accessed on 15 February 2022).

_____ (2021). Meghalaya Government and WFP partner on transforming targeted public distribution system to improve food security. (19 November). Available at www.wfp.org/news/nglisha-government-and-wfp-partner-transforming-targeted-public-distribution-system-improve (accessed on 4 January 2022).

World Health Organization (2010a). *The World Health Report: Health Systems Financing – the path to universal coverage*. Geneva: World Health Organization.

_____ (2010b). Improving health system efficiency as a means of moving towards universal coverage. World Health Report 2010, Background Paper, No. 28. Geneva.

_____ (2019). Government-sponsored cash transfer scheme to benefit poor women and children and improve access to health services. World Health Organization, News release, Phnom Penh, 27 June. Available at www.who.int/cambodia/news/detail/27-06-2019-government-sponsored-cash-transfer-scheme-to-benefit-poor-women-and-children-and-improve-access-to-health-services (accessed on 8 February 2022).

_____ (2020). A confident health workforce strengthens Lao PDR's health system and COVID-19 response. News release, 10 December. Available at www.who.int/news-room/feature-stories/detail/a-confident-health-workforce-strengthens-lao-pdr-s-health-system-and-covid-19-response (accessed on 9 February 2022).

_____ (2021a). More than half a billion people pushed or pushed further into extreme poverty due to health care costs. News release, 12 December. Available at www.who.int/news/item/12-12-2021-more-than-half-a-billion-people-pushed-or-pushed-further-into-extreme-poverty-due-to-health-care-costs (accessed on 21 December 2021).

_____ (2021b). COVID-19 continues to disrupt essential health services in 90% of countries. News release, 23 April. Available at www.who.int/news/item/23-04-2021-covid-19-continues-to-disrupt-essential-health-services-in-90-of-countries#:~:text=The%20second%20round%20of%20a,since%20the%20first%20survey%20conducted.

_____ (2021c). ***Global Strategy on Digital Health 2020-2025***. Geneva

_____ and World Bank (2017). ***Tracking Universal Health Coverage: 2017 Global Monitoring Report***. Geneva: World Health Organization and the World Bank.

World Tourism Organization (UNWTO) (2021). New COVID-19 surges keep travel restrictions in place, November. Available at www.unwto.org/news/new-covid-19-surges-keep-travel-restrictions-in-place.

World Trade Organization (WTO) (2019). ***World Trade Report 2019: The Future of Services Trade***. Geneva.

_____ (2022). Implementation of the decision on measures concerning the possible negative effects of the reform programme on least-developed and net food-importing developing countries. Information note. Available at https://docs.wto.org/dol2fe/Pages/SS/directdoc.aspx?filename=q:/G/AG/W42R22.pdf&Open=True.

World Travel and Tourism Council (WTTC) (2021). ***Travel and Tourism Economic Impact Reports 2021***. June. Available at https://wttc.org/Portals/0/Documents/Reports/2021/Global%20Economic%20Impact%20and%20Trends%202021.pdf?ver=2021-07-01-114957-177.

Yousaf, Tahir, Ghulam Ghouse, and Atiq-Ur-Rehman (2018). Impact of monetary policy on socio economic indicators: a case study of developing Asian economies. Available at https://pide.org.pk/psde/wp-content/uploads/2018/12/Mian-Ghulam-Ghouse.pdf.

Zhang, Wei (2021). Non-State actors in education: the nature, dynamics and regulatory implications of private supplementary tutoring. UNESCO Global Education Monitoring Report, No. ED/GEMR/MRT/2020/F/3. Available at https://gem-report-2021.unesco.org/wp-content/uploads/2021/12/03-Wei.pdf.